Jean E Saindon
3/79

THE ORIGINS OF PRAGMATISM

Other books by A. J. Ayer published by Macmillan

LANGUAGE, TRUTH AND LOGIC

BRITISH EMPIRICAL PHILOSOPHERS (*editor, with Raymond Winch*)

LOGICAL POSITIVISM (*editor*)

THE FOUNDATIONS OF EMPIRICAL KNOWLEDGE

PHILOSOPHICAL ESSAYS

THE PROBLEM OF KNOWLEDGE

THE REVOLUTION IN PHILOSOPHY (*with others*)

THE CONCEPT OF A PERSON AND OTHER ESSAYS

THE ORIGINS OF PRAGMATISM

PROBABILITY AND EVIDENCE

RUSSELL AND MOORE: THE ANALYTICAL HERITAGE

Errata

page 31, line 5 from bottom
 for failed read fail

page 89, last paragraph, lines 1-2
 should read
 abduction without induction
 is blind, induction without
 abduction is empty.

page 148, line 4 from bottom
 for types read type

page 177, line 10
 for qualified read quantified

page 259, lines 25-26
 for spirits who are lodged in
 our bodies read spirits who
 are intimately conjoined with
 our bodies and the ensuing
 phrase like a pilot in a ship
 should be deleted

page 275, line 9
 for for read from

page 289, lines 8-9: the phrase should
 read
 percepts without concepts are
 blind, concepts without percepts
 are empty.

page 307, line 11
 for ben read been

THE ORIGINS OF
PRAGMATISM

STUDIES IN THE PHILOSOPHY OF
CHARLES SANDERS PEIRCE
AND WILLIAM JAMES

A. J. AYER

Wykeham Professor of Logic in the University of Oxford and Fellow of New College, Oxford Fellow of the British Academy

MACMILLAN

First edition 1968
First published in paperback edition 1974

Published by
THE MACMILLAN PRESS LTD
London and Basingstoke
Associated companies in New York Dublin
Melbourne Johannesburg and Madras

SBN 333 17270 1

Printed in Great Britain by
ROBERT MACLEHOSE AND CO LTD
The University Press, Glasgow

TO
ELIZABETH
AND
RAIMUND VON HOFMANNSTHAL

CONTENTS

WILLIAM JAMES

PREFACE

This book owes its existence to my having been invited by the trustees of the Sulgrave Manor Board to give the Sir George Watson lectures for 1957. According to the terms of their endowment, these lectures, which are given annually, are intended to deal with 'the history, literature, and institutions of the United States'. The trustees informed me that this might be taken to cover a comparison of British with American philosophy. In a series of four lectures, which were delivered at University College London in November 1957, under the overall title of 'Pragmatism and Analysis', I accordingly attempted to trace the course of the main stream of American philosophy from Peirce and James to Quine and Goodman, alongside that of the main stream of British philosophy from Moore and Russell to Austin and Ryle. I believe that the lectures contained some points of interest, but the breadth of their subject and the pace at which they covered it prevented them from being very much more than a series of vignettes.

Having delivered the lectures, I put the manuscript aside for some years, partly because I was engaged in other work, but partly because I was not sure how I wanted to develop it for publication. Deciding eventually that I ought to go into the subject a little more deeply, I soon gave up the idea of trying to compress the better part of a century of British and American philosophy into one volume. I still meant to adhere to the theme of Pragmatism and Analysis but decided to concentrate on the originators of these two movements. My plan was to give a critical account of the philosophical views of Peirce and James on the one side, and Moore and Russell on the other. Both for historical reasons, and because I knew least about him, I started with Peirce. In going through his works in detail I found so many points of difficulty and interest that I was drawn into writing about him at much greater length than I had intended. When the same turned out to be true of James, I decided that the first half of my plan was enough to be going on with; a critical examination of the philosophy of these two great pragmatists would make a large enough book on its own. I have not, however, entirely given up the idea of publishing a comparable study of the philosophy of Moore and Russell at some later date.

It has not been my aim to produce a work of historical scholarship. I have read the works of Peirce and James attentively, but I have not tried to situate them in the history of philosophy, nor have I studied the writings of other commentators, to see how far their interpretations agree with mine. If this book contains passages in which other commentators discover an echo of their own published views, I can, therefore, only ask them to accept my assurance that the plagiarism is unconscious. I have tried to make up my own mind about what Peirce and James were saying and I have also felt free to develop my own theories on some of the main issues which they raise.

Finally, my thanks are due to Professor Richard Wollheim for saving me from an inconsistency in my account of Peirce's theory of probable inference, to Mrs. Rosanne Richardson for typing the first three sections of this book and to Mrs. Guida Crowley both for typing the remainder and for her help in compiling the index and correcting the proofs.

A. J. AYER

10 Regent's Park Terrace
London, N.W.1
5 November 1967

CHARLES SANDERS PEIRCE

CHAPTER ONE

INTRODUCTION

THOUGH the philosophical movement which is known as Pragmatism is thought to be a distinctly American product of the late nineteenth century, it has fairly deep roots in the history of philosophy. In one form, indeed, it may be said to go back to Protagoras. It was, however, the American philosopher, Charles Sanders Peirce, who introduced the term 'pragmatism' into philosophical literature: and he was the first to develop Pragmatism into a comprehensive system.

Peirce, who was born in 1839 and died in 1914, was the son of Benjamin Peirce, a professor of mathematics and astronomy at the University of Harvard. His work attracted little attention in his own lifetime, though he published quite a large number of articles and reviews in various philosophical and scientific journals. But none of the many books which he planned were brought to completion except for an early work on photometrics, and a treatise on logic for which he was unable to find a publisher; and he failed to secure a permanent academic position, though he held a lectureship in logic for five years at Johns Hopkins University, and occasionally gave lecture courses at Harvard. His main employment was as an official in the United States Coast and Geodetic Survey. He was a fellow Harvard undergraduate and life-long friend of William James, on whom he had a strong philosophical influence, and it was through James that his ideas became more widely known, though, as we shall see, James misunderstood or at any rate transformed them to a serious extent. It was, indeed, because the term 'pragmatism' had come to be associated with the views of William James and with those of such publicists of the movement as John Dewey, the Italian Papini, and the Oxford Humanist F. C. S. Schiller, that Peirce decided in his later years to give his system the name of 'pragmaticism', remarking that this name was ugly enough to be safe from kidnappers. In fact, not only has the name not been kidnapped, but it has failed to gain currency even in the use for which Peirce designed it. Accordingly, I shall follow the example of other writers in preferring Peirce's earlier to his later coinage, and continue to classify him as a pragmatist.

After Peirce's death, his manuscripts, of which there was a great quantity, came into the possession of the department of philosophy at Harvard, which eventually undertook to bring out a complete edition of his works. Six large volumes of the *Collected Papers* appeared between 1931 and 1935, under the editorship of Professors Hartshorne and Weiss, and the undertaking has now been completed with the appearance in 1958 of two further volumes, edited by Professor Burks. If these volumes do not make easy reading, it is not the fault of their editors but rather a consequence of Peirce's crabbed style, his predilection for coining his own technical terms, and his practice of giving many different versions of the same argument and making repeated attempts at the same set of problems. In all these respects Peirce is reminiscent of Jeremy Bentham. For those who are daunted by the bulk and prolixity of the collected works, a selection of twenty eight of the most characteristic and important papers is to be found in a book called *The Philosophy of Peirce* and edited by Professor Buchler. An earlier selection called *Chance, Love and Logic*, which appeared in 1921, is also of historical interest since it first brought Peirce's work to the notice of English philosophers, who had until then derived their mainly unfavourable ideas of pragmatism from the more popular and polemical writings of James and Schiller.

One of the qualities for which Peirce is most distinguished, again like Jeremy Bentham but on an even broader scale, is his great versatility. He thought of himself primarily as a logician, in a sense in which logic comprehended the analysis of all processes of thought and an enquiry into the conditions of their significance and truth, rather than just the formal theory of valid deductive reasoning. But whereas other pragmatists, like James and Dewey and Schiller, were indifferent or even hostile to logic in its purely formal aspect, Peirce, who regarded formal logic as a branch of mathematics, was one of the pioneers in its modern development. He was among the first to see the possibilities of Boolean algebra, he anticipated Sheffer in the discovery of the stroke-function and Wittgenstein in the idea that the laws of logic had no factual content, and he did original and very influential work in the logic of relations. As a logician in the broader sense, he improved upon earlier versions of the frequency theory of probability, he invented the idea of justifying induction as a method which must lead to success in the long run, if success is attainable at all, and he developed a highly original, intricate and comprehensive classification of signs. He was familiar, to an extent that few philosophers are, with the methods and conclusions of the natural sciences and himself engaged in scientific research. We shall indeed find that the theory of scientific method for which Professor Popper has become justly celebrated in our own times was very largely anticipated by Peirce. Finally, he had his own branch of metaphysics, which was based on a deep and wide knowledge of the history of philosophy. The originality and many-sidedness of his work make him difficult to label, but I think that those commentators who treat him as a radical empiricist are mainly in the right. It is, however, worth noting that the philosophers whom he himself most greatly admired, next to Aristotle, were Duns Scotus, Kant and Hegel. As we shall see, he actually professed to follow Duns Scotus in accepting a form of scholastic realism, and at the same time agreed with Kant in making knowledge relative to the constitution of the human mind and limiting it to the field of possible experience. I do not know that he took over any specific doctrines from Hegel whose system he regarded as being very largely vitiated by Hegel's incompetence in logic, but he had respect for Hegel's insight into the nature of phenomena, and shared what one might call the historicity of his outlook. One of the main features of pragmatism, which comes out not only in Peirce, but also in James and Dewey and their followers, is that it is a dynamic philosophy. In contrast to philosophers like Plato and Descartes who adopt the standpoint of a pure intelligence in contemplation of eternal verities, the pragmatists put themselves in the position of an enquirer adapting himself to and helping to modify a changing world. This is a point which has always to be borne in mind, if their work is to be sympathetically understood.

I shall not here attempt to cover the whole range of Peirce's thought. I shall say nothing about the technical aspects of his contributions to formal logic and the theory of probability; I shall not go very thoroughly into the more speculative parts of his metaphysics, nor shall I enter into all the details of his elaborate theory of signs. My object is to expound and criticize what I take to be the central themes of his pragmatism. The picture which I shall present of his philosophical work will therefore be incomplete, but since its pragmatic elements, when taken as incorporating his theory of scientific method, seem to me to constitute the structure of an edifice for which the formal logic provides the cement and the metaphysics a somewhat florid decoration, I do not think that it will be seriously distorted.

CHAPTER TWO

THE BASES OF PEIRCE'S PRAGMATISM

A. HIS THEORY OF TRUTH

Peirce began to develop his Pragmatism in the eighteen-seventies. He brought it to the notice of the world in the first two of a series of papers, entitled 'Illustrations of the Logic of Science', which he started contributing to the *Popular Science Monthly* in 1877. The first of these papers is called 'The Fixation of Belief' and the second 'How to Make Our Ideas Clear'. Since they lay down the central lines which Peirce continued to follow, I shall summarize them in some detail. We shall in fact find that all his later philosophy, at least in its pragmatic aspect, is a development or modification of the ideas which they contain.

In 'The Fixation of Belief', after some remarks on scientific method in which he disparages Bacon, quoting the dictum of Harvey's 'a genuine man of science' that Bacon wrote on science like a Lord Chancellor, Peirce declares that 'the object of reasoning is to find out, from the consideration of what we already know, something else which we do not know'. Consequently, the criterion of good reasoning is that given true premises, we employ it to arrive at true conclusions. It follows that the question of validity is a question of fact and not just a matter of what we happen to think. 'A being the facts stated in the premisses and B being that concluded, the question is, whether these facts really are so related that if A were B would generally be. If so, the inference is valid; if not, not. It is not in the least the question whether, when the premisses are accepted by the mind, we feel an impulse to accept the conclusion also. It is true that we do generally reason correctly by nature. But that is an accident; the true conclusion would remain true if we had no impulse to accept it; and the false one would remain false, though we could not resist the tendency to believe in it.'[1]

This is a remarkable passage in that it runs counter to what, thanks to William James, is commonly thought to be the main feature of the pragmatic theory of truth, namely the equation of true propositions with those that we find it useful to believe. In fact, Peirce never makes this equation and is inclined rather to contrast utility with truth. Even so we shall find that he does not look upon truth as being quite so objective as this passage might be taken to suggest. He does hold the validity of inference to be objective, in the sense that a form of inference is validated by its power to convey truth from premises to conclusion, whether we recognize that it has this power or not. Thus he repeatedly pours scorn on the German logicians of his time for appealing to self-evidence, pointing out that the fact that one may 'feel' an inference to be valid is by no means a guarantee that it really is so. At the same time he does not treat the truth of the premises and conclusions themselves as something altogether independent of our acceptance of them. He does hold it to be independent of their acceptance by any given person, or even by the generality of persons at any given time. But this is only because a proposition which is accepted by one person may not be accepted by others, or because a proposition which is generally accepted at one time may not be generally accepted at a later time, or at the very least because a proposition which is generally accepted at one time and never subsequently rejected might nevertheless be rejected in the long run if it continued to be made subject to scientific scrutiny. As we shall see in a moment, the extent to which Peirce wishes to tie the truth of a proposition to its acceptance is a matter on which he is not entirely clear, and perhaps not wholly consistent, but I think it fair to say that he does not hold truth to be objective if this is taken to imply that the question whether a proposition is true can be entirely dissociated from the question whether it is believed.

For anything to be an inference it is essential, in Peirce's view,

[1] V 365. References are to volumes and numbered paragraphs of the *Collected Papers*.

that it be determined by some habit of mind. This is his way of making the point that when a conclusion is inferred from given premisses, the passage from premisses to conclusion must be governed by some general principle. As he puts it, 'the particular habit of mind which governs this or that inference may be formulated in a proposition whose truth depends on the validity of the inference which the habit determines: and such a formula is called a *guiding principle* of inference'.[1] These guiding principles need not be principles of logic: they may be generalizations of any kind. An example that Peirce gives is that of observing that a rotating disk of copper comes quickly to rest when placed between the poles of a magnet, and inferring that this will happen with every disk of copper. The guiding principle in this case, he says, is that what is true of one piece of copper is true of another, and this is plainly not a principle of logic. On the other hand, it would also be possible for us to take the proposition that what is true of one piece of copper is true of another, not as a principle of inference but as a premiss of the argument, and in that case our principle of inference would be formal; it would be the necessary proposition that if what is true of one member of a class is true of any other and some predicate is satisfied by one member of the class, the same predicate is satisfied by all of them. In the case where the guiding principle of the inference is a formal principle of logic, the premisses themselves necessitate the conclusion, so that Peirce is able to make it the distinctive mark of a logical or formal principle that the premisses of the valid arguments which it governs are complete without it.[2] This differentiates them effectively from material principles, which have to be added to the premisses of the arguments which they govern if their conclusions are to be necessitated. In either case it may be said that what is required for the inference to be valid is just that its guiding principle be true, though the sense in which logical principles can be true is held by Peirce to be degenerate. His reason for this, in his own words, is that 'every logical principle considered as an assertion will be found to be quite empty. The only thing it really enunciates is a rule of inference; considered as expressing truth, it is nothing.'[1] Nevertheless, for the purpose of expounding his theory of inference, he finds it convenient to speak of logical as well as of material principles as being true.

In the domain of formal logic, there is no approximation to validity. We have no use at all for principles of inference which are logically false. But the position is rather different when the principle is a material one. An empirical generalization which is not universally true may still be serviceable if the exceptions to it are rare. Admittedly, the inferences on which such a generalization operates as a guiding principle are not strictly valid: but we may still be able to rely on them to a considerable extent. This would apply, for instance, to the guiding principle in Peirce's example, which in the unrestricted form in which he states it is no doubt false. Nevertheless, as he remarks, 'such a guiding principle with regard to copper would be much safer than with regard to many other substances – brass, for example'.[2] The implication is that in the case of material inferences, it is not a question of all or nothing: a reasonable degree of safety is not to be despised. We may even allow our guiding principles to take the form of generalizations which are explicitly stated to hold not for all but only for most instances. In Peirce's view, the inferences which they govern can actually be valid, so long as we take the precaution of casting their conclusions into the form of statements of probability.

It is to be remarked that Peirce makes a very extended use of the concept of inference, since he employs it to cover any transition from one belief to another. Indeed, he goes even further to the point of maintaining that every sort of modification of consciousness is an inference. His ground for this, as we shall see, is that every experience embodies some interpretation, which itself must rest upon some general principle. We shall also see, however, that such a general principle is not always one that we are capable of making explicit.

Ideally then, we seek to pass from true premises to true conclusions, by means of true principles of inference. But the best that this comes to in practice is that we infer from premises which we

[1] II 467.   [2] V 367.

wholeheartedly believe to be true, in accordance with principles which we accept as valid, to conclusions which we also believe to be true. And even this standard cannot always be sustained. We fall prey to doubt, whether doubt of the premisses, or doubt of the principle of inference, or doubt of the conclusion, which in its turn casts doubt on either the premisses or the principle of inference. And then we wish to remove the doubt. For a state of belief, according to Peirce, is calm and satisfactory, whereas doubt is an irritant. Doubt causes a struggle to attain belief. And it is this struggle to attain belief that Peirce terms Inquiry.

It follows that the sole object of Inquiry is to allay doubt or, as Peirce puts it, to settle opinion. One might have thought that the object of Inquiry was to arrive not so much at settled opinions as at true opinions, but Peirce dismisses this objection as a fancy. 'Put this fancy to the test', he says, 'and it proves groundless; for as soon as a firm belief is reached we are entirely satisfied, whether the belief be true or false. And it is clear that nothing out of the sphere of our knowledge can be our object, for nothing which does not affect the mind can be the motive for mental effort. The most that can be maintained is that we seek for a belief that we shall *think* to be true. But we think each one of our beliefs to be true, and, indeed, it is mere tautology to say so.'[1]

The sense of this passage is not immediately clear. It might be taken to imply that we do not, or should not, allow our opinions to be disturbed by any qualms about their truth, but such a thesis would be quite foreign to the spirit of Peirce's thought. It is contradicted by his inveterate hostility to any form of dogmatism, and by his repeated exaltation of the disinterested pursuit of truth as one of the greatest of scientific virtues. Again, it might be supposed that Peirce was saying that the truth of a proposition consisted in its being believed, were it not that this is a position which he persistently rejects. Its denial is implied by his saying that we are satisfied with a firm belief, whether it be true or false, since this plainly allows for the possibility that a proposition which is firmly believed may not be true. But then how can he consistently maintain that the idea 'that we seek, not merely an

[1] V 375.

opinion, but a true opinion' is a fancy? The answer is that he is combining two theses which are indeed logically compatible, yet do in a manner pull in opposite directions. On the one hand he sees clearly enough that the truth of a proposition cannot consist in anybody's believing it. On the other hand, he also wishes to make the point that the distinction between what is true and what we believe to be true is one which we cannot actually apply to any of our own current beliefs.

I will try to explain this more fully. In support of the first thesis, it could be argued that there is an obvious logical objection to identifying the truth of a proposition with its being firmly believed, whether by oneself, or by most people, or even by everybody who ever considers it. For what account are we to give, on this view, of the truth of the proposition which states that some proposition *is* firmly believed by the persons in question? Shall we not want to say that this second-order proposition is true in an objective sense? But if we do say this, we shall be making an exception to the theory. And if an exception is to be allowed in this case, why not in others? Why should propositions to the effect that something is believed be the only ones that are allowed to be objectively true? To be consistent, therefore, it seems that we would have to say that the truth of the proposition *q*, which states that the original proposition *p* is firmly believed, consists in its being firmly believed in its turn. But then we are launched upon an infinite regress. For the proposition that *q* is firmly believed, or in other words that it is firmly believed that it is firmly believed that *p*, is itself a proposition the truth of which will have to consist in its being firmly believed, and so *ad infinitum*. At this point it might be objected that we get a similar regress if we make truth independent of belief. For having begun by saying that it is true that *p*, we can be asked whether it is true that it is true that *p*, whether it is true that it is true that it is true that *p*, and so once more *ad infinitum*. But here the regress is harmless, for the very good reason that nothing obliges us to embark upon it or prevents us, if we do embark upon it, from stopping at any point we choose. If we are in a position to assert that *p* is true in an objective sense, we

set it up, as it were, on solid ground. To go on to assert that it is
true that it is true that p would add nothing to p's security, since
it would take us no further than the point from which we started.
The propositions which we should successively reach in this way
would be technically different from one another but the material
content of each member of the series would be exactly the same
as that of its predecessor; to be told that it is true that p is true is
to be told no more than that p is true. Consequently, from the
point of view of certifying the proposition on which it starts to
operate, the prolongation of this series neither secures any advantage nor fulfils any need. On the other hand, if we have taken the
view that the truth of a proposition p consists in its being firmly
believed, then we can only certify p to the extent that we are in a
position to say that it *is* firmly believed, and since our theory puts
us in the same difficulty with regard to the truth of this further
proposition, the infinite regress is forced upon us. What makes
it vicious is that however far we advance along it, we never reach
the solid ground of fact.

This is a standard form of argument against anything other than
what I have called an objective theory of truth, and I have no
doubt that it is valid. Even so we must be careful not to over-
estimate its force. What it establishes, in this instance, is that to
say that a proposition is believed, no matter by whom, can never
be formally equivalent to saying that it is true. What it does not
establish is that this can never in practice come to the same thing.
It debars us from holding that what we mean by saying that a
proposition is true is just that we believe it, but, as we shall see in
a moment, it does not debar us from holding that, so far as we
are concerned, the question what propositions are true comes
down to the question what we are to believe.

Peirce himself takes a shorter way to reach the same conclusion.
One of his fundamental tenets is that all our beliefs are fallible,
and from this it follows immediately that the fact that a proposition is believed, however strongly and by however many people,
is never sufficient to establish its truth. Not all philosophers,
indeed, would take this quite so far as Peirce. There are those who
think that we cannot be mistaken about the character of our

current thoughts and feelings, or of what is immediately present to our senses: and others have held that we have an infallible apprehension of the truth of such necessary propositions as those of simple arithmetic. But Peirce's view, as we shall see, is that even the most primitive judgements of perception, or the simplest characterizations of one's own thoughts and feelings, depend on processes of interpretation; and where there is interpretation, the possibility of misinterpretation can never be excluded. He does hold that we are well entitled to feel certain about the truth ot such necessary propositions as that two and two make four. For what makes such propositions necessary is that mathematics is our own construction; and if we are careful, we ought not to go astray in surveying the details of our own handiwork. Nevertheless it is an established fact that people do make mistakes in mathematics, and there is theoretically no limit to the extent to which such mistakes can go. It is not inconceivable that future experience should show us that we had been deluded in supposing that two and two invariably make four. This does not mean that we ought to regard such propositions as seriously open to doubt. Peirce is very scornful of the philosophical technique of feigning doubts which we do not genuinely feel. It is one of the many charges that he brings against Descartes. His point is just that there can be no such thing as an absolute guarantee of truth and therefore no virtue in appealing to self-evidence. Even the propositions in which we feel the most complete confidence are not sacrosanct.

But while he recognizes and indeed insists that propositions are not made true by our believing them, this does not lead Peirce to the conclusion that we can have a concept of truth which is altogether independent of the concept of belief. For now the opposing thesis comes into play. We can find a use for the distinction between what is true and what is believed to be true in the case of beliefs which are held by others, or in the case of beliefs which we ourselves have held in the past; I can say of someone else that he believes that P but he is mistaken; I can say of myself that I used to believe so and so but I now realize that I was wrong. But what this comes to in practice is that I hold a belief which is incompatible with his, or that I now disbelieve what I believed in the past. In the case of my present beliefs, the distinction is quite inoperative. For what I believe, I believe to be true, and what I take to be true is what I believe. I can, and indeed must, allow for the possibility that even my present beliefs are mistaken. But again all that this comes to in practice is that I can envisage having occasion to revise them.

An illustration may bring this out more clearly. Suppose that someone were asked to take two sheets of paper and write down on one of them a list of true propositions and on the other a list of propositions which he firmly believed, with the proviso that the lists were to be mutually exclusive, that is, that no true propositions were to figure on the list of those that he firmly believed, and none that he believed on the list of true propositions, the assignment is one that he could not rationally carry out. What he is asked to do is not self-contradictory. For it is conceivable, and indeed probable, that among the propositions which he firmly believes there are some that are false, and certainly there will be a great many true propositions which he does not believe, if only because he has never considered them or never made up his mind about them. So he might fulfil his task by accident. In compiling the list of propositions which he firmly believed, he might happen to choose only those that were in fact false, and in compiling the list of propositions which he did not believe he might happen to choose only those that were true. But the point is that he could do it only by accident: he could not be following any rational procedure. He could not say, or rather he could not judge that 'Such and such propositions, which I firmly believe, are false' or 'Such and such propositions are true, but I don't believe them'. Not that either of these judgements would be self-contradictory. In each case, it may well be that both components of the conjunction are true, that the man does firmly believe the propositions which he mentions and they are false, or that they are true and he does not believe them. But while we can say this about him, he cannot significantly say it about himself, or rather, he can say it only retrospectively. And this is not just because of

the social convention which ensures that if one makes an assertion
in a certain tone of voice one is letting it be understood that one
believes it, so that if I were to open a conversation by saying 'It
will rain this morning but I don't believe that it will', my auditors
would consider me eccentric even though I might be telling them
the truth. It is rather that if anyone is asked for examples of true
or false propositions, the best that he can do to satisfy the request
is to mention propositions which he firmly believes or dis-
believes.

The fact that the task of compiling my two lists could be
achieved by accident shows one again that the question whether
a given proposition is true is logically independent of the question
whether anyone believes it: but the fact that it could not be
achieved by any rational procedure shows also that the distinction
between what is true and what we believe to be true is one to
which we cannot ourselves give any practical effect. And Peirce
is inclined to make even more of the second point than he does
of the first. This comes out most forcibly in one of the last pieces
that he published, an article called 'What Pragmatism Is', which
appeared in the Monist in 1905. He remarks that there are one or
two doctrines 'without the previous acceptance of which pragmaticism itself would be a nullity' and goes on to say that 'they
might all be included under the vague maxim, "Dismiss make-
believes" '. 'Philosophers of very diverse stripes', he continues,
'propose that philosophy shall take its start from one or another
state of mind, in which no man, least of all a beginner in philosophy, actually is. One proposes that you shall begin by doubting
everything, and says there is only one thing that you cannot
doubt, as if doubting were "as easy as lying".' This is, of course,
a malicious reference to the Cogito of Descartes. 'Another proposes that we should begin by observing "the first impressions
of sense", forgetting that our very percepts are the result of
cognitive elaboration. But in truth, there is but one state of mind
from which you can "set out", namely, the very state of mind
in which you actually find yourself at the time you do "set out" –
a state in which you are laden with an immense mass of cognition
already formed, of which you cannot divest yourself if you

would: and who knows whether, if you could, you would not have made all knowledge impossible to yourself?'[1]

In short, there are practical limits to what anyone can really bring himself to doubt; and what a man does not doubt, he takes to be incontrovertibly true. But surely he must admit that he is fallible; it is at any rate possible that some of the propositions which he doubts are true and that some of those which he does not doubt are false. Yes indeed, but unless he seriously expects to discover that his assessment of these propositions is mistaken, this admission is only a piece of make-believe. 'You only puzzle yourself', says Peirce, 'by talking of this metaphysical "truth" and metaphysical "falsity", that you know nothing about. All you can have any dealings with are your doubts and beliefs, with the course of life that forces new beliefs on you and gives you power to doubt old beliefs. If your terms "truth" and "falsity" are taken in such senses as to be definable in terms of doubt and belief and the course of experience (as for example they would be, if you were to define the "truth" as that to a belief in which belief would tend if it were to tend indefinitely towards absolute fixity), well and good: in that case you are only talking about doubt and belief. But if by truth and falsity you mean something not definable in terms of doubt and belief in any way, then you are talking of entities of whose existence you can know nothing, and which Ockham's razor would clean shave off. Your problems would be greatly simplified, if, instead of saying that you want to know the "Truth", you were simply to say that you want to attain a state of belief unassailable by doubt.'[1]

But how is this state of confidence to be attained? In 'The Fixation of Belief', Peirce declares that there are just four methods of stabilizing one's opinions. He calls them the method of tenacity, the method of authority, the *a priori* method, and the method of science. His procedure is to discredit the first three of these methods in the interests of the fourth.

The method of tenacity, which is quite widely practised, is that of holding on to one's beliefs, for example, the beliefs that one has acquired through conditioning in childhood, and shutting one's eyes to any evidence that might tend to weaken them. Peirce's objection to this is not that it is an improper proceeding in itself. If someone succeeds in 'keeping out of view all that might cause a change in his opinions' Peirce says that he does not see what can be said against his doing so. 'It would be an egotistical impertinence to object that this procedure is irrational, for that only amounts to saying that his method of settling belief is not ours. He does not propose to himself to be rational, . . . so let him think as he pleases.'[1] What is wrong with this method, in Peirce's view, is that except perhaps for hermits it is ineffective. If one comes into contact with other people, one is bound to discover that some of them at least think differently, and then one's confidence in one's beliefs will be shaken.

This will happen much less easily, however, if one's beliefs are conventional and backed by social sanctions, and for this reason the second method, the method of authority, is greatly superior to the first. It is, indeed, the traditional method of securing agreement on matters of religious, political and moral doctrine, and in the hands of Church and State, with an adequate provision of force and fraud, it has achieved very considerable results. The fatal defect which Peirce ascribes to it is that 'no institution can undertake to regulate opinions on every subject'.[2] There must be some matters on which men are left free to think for themselves and this will lead some of them, and in the end enough of them, to question the dogmas which have been forced upon them. It seems to me that this conclusion may be a little over-optimistic, especially with modern techniques of propaganda, but there is some historical justification for it.

The third, or *a priori*, method has been mainly practised by philosophers. It is that of accepting systems of beliefs on the ground that 'their fundamental propositions are "agreeable to reason".'[3] This is the method of Descartes with his reliance on clear and distinct perception, a theory of which Peirce remarks that the world 'has quite distinctly come to the conclusion that it is utter nonsense'. It is also to some extent the method of Kant who is scorned by Peirce for maintaining that what there is a

[1] V 377.   [2] V 381.   [3] V 382.

very decided and general inclination to believe must be a necessity of thought. 'The dry-rot of reason in the seminaries has gone to the point where such stuff is held to be admirable argumentation.'[1] This is undoubtedly unfair to Kant if not to the seminaries, though I think that Peirce is right in being distrustful of *a priori* anthropology.

In spite of these harsh judgements of the philosophers who have employed it, Peirce admits that the *a priori* method is 'far more intellectual and respectable from the point of view of reason' than its predecessors. It is, however, even less effective as a means of fixing beliefs. For it subjects Inquiry to the fluctuations of taste, which is no more stable intellectually than it is in other fields. What seems self-evident to one man does not to another: what seems self-evident at one period does not at another. 'The opinions which today seem most unshakeable are found tomorrow to be out of fashion.' They are even more changeable than we realize, because we still go on using phrases when the opinions which they were tailored for have become defunct. Here Peirce gives the interesting example of our persisting in talking about cause and effect 'although in the mechanical world the opinion that the phrase was meant to express was shelved long ago'.[2] He is thinking of the fact that, according to the laws of classical mechanics, there is no ground for stipulating that the cause must precede the effect in time; if the past determines the future, the future equally determines the past. It should, however, be noted that this very fact that all mechanical processes are reversible was one of the main reasons why Peirce came to hold that not all the processes in nature are governed by mechanical laws.

Its rivals having been shown to be inadequate, as a means of ensuring the fixity of belief, the way is now left open for Peirce's own candidate, the method of science. Its great merit, in his eyes, is that it is the only one of the four methods which sets a public standard of truth and frees it from dependence on our individual fancies and caprices: for whether you call them rational insights, or mystical intuitions, or religious revelations, they are still fancies

[1] Ibid.   [2] Ibid.

and caprices. The fundamental hypothesis, on which the method rests, is this: 'There are Real things, whose characters are entirely independent of our opinions about them: these Reals affect our senses according to regular laws, and, though our sensations are as different as are our relations to the objects, yet, by taking advantage of the laws of perception, we can ascertain by reasoning how things really and truly are; and any man, if he have sufficient experience and he reason enough about it, will be led to the one True conclusion.'[1]

But how is this hypothesis to be justified? How can we know that there are real things? To many contemporary philosophers, this would seem an improper question. For what would it be like, they would ask, for there not to be real things? The mere fact that we have a use, or rather several uses, for the word 'real', that we are able to contrast what is real with what is imaginary, or illusory, or spurious, or artificial, shows that in one sense or another there must be real things. But, as I have tried to show elsewhere,[2] this short way with the sceptic is very far from achieving all that its advocates have supposed. The most that it can be held to prove is that the word in question corresponds to something in the experience of those who use it; but the interpretation which they put upon this experience, the theory or the conceptual system in which the word is embedded, remains entirely open to criticism. We are surely not obliged to swallow any form of superstition, merely because it has secured a foothold in the 'ordinary language' of its devotees.

In short, when it comes to conceptual questions, and especially the kind of conceptual questions which are raised by philosophers, the appeal to customary usage is generally found to be beside the point, and this is so in the present instance. For what Peirce is seeking is not a justification of the hypothesis that there are real men, as opposed to characters in fiction, or real snakes as opposed to those which appear in the illusions of drunkards, or real coins as opposed to counterfeits; if he were, it would be sufficient to call

[1] V 384.
[2] See my essay on 'Metaphysics and Common-Sense' in *Metaphysics*, ed. W. E. Kennick and Morris Lazerowitz (New Jersey, 1966).

his attention to the empirical facts. What he wants to justify is the use of a conceptual system which makes provision for external objects, in the sense that it admits the postulate that things exist independently of our thinking about them or perceiving them. Now this is something for which a justification can reasonably be asked. For it cannot be taken for granted that this is the only, or even, from all points of view, the most satisfactory way of interpreting our experiences. In a system, like Berkeley's, where the existence of what we ordinarily regard as external objects is made to depend upon their being perceived, the empirical distinctions which the word 'real' is used to mark can equally well be made. It may be, indeed, that Berkeley's system is incoherent. It may be that the postulation of real things, in Peirce's sense, is an indispensable feature of any adequate interpretation of our experience. But this is not something that can simply be assumed without question. It is a philosophical thesis which needs to be supported.

In favour of the hypothesis that there are real things, Peirce himself adduces four not very convincing arguments. The first of them, which is perhaps the strongest, is that while scientific investigation cannot prove this hypothesis to be true, for the reason that it presupposes it, it also will not work against it. Investigation can show that this or that thing is not real, but not that nothing is real. But this means that practice of the scientific method does not lead to doubt of it, whereas it is inherent in the other methods that the practice of them does lead to a loss of confidence in them.

The logical point on which Peirce is relying here is that what a method presupposes it does not put in question. If it is a presupposition of scientific method that 'Reals affect our senses according to regular laws', the employment of it may indeed reveal to us at any stage that the laws are not what we had taken them to be, but it cannot consistently lead us to the conclusion that there are no such laws at all. If we failed to find them we are bound to conclude, so long as we adhere to the method, that they still remain to be discovered. But while this argument is formally sound, it does not bear the weight which Peirce lays on it. For even if the use of the method could not strictly refute its presuppositions, it might still work in such a way as to discredit them. Suppose that our experiences were such that the regularities in the behaviour of things which we thought that we had discovered constantly broke down in unpredictable ways; we surely then might come to doubt scientific method through the practice of it. Finding that it consistently disappointed our expectations, we might be led to rely more strongly on our fancies. The situation which might lead to such a result is not easy to envisage, especially in any detail, but I am not persuaded that the possibility of it can be excluded *a priori*; and if it cannot be excluded, Peirce's argument fails. I shall, however, return to this point when I come to examine his philosophy of science.

The second argument is that the only reason why we need a method for fixing belief is that our inability to decide between conflicting propositions is a source of dissatisfaction to us. But this itself implies that we think there is a truth to be discovered. Unless we believed that there was a correct answer of which we were ignorant, we should not feel dissatisfied. It follows that nobody can seriously doubt that there are real things. So the hypothesis is not one which we shall be led to doubt through the workings of the social impulse.

This is a curious argument, and I think a fallacious one. It begs the question by assuming that it is only within a conceptual system of the sort which Peirce is advocating that propositions can be assigned a definite truth-value. But it is certainly not obvious that philosophers who deny that there are real things, in Peirce's sense, are thereby debarred from holding that there can be true or false answers to questions about matters of fact. And in any case why should it be assumed that doubts which relate to matters of fact are the only serious doubts that we can feel, or the only ones that can cause dissatisfaction? Do we not have serious doubts on matters of taste or policy? In the domain of ethics or aesthetics, people who hold that judgements of value are objectively neither true nor false may still be in serious doubt concerning the principles or standards that they should adopt. Indeed this applies to Peirce himself, since, here again anticipating modern thought, he holds that the 'fundamental problem of ethics is: "What am I prepared deliberately to accept as the statement of what I want to do, what am I to aim at, what am I after?" [1] Surely such questions can give rise to doubt. It is true that our attempts to resolve them are bound up with our beliefs about matters of fact. Even so, the fundamental decisions have to be taken: and when one is trying to take them, it may be a source of great dissatisfaction that one finds it difficult to make up one's mind.

The next of Peirce's points is somewhat trifling. It is that 'everybody uses the scientific method about a great many things, and only ceases to use it when he does not know how to apply it'.[2] But it is not only lack of skill or knowledge that prevents people from approaching questions scientifically. There are also such other factors as conservatism, timidity and prejudice. And, even if it were now true that everybody employed scientific method to the extent of his ability, this has not always been the case and might not always continue to be so.

Finally, Peirce argues that 'experience of the method has not led us to doubt it, but, on the contrary, scientific investigation has had the most wonderful triumphs in the way of settling opinion'. It would be hard to quarrel with this as a statement of historical fact, but in the present context it does raise two contentious questions. The first, to which I shall return in a moment, is that if a method of fixing belief is to be justified by an appeal to fact, then we have to consider how the existence of the facts themselves is being determined. The second, which will come up in our examination of Peirce's philosophy of science, is that we have also to consider whether the fact that a method has been successful in the past is a sufficient basis for concluding that it will also be successful in the future.

In reviewing this whole discussion, one is left with the impression that Peirce is being slightly disingenuous. His insistence that all that is in question is the most effective method of fixing belief does not ring entirely true, and the credit which he gives to the methods of tenacity and authority and to the *a priori* method appears largely ironical. And in the end he comes out into the

[1] II 198.   [2] V 384.

open. Having noted the advantages of the other methods, the strength, simplicity and directness of the method of tenacity, the social security which is obtained by the method of authority, the comfortable conclusions of the *a priori* method, he remarks that a man should then consider 'that, after all, he wishes his opinions to coincide with the facts, and that there is no reason why the results of those three first methods should do so. To bring about this effect is the prerogative of the method of science.'[1]

But what meaning can Peirce attach to the statement that an opinion does, or does not, coincide with fact? Or to put it another way, how does he suppose that we can discover whether our opinions coincide with fact or not? By pursuing scientific method. But the other methods also result in beliefs which coincide with what they would lead us to accept as fact, and the scientific method does no more. The difference is that if we follow one of the other methods we may have to shut our eyes to a great deal that we should otherwise be led to believe. We may have to inhibit our inclinations to form certain beliefs on the basis of our sense-experiences. To the extent that we cannot avoid having the sense-experiences which would naturally give rise to such beliefs, we shall have to interpret them differently. But this can be done, and in some measure *is* done, as Peirce acknowledges. We may concede to him that it cannot be done *ad libitum*. Some unwelcome facts will force their way in. Indeed, without a modicum of science, we could not keep ourselves alive. But this concession does not commit us to very much, certainly not to the acceptance of the scientific method in every field of thought. It is true also that if we adhere to one of the other methods we shall find ourselves believing many things which, if we were to investigate them, we should discover to be false. But again, why should we investigate? Why should we make experiments? Because that is the way to discover what the world is like. But this begs the question. All that we are entitled to say is that it is the scientific way to discover what the world is like.

What this comes to, in short, is that the method of science is victor in its own cause. We can safely conclude that the scientific method is the only one that gives us a good chance of having our opinions coincide with fact, provided that we have already accepted the scientific point of view, which means, among other things, that we are using scientific method to determine what are the facts with which our opinions have to coincide. But then the acceptance of the scientific point of view is itself a decision. In the broad sense, in which any fundamental decision which affects the conduct of our lives can be said to come within the sphere of morals, it is a moral choice.

This conclusion might not have been unwelcome to Peirce since he held that logic, in which he included the determination of the criteria of truth, was a normative science, and that as a normative science it was subordinate to ethics, which lays down principles of conduct, ethics in its turn being subordinate to aesthetics which, in Peirce's somewhat peculiar usage, is the normative science that concerns itself with ultimate ends. He does not, however, indicate in any detail how he thinks that logic is governed by ethics, beyond saying that the practice of logic requires self-control, which is a moral quality, and that there is a moral value in the pursuit of truth. But this does not explain why morality should require that truth be assessed in scientific terms.

Nevertheless, if we look at what he says about the character of scientific research, I think it comes out fairly clearly that the main reason why he thinks we should decide in favour of the method of science is that it is the one best adapted to our social needs. The assumption is that we wish to find ourselves in agreement with one another. Now not only is it characteristic of the method of science that nothing is acceptable even as a fact of observation unless it is, or at least is capable of being, publicly attested, but, according to Peirce, the practice of the method by all inquirers must in the long run lead to all disputed questions being settled. They will be settled in the sense that we shall eventually come to the point where there are no hypotheses but those that are generally accepted, and all the generally accepted hypotheses agree as a body with all the accredited experimental facts. Thus, that truth will prevail is a logical necessity; and for this reason truth can be defined as that which will prevail, and reality as its correlate. So Peirce is able to say: 'The opinion which is fated to be ultimately agreed to by all who investigate, is what we mean by the truth, and the object represented in this opinion is the real.'[1]

This last point is very dubious. Briefly, the idea is that the practice of scientific method ensures that theories are constantly put to the test of observation and that they are constantly adjusted so as to stand in accordance with the known empirical facts. Consequently, if there are any laws which hold in the field of our experience – and what is totally outside the field of experience does not concern us, there is no sense indeed in our even supposing it to exist – we are eventually bound to come upon them. Moreover, it is a condition of our being able to raise this question at all that there should be such laws. For any world that is conceivable must be capable of being described in general terms, and whatever can be described in general terms is subject to law.

But, quite apart from the assumption that the laws are not too complex for us to grasp, we can only be sure that they will not evade us, if the process of inquiry is indefinitely prolonged. If no term is set to the length of the inquiry, then it is trivial to say that we shall end by discovering the laws, simply because it is assumed that the inquiry will continue until we do. But this is consistent with our failing to reach this end in any finite period that one cares to name, however long.[2] So if it is said that this end is unavoidable, it must be implied that the process of scientific inquiry is bound to continue indefinitely: that the human race will not cease to exist, or even relapse into barbarism, before this goal is attained. But of this there is no guarantee at all.

However, though Peirce sometimes seems to commit himself, as in the passage quoted, to the view that the scientific millennium is bound to come about in fact, he also very often writes as though he held its achievement to be no more than a hopeful possibility, or even something like a Kantian ideal of reason. Thus, in one of his later contributions to the *Monist*, he admits that 'we cannot be quite sure that the community will ever settle down to an unalterable conclusion upon any given question. Even if they do so for the most part, we have no reason to think the unanimity

[1] V 407.   [2] See below, Ch. 3 B.

will be quite complete, nor can we rationally presume that any overwhelming *consensus* of opinion will be reached upon every question. All that we are entitled to assume is in the form of a *hope* that such conclusion may be substantially reached concerning the particular questions with which our inquiries are busied.'[1] And in an unpublished *Survey of Pragmaticism* which he wrote towards the end of his life he declares himself to hold that 'truth's independence of individual opinions is due (so far as there is any "truth") to its being the predestined result to which sufficient inquiry *would* ultimately lead.'[2]

The idea that true propositions are those that we should agree in accepting if we were able to pursue our inquiries to their ideal limit is clearly a great improvement on the idea that true propositions are those that our descendants will in fact accept, but it still faces one obvious objection if it is to be taken as supplying a definition of truth. The objection is that if truth is made a matter of future agreement, even though this agreement be treated as an ideal which is never actually realized, an enormous number of propositions, which we shall wish to characterize as true or false, will not be able either to pass or fail the test, simply because their candidature will have lapsed. For it can hardly be supposed that even in the scientific millenium a complete historical record will have been kept of every particular event. Such humdrum questions as how many people there were on the beach today, what clothes I am now wearing, what my neighbour is having for his dinner, and countless others of this kind, to which there are in fact true answers, will not be a matter of future agreement or disagreement, simply because they will be quickly forgotten even by those whom they now concern. To keep a perfect record of the answers to them would not even be good scientific practice. It would be far too uneconomical.

Peirce does notice this objection in passing, but I cannot find that he offers any reply to it. I have the impression that he did not think it worth a serious reply. And the explanation of this is, I believe, that he was not much concerned with the truth of particular propositions of this kind: or rather, he thought that

[1] VI 610.   [2] V 495.

the determination of their truth did not present any awkward problem. He held, as we shall see, that our judgements of perception were virtually forced upon us. We might be led to revise them, but only because they could not hold their own against the weight of other judgements of perception which we were forced to accept. The only question that arises for us, therefore, is how these judgements are to be interpreted; that is, what inferences we are to draw from them; and the success or failure of an inference can only be measured by what happens in the future. The question of truth resolves itself accordingly into a question of method. What method will afford us the best chance of making our inferences accord with future facts? But what these facts turn out to be depends not only on one's own observations but also on those of other people. To put it another way, the experiences by which my inferences are tested will be not only those which I take to be indicative of the properties of physical objects, but also those which I interpret as proving that other people are having similar, or it may be different experiences; and I can only have confidence in the judgements which I make about physical objects, or indeed, as Peirce would say, in any judgements at all about matters of fact, if I have reason to think that they conform to the corresponding judgements that other people are making, or at any rate would make if they were placed in similar conditions. But this requires not only that our experiences be broadly similar but also that they be interpreted in similar fashion. Consequently, the method which we are seeking is one which if applied collectively to similar experiences will furnish similar results. And only the method of science satisfies this condition.

But, if this is what Peirce had in mind, it becomes more clear than ever that he is allowing the method of science to be judge in its own cause. For why should I make my judgements depend upon those which are made by other people? Or, if I do attach a value to this, why should I not insist on interpreting my experiences in such a way that the judgements which I ascribe to others coincide with mine? The answer is that if I take either of these courses, I shall be punished by the facts. Perceptual judgements will be forced upon me which my methods have not put me in a position to predict. In short, the world is so constituted that it is only on the basis of phenomena which are publicly attested, by relying on laws which are valid for everybody's experience, that my predictions can be assured a fair measure of success. So, fundamentally, the reason for relying on the method of science is that it corresponds to reality in a way in which its rivals do not. Peirce does his best to disguise this assumption by insisting on defining reality as what we shall, or should, ultimately agree in thinking; but the truth is that he is able to give this definition only because he tacitly assumes that the nature of our experience, and so of the world which it reveals to us, is such that it cannot withhold its secrets from a scientific approach. And in one significant passage he allows this to become explicit. In the sixth of the seven lectures on Pragmatism which he delivered at Harvard in 1903, lectures which William James described with some justification as 'flashes of brilliant light relieved against Cimmerian darkness', Peirce declares his faith that there is 'in experience, an element of Reasonableness to which we can train our own reason to conform more and more. If this were not the case, there could be no such thing as logical goodness or badness; and therefore we need not wait until it is proved that there is a reason operative in experience to which our own can approximate. We should at once hope that it is so, since in this hope lies the only possibility of any knowledge.'[1]

Why then was he not content to define truth, in the classical manner, as correspondence with reality? The answer, as should by now be clear, is that he was not interested in obtaining an adequate formal definition of truth. He thought that such a concept would be idle, that it would do no work for us; and, as we shall see in a moment, he assesses concepts wholly in terms of the work that they do. We must remember here, as I said at the outset, that the position which Peirce takes is that of a man engaged in a process of inquiry. It is of no help to such a man to be told, with classical propriety, that a proposition is true if what it states is so. He wants to know what is so, or rather he wants to know how best to find out what is so; which means, in concrete terms, how to

[1] V 160.

select his hypotheses and how to test them. It is not surprising, therefore, that Peirce's theory of truth should devolve into a theory of scientific method.

B. HIS THEORY OF MEANING

1. *What is Belief?*

At this point it will be instructive to turn to the second of Peirce's 'Illustrations of the Logic of Science', the paper entitled 'How to Make Our Ideas Clear', since it brings us a step nearer than the first to what are usually regarded as the characteristic doctrines of Pragmatism.

After making some more derogatory remarks about the use which Descartes, and also Leibniz, attempted to make of the notion of clear and distinct perception, Peirce reiterates the point which he made in the preceding paper 'that the action of thought is excited by the irritation of doubt, and ceases when belief is attained; so that the production of belief is the sole function of thought'.[1] But now he asks: 'What is belief?' This is an important question for him, since the notion of belief plays a central part in his philosophy, but he never goes to any great pains to answer it. All that he says here is that belief has just three properties: 'First, it is something that we are aware of; second, it appeases the irritation of doubt; and third, it involves the establishment in our nature of a rule of action, or, say for short, a *habit*.'[2]

Neither of the first two of these properties is of much assistance to us in arriving at an analysis of belief. To say that belief is something that we are aware of does not distinguish it from the many other things that we are aware of, quite apart from the fact that the notion of awareness itself stands in need of explanation. Moreover, it is doubtful whether it should be made a necessary condition of anyone's holding a belief that he be aware of it; and in the main it would appear that Peirce himself did not wish to make it so. Thus in the essay on 'What Pragmatism Is' he says that

[1] V 394.   [2] V 397.

'belief is not a momentary mode of consciousness: it is a habit of mind essentially enduring for some time, and mostly (at least) unconscious';[1] and in an article called 'A Neglected Argument for the Reality of God', which he contributed to the *Hibbert Journal* in 1908, his aim being to show that any normal man who pursues the right course of reflection will come to act as if God were real, he claims that 'to be deliberately and thoroughly prepared to shape one's conduct into conformity with a proposition is neither more nor less than the state of mind called Believing that pro-position, however long the conscious classification of it under that head be postponed'.[2] This would still allow him to make it a necessary condition of the existence of a belief that the person who holds it can become aware of it, even though he never in fact may be so: but clearly this does not take us very far.

It is even less helpful to try to define belief in terms of doubt: for how is doubt to be characterized in this connection, except in terms of one's not knowing what to believe? Neither is it a distinctive property of belief that it appeases the irritation of doubt; for this might be brought about in other ways, for instance by the use of drugs.

But in any case, it is the third property that Peirce takes to be the important one: 'The essence of belief', he says in the next paragraph, 'is the establishment of a habit; and different beliefs are distinguished by the different modes of action to which they give rise. If beliefs do not differ in this respect, if they appease the same doubt by producing the same rule of action, then no mere differences in the manner of consciousness of them can make them different beliefs, any more than playing a tune in different keys is playing different tunes.'[3]

Remarks of this kind are scattered throughout Peirce's work, and it is not easy to see exactly how we are meant to take them. One proposition which he certainly wishes to maintain is that it is a necessary condition of a belief's being sincerely held that the person to whom it is ascribed should be prepared to act upon it if the occasion arises. I think that this proposition would be generally accepted, with two reservations which take away much

[1] V 417.   [2] VI 467.   [3] V 398.

of its interest. The first is that there are many beliefs to which it would be inapplicable, since the occasions for acting on them never would arise. The second is that even in cases where a belief is sincerely held, the action which one would expect to follow from it may be inhibited because of the subject's timidity or moral scruples, or a temporary or habitual paralysis of the will. This might, however, be met by saying that even in this case the belief would have to make its presence felt by setting up some sort of conflict. There would have to be some signs of frustration, or some effort of repression, which might be counted as practical consequences of the belief. But of course the more widely we extend the concept of action, the less interesting the proposition is.

This applies also to the stronger and much more controversial thesis to which Peirce most often appears to be committed. On this view, the existence of a belief is taken not merely as entailing but as being simply equivalent to a propensity to action. It is maintained, in other words, that to say of someone that he believes such and such a proposition is to say no more and no less than that he is disposed to act in such and such ways. This is in many ways an attractive theory; much more so than its lazy competitor, that belief is a distinctive attitude of mind which is directed towards a proposition as its intentional object: but it does encounter rather serious objections.

To begin with, it is clear that one cannot properly define a belief in terms of the actions to which it actually gives rise: for a great many beliefs, beliefs which one holds about the past, for example, may never in fact give rise to any action at all. We have to put it hypothetically. We have to say that A's believing that p consists in the fact that he would act in the appropriate fashion, if the requisite conditions were fulfilled. This is not an objection in itself: or rather it would not be if we had a satisfactory analysis of contrary-to-fact conditionals: and this may be thought to be attainable.

But now comes the difficulty that the way in which a person would act under a given set of conditions depends, not only on his beliefs, but also on the sort of person that he is. Two persons may believe the same propositions and yet be disposed to act very differently under the same external conditions, because of their different purposes or characters. Consider, for example, the very different reactions upon different persons of a common belief in the imminence of war.

The only way that I can see of overcoming this obstacle, if we are to arrive at a general analysis of belief in purely behavioural terms, is to introduce the notion of utility and construe it in such a way that an action is said to be useful to a person A, in a given set of circumstances, if and only if it conduces to the fulfilment of whatever purposes, or set of purposes, he is then pursuing. This would have to be made much more precise. We might have to stipulate that A himself need not be conscious of the purpose in question: we should have to distinguish between more immediate and remoter ends: and we should have to make special provision for what might be called the standing factors in any given situation, that is, those that are equally conducive both to the achievement of one's purpose or to its frustration, in the sense that the fact that the earth is still warm enough to support human life is equally conducive to my catching my train or to my missing it, since it is a necessary condition of my doing anything at all. It is not at all clear to me that all such loopholes could be stopped: but if they could be we might attempt to analyse belief in some such terms as this: 'A believes that p' is equivalent to 'A is disposed to behave in a way that is useful to him if p and not useful if not p'.

But now an even more serious difficulty arises. For not only is the utility of A's behaviour quite likely to be affected by a number of factors of which he is entirely ignorant, but his behaviour in any actual situation will almost invariably depend not only on his belief in a given proposition p, but also on his belief in various other propositions. And then we have to reckon with the possibility that his purpose is frustrated, in spite of the truth of p, because one or more of these other propositions is false. Consider, for example, the case of a doctor who believes that his patient has such and such a disease and wishes to cure him of it, but being an unskilful doctor applies the treatment which would be appropriate to a different disease and makes the patient worse. If the analysis of belief which I have been sketching were correct we should have to conclude that the doctor really believed that his patient was suffering not from the disease which he ascribed to him but from that to which his treatment was appropriate; a way of reasoning which would go a long way towards enhancing the prestige of doctors, were it not manifestly absurd. It is clear that we could find a great many counter-examples of this type, and I do not see how the theory could be modified to meet them.

This does not mean, however, that we are forced entirely to abandon this method of approach. Even if it is not possible to find a satisfactory general formula for the analysis of belief in behavioural terms, it could still be held that a purely behavioural account could be given of any belief which a particular person held in a particular situation. For to the extent that we are able to specify the subject's other relevant beliefs, we can provide for their being false by making the utility of his action depend upon the states of affairs that would exist if they were true. Thus, in our example of the inefficient doctor, we could say that his belief that his patient had the disease in question consisted in the fact that he behaved in a way which was useful if the patient had the disease and not useful if he had not, this being subject to the further condition that the given treatment does in general cure this disease. Since the equation is not supposed to hold unless the further condition is satisfied, the fact that it is not satisfied does not ruin the analysis. This is clearly no way of obtaining a general definition of belief, but it might enable us to deal severally with A's belief that p, A's belief that q, B's belief that p and so forth. Since there is no definite limit to the number of wayward beliefs which might have to be provided for, I do not think that, even in particular cases, we could expect to tell a behavioural story of which we could say that it was necessary that this be true for A to believe that p, but we might expect to be able to tell one that was sufficient. If this is correct, the strongest claim that can reasonably be made for the behavioural theory is that it is in a position to furnish specimen cases of any type of belief. Though this is less than most of its advocates have hoped for, it would be quite a significant result. It is, however, still far from being established that even this more moderate ambition can be satisfied.

One well-known objection, to which I am not clear how much weight should be attached, is that whereas one may have to find out what other people believe by noting their behaviour, this does not appear to be necessary in the case of one's own beliefs. It does not seem that I have to consider how I should behave in various hypothetical situations in order to discover what I believe, and when I do know what I believe it does not seem that what I know is a set of hypothetical facts about my behaviour. Against this, it may be argued that the proof that the accounts which one gives of one's own beliefs refer at least partially to one's potential behaviour is that they may be overridden if one's behaviour does not bear them out. Thus, someone may think he believes that people who infringe certain moral rules will go to hell, but when we find him infringing them quite cheerfully and showing no apprehension even when he is seriously ill, we conclude that, whatever he may think about it, this is not a belief that he genuinely holds.

But even if this example were typical, it would prove no more than that one's disposition to behave in certain ways is one of the criteria for the assessment of belief, and that in some cases at least it is the dominant criterion. It would not prove that there is nothing more to a belief than its effect on one's behaviour, or even that this criterion is always dominant. An obvious class of cases in which it appears not to be dominant is that of one's beliefs concerning one's present sensations. Even if such beliefs are fallible, as we have seen that Peirce holds, it seems strange to regard them as even partial predictions of one's future behaviour. But the whole topic of immediate perception raises a special set of problems, to which we shall recur.

A common weakness in behavioural theories of belief is that the crucial term 'behaviour', or in Peirce's case 'action', is allowed to remain unduly vague. It is not made clear whether its range is meant to be restricted to physical movements or, if not, how much more it is permitted to comprise. It seems to me, however, that it would need to comprise a great deal more, if a theory of this kind is to make any show of being viable. For not only is it true, as we have already remarked, that we hold a great many beliefs on which we never do have any occasion to act in any full-blooded sense, but many of these, for example beliefs about events which are very distant from us in space or very remote from us in time in one direction or the other, are such that we never should have occasion to act on them under any realizable conditions. It would seem, therefore, that on a behavioural theory our belief in the existence of such events would have to be analysed in terms of our disposition to perform such 'actions' as writing down the appropriate words in an examination paper, or using them in conversation with others or even merely with one-self.

It is notable, however, that when Peirce considered this suggestion in the first of the Harvard lectures on Pragmatism, he decisively rejected it. 'A thinker must be shallow indeed,' he says, 'if he does not see that to admit a species of practicality that consists in one's conduct about words and modes of expression is at once to break down all the bars against the nonsense that pragmatism is designed to exclude. What the pragmatist has his pragmatism for is to be able to say: here is a definition and it does not differ at all from your confusedly apprehended conception because there is no *practical* difference. But what is to prevent his opponent from replying that there is a practical difference which consists in his recognizing one as his conception and not the other? That is, one is expressible in a way in which the other is not expressible. Pragmatism is completely volatilized if you admit that sort of practicality.'[1] Unfortunately, he does not then go on to say how else he would dispose of the difficulty which this suggestion was designed to meet.

It may indeed have been his inability to answer this question that led Peirce in an unpublished paper on Belief and Judgement, which he wrote in 1902, to draw a distinction between theoretical and practical beliefs. He still insists that 'every proposition that is not pure metaphysical jargon and chatter must have some possible bearing upon practice',[2] but he no longer wishes to maintain

[1] V 33.   [2] V 539.

that their actual or possible bearing upon practice, which may in some cases be extremely tenuous, constitutes the whole meaning of theoretical beliefs. What is essential to every type of belief, with the possible exception, which Peirce here admits, of beliefs concerning 'direct perceptual facts', is that it 'involves expectation'. But whereas in the case of practical beliefs, the expectation consists in a readiness to perform certain actions if ever the occasion arises for them, in the case of theoretical beliefs it mainly consists in anticipations of experience: what is expected is that under the relevant conditions a certain set of observations will or would be made. Peirce sums up the difference epigrammatically by saying that the practical belief is expectant of muscular sensation, and the non-practical belief is expectant of sensation which is not muscular: but this should not be interpreted as a concession to phenomenalism: if he can speak in this context of our looking forward to having different types of sensation, it is only because he thinks of these sensations as the means by which we respectively become aware of our actions or of physical facts.

I find this theory much more plausible than that which would resolve beliefs of every kind into 'habits of deliberate action'. In the case of theoretical beliefs – and I take it that there are very few beliefs that would not be found to include some element of theory, in Peirce's sense – it amounts to saying that one's belief in a proposition consists in one's expectation of the results that one would obtain if one were able to test it. The belief is positive if these results are expected to be favourable to the proposition, negative if they are not. But what of our belief in propositions which we cannot reasonably expect to be able to subject to any further tests, propositions of history, for example, in cases where there is no serious hope of our discovering any additional evidence? It would be open to Peirce to reply that in such cases our expectations bore upon what we should find if we looked up the existing evidence. The repetition of these experiments would be a waste of time, given at least that the history books were not being tampered with, but this would not be an objection to the theory. Peirce, however, wishes to go further. He takes as one of his examples the allegation made by Diogenes Laertius,

Suidas, Plutarch and an anonymous biographer, that Aristotle was unable to pronounce the letter R. If there were any reason to believe in a general connection between the inability to pronounce the letter R, and outstanding ability in logic, this would be confirmatory evidence, but unfortunately there is not. So Peirce speaks of the possibility of meeting Aristotle in the Elysian Fields, and more seriously remarks that if we 'give science only a hundred more centuries of increase in geometrical progression', it will somehow find means to pick up the sound waves of Aristotle's voice.[1] This is indeed to take the notion of possible observation rather far, and that of expectation even further if we can be said to expect things that are not likely to happen for another hundred centuries. Even so, the example serves its purpose, which is to illustrate the point that even if we have some evidence in favour, say, of a historical proposition, our belief in the proposition is not serious unless we think that there is some likelihood of its being further confirmed.

This is a stronger and also, I think, a more dubious thesis than that which would require of any factual proposition which might be a candidate for belief merely that it be empirically testable. It is in fact a consequence of the even stronger and still more dubious thesis, which is bound up, as we shall see, with Peirce's theory of signs, that the meaning of every proposition extends indefinitely into the future. For what this involves, in the case of historical propositions, is not merely that there must always be a serious possibility of obtaining further evidence in their favour, but that their meaning is equated with this endless supply of evidence.

I said a moment ago that I thought it more plausible to resolve theoretical beliefs into expectations than into habits of action. But here it may be objected that the reason why this appears more plausible is that it is covertly circular. For what is an expectation but a form of belief? If this circle is unavoidable, we shall have to conclude that all that Peirce is doing at this point is to advance the proposition that all belief looks towards the future. This is an interesting and controversial thesis, but it could hardly be regarded as supplying an analysis of belief. I think, however, that there may

[1] V 542.

be a way in which the circle can be avoided. This would be to treat expectation as consisting ultimately in a readiness to confront the relevant facts: we should be 'set' to confront them in the sense that the observation of them in the appropriate circumstances would not come as a surprise; the stimuli which they afforded would find us psychologically prepared. This interpretation would also have the effect, which would be consonant with Peirce's general view, of narrowing the gap between theoretical and practical beliefs: for one way in which our expectations would be manifested would be through our disposition to act, in the relevant conditions, in ways that were consistent with the fulfilment and not with the disappointment of our theoretical beliefs.

2. Operations on Concepts

The connection of thought with belief and of belief with action which Peirce first attempts to establish in the paper on 'How to Make Our Ideas Clear' leads him to formulate his pragmatic maxim: 'Consider what effects, that might conceivably have practical bearings, we conceive the object of our conception to have. Then, our conception of these effects is the whole of our conception of the object.'[1]

This is not a very clear saying, mainly because it is not immediately obvious in what sense an object is to be conceived of as having effects; but Peirce goes on to give a series of examples which sufficiently illustrate the meaning which he attaches to it. I shall go through these examples, because they raise a number of points of philosophical interest. It must, however, be borne in mind that they represent a 'tougher', more strictly pragmatic, theory of meaning than that which Peirce adopted in most of his later work. We shall see that the reason why he came to modify the original theory was to make room for his scholastic realism; but also that this makes a smaller difference than one might expect.

The first example is that of our use of the word 'hard'. What do we mean by calling a thing 'hard'? 'Evidently', answers Peirce, 'that it will not be scratched by many other substances. The whole

[1] V 402.

conception of this quality, as of every other, lies in its conceived effects. There is absolutely no difference between a hard thing and a soft thing so long as they are not brought to the test.'[1] But surely things may be hard even though their hardness is never directly tested. Peirce considers this objection. 'We may ask' he says, 'what prevents us from saying that all hard bodies remain perfectly soft until they are touched, when their hardness increases with the pressure until they are scratched.'[2] His rather startling reply is that 'there would be no *falsity* in such modes of speech. They would involve a modification of our present usage of speech with regard to the words hard and soft, but not of their meanings. For they represent no fact to be different from what it is; only they involve arrangements of facts which would be exceedingly maladroit. This leads us to remark that the question of what would occur under circumstances which do not actually arise is not a question of fact, but only of the most perspicuous arrangement of them.'[3]

There are several very interesting points here. In the first place, it is to be noted that Peirce does not attempt to define hardness in terms of our sensations. The effects to which he is referring are publicly observable, physical events. His pragmatism, at least in this version of it, is uncompromisingly reductive: but he does not push the reduction to the level of sense-data, for the sufficient reason that he thinks it a mistake to treat sense-data as primitive. This is one of the important ways in which we shall find that his position differs from that of William James.

Secondly, it would surprise and no doubt shock some modern philosophers that Peirce should so sharply distinguish usage from meaning. The usage of a word, in his terminology, is fixed by the contexts in which it is proper to employ it and by the nature of the verbal combinations into which it can significantly enter. This is partly a matter of linguistic convention, but partly also a matter of scientific theory. Thus, it is not a misuse of language to say that diamonds are soft when no other body is in contact with them, as it would be a misuse of language to say diamonds are sums of cube numbers, but it is semantically improper in that it

<hr>

[1] V 403.　　　　[2] Ibid.　　　　[3] Ibid.

runs counter to the accepted theory that the members of a certain class of physical properties, which are accessible to observation, are retained by the things which manifest them, even at times when the relevant observations are not being made, so long as the things in question are not divested of these properties by processes of physical change. I call this a theory because I cannot think what else to call it, but of course it is not a theory in the sense that it is a matter of theory whether a diamond would or would not be scratched if such and such another substance were brought into contact with it. It is not a theory in this sense, because it does not lead to any predictions. There is no experiment which can decide whether a diamond is hard or soft when it is not being tested. It is a theory only in another, perhaps less familiar, but still legitimate sense of the word, as being a way in which we choose to systematize a set of data. And since our methods of systematizing data are articulated in a conceptual system which is embodied in our language, I think that it is permissable for Peirce to treat this as a question of linguistic usage. In this sense, indeed, it is a matter not of fact but of linguistic usage that physical objects themselves exist unperceived.

The meaning of a word, on the other hand, is obtained, in Peirce's view, to put it summarily, by listing the facts to which the word applies. Thus, if someone says of a diamond that it is hard, he means that it is never the case that some substance which is brought into contact with the diamond scratches it. And the meaning, as opposed to the usage, of the sentence 'this diamond is soft, but becomes hard when it is brought into contact with another substance' is exactly the same. For the acceptance of either statement leads to the same expectation, the expectation that when the diamond is brought into contact with some other substance, it will not be scratched. The only difference is a difference in the pictures which accompany this belief. On the one hand we have a picture of the diamond lying there, as it were, with its muscles tensed, all ready to repel any attempt to scratch it, and on the other a picture of the diamond lying limp and relaxed, and only putting forth its effort when the emergency arises. But the difference in these pictures does not correspond to any difference in the facts. In the same way, I have sometimes thought that the point at issue between different philosophical theories of perception comes down to a preference for one or other of a set of rival pictures. The naïve realist pictures things as continuing to exist in very much the same form as that in which we perceive them: the causal theorist pictures them as skeletons, to which our senses intermittently contribute flesh: for the phenomenalist the world is a cinema which never plays to empty houses; it is only in the presence of an audience that images are thrown upon the screen; if he is a Berkeleyan he will bring in a deity to work, or rather to constitute, the film projector. And here again it can be argued that the very considerable difference in these pictures does not correspond to any difference in the facts.[1]

It may be objected that this is an odd use of the word 'meaning': and indeed it does oblige us to treat certain sentences as equivalent in meaning, which would not ordinarily be thought to be so. But this is not a point of any great importance. If we think it worth while to appease the linguistic purist, we can substitute for the word 'meaning' some more anodyne expression such as 'factual content' without doing injury to the theory. But even if we make this substitution, the theory has consequences which are not easy to accept. For instance I feel some reluctance to allow that the table at which I am writing is soluble, just on the ground that it never is immersed in water. But the factual content of the proposition that the table is soluble is the same as that of the disjunction 'either the table is not immersed in water or it dissolves' and if the table is not immersed in water, this is true. Of course this is not the only way in which such dispositional statements can be interpreted, but it is the only way that is consistent both with Peirce's assumption that every proposition is either true or false, and with the limitations which his theory places on the domain of fact. We shall see later on that the main effect of what he calls his scholastic realism is to bring possibilities within the range of facts and so permit him to give an account of dispositional statements which is more in accord with common sense.

[1] This suggestion is developed a little further in the last section of this book.

Since Peirce's whole treatment of the example of the diamond depends on the distinction between facts and their arrangement, it is unfortunate that he takes no steps to make this distinction precise. It is clear enough that he is confining the range of facts to physical states of affairs which are actually observed: but what is to count as such a physical state of affairs itself stands in need of definition. The trouble is that every account of what has been observed is the result of some process of interpretation: and it is not clear how far this process can extend before it takes us out of the domain of facts into questions about their arrangement. Since the fixing of any line of demarcation is bound to be somewhat arbitrary, the best procedure might be simply to draw up a list of terms which are, for the purposes of the theory, to count as terms of observation. Peirce, however, seems to have thought it sufficient for his purposes to rely on our rough intuitive idea of what is, or is not, directly observable.

His next example is that of the concept of free-will. 'I have done something of which I am ashamed. Could I, by an effort of the will, have resisted the temptation, and done otherwise?'[1] The answer is that since what we have to pronounce on is an unfulfilled conditional, 'this is not a question of fact but only of the arrangements of facts', or, as I should prefer to put it, the choice of a conceptual picture. The fact is that when the temptation came I did not make an effort to resist it. To say that I could have resisted it is equivalent, in Peirce's view, to saying that I should have resisted it, if I had tried: and the factual content of this statement is that either I resisted the temptation or I did not try to. Correspondingly, the factual content of the statement that I could not have resisted the temptation is that either I did not resist it, or I did not try to. But since in fact I did not try to resist it, both these statements are true. They are, however, pictorially contradictory, and I have, therefore, to decide which one I prefer to accept. If I picture myself as being equipped to resist temptations of this sort, or indeed as being disposed to resist them in the event of their assailing me, then I shall tell myself that I could have resisted on this occasion, and blame myself for having done

[1] V 403.

wrong. And I may well find this preferable on personal and social grounds to picturing myself as being caught in the toils of necessity, and consequently free from blame, since the temptation was one that I could not have resisted. But this second picture, whatever its moral shortcomings, is no less true than the other. It is equally conformable to the facts.

Peirce admits that the free-will problem is rather more complex than this would make it appear, and in particular that something needs to be said about the issue of determinism: but he thinks that the source of the whole controversy does lie in the question whether we could have acted otherwise than as we actually did, and he claims that this question is perfectly solved in the manner he has indicated. For rather different reasons, I am inclined to think that this solution is along the right lines, but it would need much stronger support than this far too simple analysis of unfulfilled conditionals.

There is little interest in the next example, which is that of the concept of weight, since it merely duplicates the previous example of the concept of hardness. 'To say that a body is heavy simply means that, in the absence of opposing force, it will fall.'[1] No doubt this needs some further refinement, but the principle is clear. The meaning of these theoretical terms is to be identified with the observed effects by which the presence of what they are supposed to designate is actually detected.

A more complicated but parallel case is that of the concept of force. What purpose does this concept serve for us? We use it, says Peirce, to account for changes of motion. 'If bodies were left to themselves, without the intervention of forces, every motion would continue unchanged both in velocity and direction.'[2] This is not, or anyhow should not be, put forward as a statement of fact in Peirce's sense, but only as a feature of Newtonian theory; though he does not make this explicit, he is thinking of the concept of force as operating solely within this theory. So, changes of motion which are always continuous, at least so long as we are dealing with macroscopic bodies, are pictured as being compounded according to the rules of the parallelogram of forces.

[1] V 403.   [2] V 404.

This makes it possible for Peirce simply to identify forces with the accelerations which they are said to cause.

It should by now be clear that what we are being offered here is a hard-headed version of the theory of operationalism, a theory which has gained fresh popularity since Professor Bridgman revived it in his book *The Logic of Modern Physics*. It should be clear also that the reason why I call Peirce's version of the theory hard-headed is that it stipulates that the basis to which theoretical statements are to be reduced consists not of statements referring to what is observable, but of statements referring to what is actually observed.

A theory of this kind has obvious attractions. It puts all the cards on the table and thereby frees us from such tiresome complaints as: 'We know what the effects of electricity are, but we do not know what electricity is'. Electricity is what electricity does. With everything brought into the open, we are spared any nonsense about occult qualities. The theory forbids us to search for the current in the wire, or the leprechaun in the watch.[1] In short, it allows no truck with metaphysics. Its standpoint is very closely akin to that which was later to be adopted by the logical positivists. Peirce's pragmatic maxim is indeed identical, for all practical purposes, with the physicalist interpretation of the verification principle.

All the same there are difficulties, especially when one tries to work the theory out in detail. I shall briefly mention a few of the more important ones, and make one or two suggestions as to how they might be met.

To begin with, complaints like 'We don't know what electricity is' need not be entirely metaphysical. They are very often requests for the explanation of certain effects, as, for example, that of electrical phenomena in terms of waves or in terms of particles. This is partly, but not entirely, a matter of associating the facts with different pictures, and in any case the heuristic value of pictures, or models, should not be underrated. An explanation of this kind may also yield a more powerful, because more comprehensive, theory. Indeed, the tendency of science is to explain

[1] Cf. John Widsom, *Other Minds* (1952).

functions in terms of structures, to try to find agents for agencies. Such agents are indeed known only through their operations, but the effect of introducing them is to widen the field of operations which our theories bind together. Too rigid a positivism, which would tend to discourage even the provisional admission of unobservable entities, might therefore be scientifically inhibiting. This is, however, only a psychological point. It does not bear on the correctness of Peirce's interpretation of what scientists are doing.

A more serious objection, which we have already touched on, is that the distinction which figures so largely in any view of this kind between the experimental facts and the theories which serve merely to arrange them is wholly artificial. For even in the simplest cases, as when we make use of a ruler to measure length or a spring-balance to measure weight, the operations which are supposed to give us our records of fact presuppose a considerable amount of theory; for example, the whole of the theory of rigid bodies. As I have said, this is not a point that Peirce himself would have wanted to deny. It does not seem to me, however, any more than it can have done to him, that this admission is fatal to his view. For even if it be granted that there can be no such thing as a 'pure' statement of fact, it is still open to us to lay down a criterion of relative purity, on the basis of which we can distinguish between those propositions which refer to states of affairs whose existence or non-existence can be directly checked by observation and those which do not. Indeed this is tacitly admitted even by those like Professor Popper and his followers who press this argument against the operationalists[1]: for Popper's own system depends on his marking out a class of 'basic state-ments' in terms of which the truth or falsehood of all higher-order statements is to be checked, and the restriction which he places on the predicates that are allowed to figure in these basic state-ments is just that the properties for which they stand must be observable. The difference between Popper and the operational-ists is not, then, that they rely upon a distinction between fact

[1] Cf. P. K. Feyerabend, 'An Attempt at a Realistic Interpretation of Experience', in *Proc. Arist. Soc.*, 1957-8.

and theory which he is able to dispense with, but that they seek in a manner to reduce all higher-order statements to their basic statements, while he does not. It is, however, also true that not all the parties to a dispute of this kind will draw the line between fact and theory in exactly the same place. Even among those who agree in taking physical situations rather than sense-data as their starting point, there may be a difference of opinion as to the range of physical situations which qualify for this role. In this respect, Peirce's approach is one of the most restrictive, since he excludes from the category of factual terms not only those which would not commonly be taken to stand for anything directly perceptible, but also those which refer to dispositions, rather than occurrences.

The result of this, as his examples show, is that a great many propositions which might ordinarily be thought to be straight-forwardly categorical are treated by him as disguised conditionals. This would not be a very serious matter if this treatment of conditionals were not itself so controversial. But an analysis which leads to such conclusions as that it is true that this table is soluble and also true that it is not soluble, so long as it is never immersed in water, is not very easy to accept. I think, however, that these paradoxes could be mitigated by making a distinction between acceptable and unacceptable arrangements of the facts. It could thus be denied that one is equally entitled to assert 'if p then q' and 'if p then not q', in all cases where p is unfulfilled; for, as in the case of 'this table is soluble', one or other of the pair might be unacceptable at the higher level. This would leave us with the problem of laying down criteria for deciding what is or is not acceptable as an arrangement of the facts, but this is a problem which is going to arise in any case with respect to the evaluation of scientific theories. We should, however, also be precluded from making the simple equation of the meaning of dispositional terms with their occurrent manifestations: for clearly we should have to allow that the meaning of a term like 'soluble' was at least partly determined by the role that it played in our arrangement of the facts.

An alternative suggestion, which has been made by Carnap,[1]

[1] See R. Carnap, *Testability and Meaning* (1950).

is that we should analyse dispositional predicates in terms of purely factual conditionals, but treat their meaning as undetermined in the case where the antecedent of the conditional is not fulfilled. But a definition which does not license us to ascribe dispositional properties to objects which do not actually manifest them, a definition which attaches no meaning to the statement that this table is soluble so long as the table never is immersed in water, cannot be regarded as wholly satisfactory. To have to say that such a statement is neither true nor false, under this condition, is no great improvement on having to say that it is true both that the table is soluble and that it is not.

It is, however, not only the difficulty about the interpretation of conditionals that might lead one to conclude that an operational analysis of scientific terms could at best yield only a partial determination of their meaning. There is also the fact that theoretical concepts have what Dr. Waismann used to call an open texture[1]: no definite limit is set to the ways in which the presence of the things or properties or processes for which they stand is capable of being manifested. We cannot, therefore, say that the operational tests which we can at present specify exhaust the meaning of the term in question, since we have to reckon with the possibility that new types of tests will be devised. This difficulty might be met by saying that the meaning of these terms was subject to enlargement, or alternatively that what appeared to be a single concept was really a family of concepts, the members of the family being distinguished from one another by the fact that they were defined in terms of different, though concordant, operational procedures; this would apply not only to such concepts as that of being electrically charged, but even to such elementary concepts as that of weight or length: there would then be no difficulty in admitting that the family was liable to increase. If, however, we follow Peirce in equating the meaning of a term with all the experimental facts by which its 'object' ever will be manifested, we face the awkward consequence that we can never be sure that the meaning of any term is fully known to us.

[1] F. Waismann, 'Analytic–Synthetic' I–VI, *Analysis*, 1949–53.

We are already finding that the operational approach is a good deal less straightforward than it first appeared, and we are not yet at an end of the technical difficulties. For instance, a point which has been made by Professor Carl Hempel in his very interesting paper on 'The Theoretician's Dilemma'[1] is that what he calls functors, that is terms expressing quantitative aspects, whose permissible values range over all real numbers, cannot be explicitly defined in terms of what is actually observable. This applies once again even to such concepts as those of length and weight. For in any physical theory which incorporates Euclidean geometry certain lengths will have irrational numbers for their values, for example, the square root of 2: and no actual operation of measurement can have an irrational number as its result. Neither can we escape this difficulty by defining the irrational number in terms of the series of rational numbers which approach it asymptotically: for this series is infinite and a series of actual observations is finite. In the case of weight, the problem is not that any weight will have an irrational number for its value but that the number of possible differences in weight is infinite, since given any two values there is another in between. But this means that there are theoretically more differences in weight than our observations can distinguish. In general, the point is that observational concepts are coarser than theoretical ones. At the level of observation, mathematics is discrete.

It would seem also that when it comes to any fairly abstract theory, we cannot find an observational counterpart, or set of counterparts, for each concept independently. The best that we can do is to explain these concepts in terms of one another and then compile a 'dictionary' which correlates statements incorporating such a set of concepts with statements of observation. That is, we define them, as it were *en bloc*. But again this is not a fully-fledged definition. The observation statements will be statements which confirm the theory, but they cannot normally be regarded as expressing both necessary and sufficient conditions of the truth of the theoretical statements with which they are correlated.

For these reasons, I think that if the thesis of operationalism is

[1] See *University of Minnesota Studies in the Philosophy of Science*, vol. II (1958).

taken to be that all empirical statements can be reduced to observation statements, in the sense that they can be translated into them without alteration of meaning, it has to be rejected. It, may, however, be possible to sustain a weaker thesis, which might have satisfied Peirce. If, as I suggested earlier, we make a distinction between the 'meaning' of an expression and its 'factual content', where the meaning is understood to go beyond the factual content in that it covers an indefinite range of possibilities, being as it were an open draft upon the facts which is honoured by the factual content, that is, by the actual observations which are made under such and such specified conditions, then the thesis, which now comes out as a tautology, is that the factual content of a theory is given by listing the experimental facts which actually verify it. The thesis comes out as a tautology because of the way in which the notion of 'factual content' has been defined, but this is not to say that it is trivial. The question then shifts to the point of introducing this notion, that is, to the merits of the assumption, which is made by Peirce and others, that its factual content, in this sense, is as it were the stuffing of any theory, while the rest is only frills.

If this view were correct, we could in principle take out the frills and just present the factual content of the theory as being what it really told us about the world. This would take the form of a possibly very long but still finite conjunction of propositions each of which would record or predict that at such and such a place and time, under such and such conditions, there obtains an observable state of affairs of the sort for which the theory provides. We could not, however, use this as a substitute for the theory because it would not supply us with a rule for adding any further predictions to those that we had already made; and we should seldom, if ever, be in a position to claim that the set of propositions which we had actually listed as making up the factual content of the theory was complete. Even if we had such a rule, we could not expect it to do more for us than enable us to devise conditional predictions; it might make it possible for us to predict not that such and such was going to be the future factual content of the theory, but only that it would be such and such if the appropriate conditions were fulfilled; but the question whether they will in fact be fulfilled will generally lie outside the scope of the theory. This has the strange and perhaps unacceptable consequence that where a theory represents one variable quantity as a function of another, its factual content is restricted to those values of the primary variable that are known to be realized. Thus the factual content, for example, of the law which makes the pressure of gas a function of its temperature and volume, would be restricted to those specimens of gases whose temperatures and volumes happened actually to be recorded.

I have tried to put up some sort of defence for the operational approach against the more obvious objections that can be urged against it, but I should not go so far as to claim that it was forced upon us by a consideration of the way that scientific theories function. It is rather, in Peirce's as in other cases, the fruit of an ontological decision: the decision to count only what is directly observable, or, in Peirce's stricter version, only what is directly observed, as having factual status. It follows that theoretical statements, which cannot be construed as referring straightforwardly to what is directly observable, do not have the function of recording facts. Their point is that they enable us to link observation statements with one another and so to predict what will be observed on the basis of what has been observed. Though it is a mistake to regard them as mere summaries of observation statements, their only function is that of generating observation statements, or, as Peirce preferred to put it, that of arranging facts.

I think that this view is tenable, at least in its more liberal form, and indeed I am disposed to hold it, but I doubt if it now amounts to very much more than the expression of a preference for what I have called a dynamic rather than a static conception of reality. The thesis that all empirical statements are translatable into observation statements was interesting and controversial, but it turns out to be false. If we now substitute for it the thesis that the observation statements are all that really count, it is not clear what this signifies beyond a stubborn determination to continue to eat the cake we cannot have. But perhaps some slices of it remain to us. It is still worth emphasizing that hypotheses are empty unless they are empirically testable, and that if two theories do not differ in their observable consequences, then, however disparate they may appear, in terms of truth and falsehood there is nothing to choose between them.

3. Concessions to Realism

That Peirce's theory of meaning has its roots in an ontological decision is borne out by the fact that when he widens his ontology he also modifies the theory. The change is not very marked and Peirce himself at times seems unaware that he has made it. Thus, as late as 1905, in the paper on 'What Pragmatism Is', we still find him claiming that 'the rational meaning of every proposition lies in the future' and expanding this into the assertion that 'of the myriads of forms into which a proposition may be translated ... that one which is to be called its very meaning ... must be simply the general description of all the experimental phenomena which the assertion of the proposition virtually predicts'.[1] He contends that this is in line with the outlook and practice of experimental scientists on the ground that whatever assertion one may make to 'the typical experimentalist', 'he will either understand as meaning that if a given prescription for an experiment can be and ever is carried out in act, an experience of a given description will result, or else he will see no sense at all in what you say.'[2] There is nothing here that might not have come out of the paper on 'How to Make Our Ideas Clear', which was written nearly thirty years before. And indeed Peirce goes on to speak of himself as having then 'framed the theory that a *conception*, that is, the rational purport of a word or other expression, lies exclusively in its conceivable bearing upon the conduct of life; so that, since obviously nothing that might not result from experiment can have any direct bearing upon conduct, if one can define accurately all the conceivable experimental phenomena which the affirmation or denial of a concept could imply, one will have therein a complete definition of the concept, and *there is absolutely nothing more in it*'.[3]

[1] V 427.   [2] V 411.   [3] V 412.

The change is very slight, merely a shift from talking of 'the effects we conceive the object of our conception to have' to talking of 'the phenomena which the affirmation or denial of a concept could imply', but it is significant. For if the meaning of a concept is now to be analysed, not just in terms of the actual observations which show it to be satisfied, but also in terms of the hypothetical observations which could do so, the way is open to allowing theoretical concepts to have a richer factual content than the mere conjunction of the observation statements which record what these concepts actually serve to predict.

The result is that in the Harvard lectures on 'Pragmatism', Peirce is able to maintain that 'general principles are really operative in nature'.[1] Suppose, for example, that I hold a stone in my hand; then I know that if I let go of it, and there is no obstacle in the way, it will fall to the ground. But 'if I *truly know* anything, that which I know must be *real*'.[2] The uniformity with which stones have fallen up to now 'has been due to some *active general principle*'.[3] And here the implication is that even if I had not let go of the stone it is still true that it would have fallen.

So, in a paper called 'Issues of Pragmaticism', which appeared in the *Monist* in 1905 as a sequel to the paper on 'What Pragmatism Is', the example of the diamond is reconsidered. Peirce sums up his earlier view by saying that he had represented it as being 'merely a question of nomenclature' whether the diamond which never in fact was tested for hardness should be said to have been hard or not. He still does not mind saying that it is a question of nomenclature, but now objects very strongly to its being said that it is *merely* so. This use of the word 'merely' contains an 'abominable falsehood' since it implies that symbols, presumably here taken in the sense of what is symbolized, are not real. 'Nomenclature involves classification; and classification is true or false, and the generals to which it refers are either reals in the one case, or figments in the other.'[4] Besides, the condition of the diamond is not 'an isolated fact'. It may have been tested for other properties which we associate by law with hardness. Its possession of some of them will be implied by its being a mass of pure carbon, which

[1] V 101. [2] V 94. [3] V 100. [4] V 453.

we know it must be if we know it to be a diamond. And any-how, even if this diamond has not been tested for hardness, other diamonds have. And 'how can the hardness of all other diamonds fail to bespeak *some* real relation among the diamonds without which a piece of carbon would not be a diamond? Is it not a monstrous perversion of the word and concept *real* to say that the accident of the non-arrival of the corundum[1] prevented the hardness of the diamond from having the *reality* which it other-wise, with little doubt, would have had.'[2]

So now we are told that: 'Pragmaticism makes the ultimate intellectual purport of what you please consist in conceived con-ditional resolutions, or their substance; and therefore, the con-ditional propositions, with their hypothetical antecedents, in which such resolutions consist, being of the ultimate nature of meaning, must be capable of being true, that is, of expressing whatever there may be which is such as the proposition expresses, independently of being thought to be so in any judgement, or being represented to be so in any other symbol of any man or men. But that amounts to saying that possibility is sometimes of a real kind.'[3]

This is the scholastic realism to which Peirce attached very great importance. His insistence on it is one of the three respects in which he maintains that his pragmatism is distinct from positivism, the others being 'its retention of a purified philosophy' and 'its full acceptance of the main body of our instinctive beliefs'.[4] It is, however, not at all easy to make out exactly what it is that he takes this scholastic realism to entail. He says, more than once, that it commits him to holding that some possibilities are real, which is itself a consequence of the proposition that general principles are really operative in nature; but it is not at all clear how this differs from his earlier view that general principles are useful devices which we employ for the arrangement of facts. In his own pragmatic terms, there is nothing to choose between them, since whichever view is taken of the status of these general principles, the concrete expectations which result from accepting

---

[1] I.e. the testing substance. [2] V 457.
[3] V 453. [4] V 423.

them remain the same. It would seem, therefore, once again, that all that this adherence to scholastic realism comes to is a preference for a certain type of picture of reality. This preference does, however, have a practical consequence within the sphere of Peirce's philosophy: for, as we have remarked, it leads him to widen his notion of fact, so that facts become capable of being stated by unfulfilled conditionals, and in this way to relax the austerity of his theory of meaning.

But since this is not a consequence to which Peirce himself draws any special attention, it is still hard to see why he regarded his scholastic realism as such an important feature of his general position. A clue to the answer may be found in a passage, written in 1871, in which he contrasts his conception of reality with that which he attributes to his nominalist opponents. Nominalism would be true, he says, if reality were to be equated with 'a thing out of the mind which directly influences sensation and through sensation thought',[1] for then to say that two things A and B had something in common would just be a way of saying that they caused similar sensations; there would be no occasion and no ground for going beyond this and attributing to them a genuine common property. There is, however, another view of reality which represents it as embracing just those things which will be thought to exist in the final opinion 'to which the mind of man is on the whole and in the long run tending', this final opinion being 'independent not indeed of thought in general but of all that is arbitrary and individual in thought', that is, 'independent of how you or I or any number of men think': and it is this view of reality that favours scholastic realism.

The first difficulty here is that there seems to be no reason why these two views of reality should not be combined, as in fact they are combined by Peirce himself in the papers which I have summarized. What he here calls the nominalistic view is there taken by him, as we have seen, to be the essential feature of the scientific method of fixing belief; and the use of scientific method is supposed to lead to the general agreement, on the prospect of which his 'realistic' view of reality depends.

[1] VIII 12.

The way in which one view leads into the other comes out most clearly at the end of the paper on 'How to Make Our Ideas Clear', where the concept of reality is taken as the final example of the operation of the pragmatic maxim. Peirce there begins by looking for what he calls an abstract definition of the real and finds it by contrasting reality with the product of one's imagination, that is, with fiction. This leads him to define the real as 'that whose characters are independent of what anybody may think them to be',[1] a definition to which he constantly recurs throughout his work. So a dream is real as a mental phenomenon: for that someone is having such and such a dream is a fact which is independent of what anybody thinks about it, including the dreamer himself, since he may dream without judging that he is dreaming. On the other hand, the events about which he dreams are not real, for they do not occur independently of his dreaming of them.

Peirce finds this satisfactory, so far as such definitions go, but maintains that no abstract definition can make the idea of reality perfectly clear. He therefore goes on to apply his pragmatic rule, and puts the rather strange-sounding question: 'What sensible effects do things partaking of reality produce?' His answer is that 'the only effect which real things have is to cause belief, for all the sensations which they excite emerge into consciousness in the form of beliefs'.[2] But this is evidently not sufficient, for hallucinations also may cause beliefs, else we should never be deceived by them. 'The question therefore is, how is true belief (or belief in the real) distinguished from false belief (or belief in fiction)?' But this brings us back to the question of the fixation of belief. Now, according to Peirce, it is only for those who follow the method of science that there can be any problem of distinguishing true from false beliefs, since according to the other methods whatever one chooses to believe is true, or in the case of the method of authority, whatever our rulers choose that we shall believe. So the true beliefs are those which survive investigation by scientific methods. And the real is the object which is represented in these beliefs.

[1] V 405.   [2] V 406.

We have already examined this chain of reasoning. The puzzling question in the present context is why its conclusion should be thought to favour any form of scholastic realism. What possible grounds could there be for supposing that the opinion to which the pursuit of scientific method would ultimately lead is that things have genuine common qualities, as opposed to their merely resembling one another in their sensible effects? Since the experimental consequences of these two views are identical, it is hard to see how the process of scientific investigation, however long continued, could ever lead us to decide between them. They both would survive it equally well.

It may be, however, that Peirce is rather strangely attributing to nominalism the view that to know things through their sensible effects is not to know them as they are in themselves, and that the view which he wishes to characterize as realistic is that real things are directly accessible to our thought. This is borne out by his saying that the realist 'will maintain a doctrine of immediate perception'. He will hold that 'the very same objects which are present in our minds in experience really exist just as they are experienced out of the mind'.[1] Then these objects can be said to have common qualities just in the sense that the same predicates may apply to them intrinsically, as opposed to merely characterizing their sensible effects. This book and that cushion are both red because that is how they normally appear; and how they normally appear is how they really are.

The emphasis then is not on the idea of reality as that in which belief is reached as the unshaken result of prolonged scientific inquiry but rather on the idea of reality as the *object* of general agreement. But this has the curious consequence that Peirce's scholastic realism turns into a version of what he calls objective idealism. This goes further than the admission, which we always find implicit in his pragmatism, that what is real, though it is by definition independent of what any given person may think about it, is not independent of thought in general. It takes him to the point of holding that 'everything we can in any way take cognizance of is purely mental',[2] which does not prevent it from

[1] VIII 16.   [2] VIII 145.

also being material since 'all mind more or less partakes of the
nature of matter'. 'Viewing a thing from the outside, considering
its relations of action and reaction with other things, it appears as
matter. Viewing it from the inside, looking at its immediate
character as feeling, it appears as consciousness. These two views
are combined when we remember that mechanical laws are
nothing but acquired habits, like all the regularities of mind,
including the tendency to take habits, itself.'[1] So elsewhere we
are told that 'matter is effete mind, inveterate habits becoming
physical laws'.[2] This idealism is objective in the sense that it
makes provision for external objects, the conditions which they
are required to satisfy being somewhat stronger than that which
anything must satisfy in order to be real. For whereas it is sufficient
for a thing to be real that it be what it is independently of what
any particular person may think about *it*, for a thing to be external
it is necessary that it be what it is independently of what any
particular person may think on *any subject*.[3] But this is still a rather
limited independence, seeing that it is required of these external
objects not only that they be possible objects of thought, but that
they be part of its nature.

The way in which this is meant to vindicate scholastic realism
at the expense of nominalism is brought out in Peirce's review of
Karl Pearson's famous book *The Grammar of Science*. Pearson had
maintained the nominalistic thesis that what we call the laws of
nature are our own intellectual constructions. In other words, he
agreed with Peirce's earlier view that propositions of law are not
themselves expressions of facts, but only of our method of
arranging them. Peirce's answer is not that Pearson was mistaken in regarding the laws of nature as intellectual constructions,
but that this did not justify his nominalistic practice of treating
them as fictions. 'If he had thoroughly accepted the truth that all
realities, as well as all figments, are alike of purely mental composition, he would have seen that the question was not whether
natural law is of an intellectual nature or not, but whether it is of
the number of those intellectual objects that are destined ultimately
to be exploded from the spectacle of our universe or whether, as

---

[1] VI 268.   [2] VI 25.   [3] VII 339.

far as we can judge, it has the stuff to stand its ground in spite of all attacks.'[1]

But again what does this come to? Merely that if the scientific millenium were ever reached some generalizations would be found to have survived. And of this indeed there can be no question, once we make the assumption that the scientific millenium is attainable. But whether these generalizations reflect the habits of nature, or whether they are merely devices which help us in the arrangement of particular facts, is a question which their power of survival goes no way to decide. It cannot possibly decide it since it is common ground to both views that the generalizations are supposed to be consonant with the observable facts, and this is all that their survival shows. Whether there is anything more to Peirce's 'objective idealism' than the necessary truth that we cannot significantly talk, or even conceive, of what lies outside the field of possible experience is a question which we must try to resolve when we come to examine his theory of knowledge. But I think it is now clear that the scholastic realism which it is meant to entail amounts to no more than the adoption of an anthropomorphic picture; physical objects are credited with propensities to action which are analogous to those that we discover in ourselves. But since to know that we have these propensities is to know nothing more than that we should act in such and such ways if such and such conditions were realized, the only difference that the adoption of the picture makes, in terms of Peirce's practical philosophy, is the addition of unfulfilled conditionals to the stock of observation statements in terms of which the meaning of theoretical concepts is supposed to be capable of being analysed.

If we waive the considerable difficulties which stand in the way of a satisfactory interpretation of unfulfilled conditionals themselves, we must allow that their inclusion in the domain of experimental facts makes Peirce's operationalism more plausible, if less exciting. Even so it remains open to some of the objections which hold against it in its stricter form. We shall still be unable to find observational equivalents for the terms of any fairly

[1] VIII 145.

abstract scientific theory, if they are taken individually, but only at best for a number of them taken *en bloc*; and even if the difficulty about the open texture of theoretical concepts can be met by some such device as that of supposing that we have all the evidence potentially at our command, the relative coarseness of our observational terms will still make it impossible for them to furnish translations of many of the theoretical statements which we are required to reduce to them. The most that could be claimed is that with the extension of the range of observation statements, the account which the theory is able to give of the factual content of theoretical statements can now be regarded as more satisfactory.

There is, however, the further difficulty in Peirce's theory that with the exception of those which describe our present or future perceptions, or our present memories, it obliges us to treat all empirical propositions as conditionals and all conditionals as forward-looking. The result is that all propositions about events which we are not and never shall be in a position to perceive, that is, not only all propositions about events which are not directly observable, but all propositions about observable events in the present which are remote from us in space, all propositions about the past, or at any rate 'that part of the past that lies beyond memory',[1] and presumably also all propositions about events which we shall not live to see, have to be construed as referring to the future evidence in their favour, which will or, under suitable conditions, would be available to us. In the case of the past, which in this respect can stand as a model for the others, Peirce tries to justify this conclusion by arguing that, so far as we are concerned, the assertion that some event has occurred and the assertion that it will be found to have occurred come to the same thing. 'It is evident that to guarantee that, if a piece of work has not already been done right, one will pay for it, and to guarantee that, *if it shall be found* not to have already been done right, one will pay for it, have one and the same meaning. One or other of them therefore must be an elliptical or otherwise uniliteral expression, or else both are so. But nobody will maintain that to

[1] V 461.

promise to pay for the work, if it should be ascertained not to have been already done right, really means to promise to so pay, if it shall in fact not have been already done right, whether it be ascertained or not. It would be equally absurd to say that there was any third meaning which should have reference to an un-ascertained past. . . . Hence there can be no meaning in making oneself responsible for a past event independent of its future ascertainment. But to assert a proposition is to make oneself responsible for its truth. Consequently, the only meaning which an assertion of a past fact can have is that, if in the future the truth be ascertained, so it shall be ascertained to be.'[1]

If this is offered as an analysis of propositions about the past, it is open to very serious objections. In the first place, it has the consequence that the meaning of any such proposition, or rather of the sentence which expresses it, is continually changing. For with the passage of time, the evidence, whether hypothetical or actual, which was future itself becomes past, so that the statements which were taken to refer to it have to be reinterpreted as referring to whatever future evidence there would be or might be in favour of *them*, and so *ad infinitum*. A second consequence, which I at least find objectionable, is that a sentence in the past tense can never express the same proposition, or even a proposition with the same factual content, as the corresponding sentence in the present or future tense. My own view is that the factual content of what is expressed by the sentence 'It will rain on June 1st 1965', said before the event, 'It is raining on June 1st 1965', said at the time, and 'It rained on June 1st, 1965', said after the event, is the same in each case. The difference in tense serves only to indicate, without explicitly asserting, a difference in the temporal position of the speaker relatively to the event which he describes. But, on Peirce's view, the proposition which is expressed by the sentence in the past tense will be of quite a different form from those which are expressed by the others. It will have to be interpreted as referring not to the occurrence of rain on the date in question but to such things as meteorological records. Finally, it seems obvious that a statement about the future evidence for a past event, however comprehensive it may be, cannot be formally equivalent to the statement that the event occurred. For we must always admit at least the logical possibility that the evidence is deceptive. In very many cases, indeed, this is not a possibility that any rational person would take seriously, but it cannot be formally excluded. However strongly the evidence which is available at some later time may support a historical proposition it can never get to the point where it entails it.

I do not think, however, that Peirce would have been much disturbed by these objections, which are indeed so obvious that they can hardly be supposed to have escaped his notice. If he had been trying to represent propositions about the past as being formally equivalent to whatever set of propositions, at any given later time, exhibited the best evidence that could then or subsequently be obtained in their favour, these objections would indeed be conclusive. But he makes it clear enough that he is not interested in finding formal equivalences. He would have been perfectly ready to admit that no amount of favourable evidence could entail a historical proposition: but he would have insisted that all that this came to, in concrete terms, was that we have to allow for the possibility, however remote, that future evidence will reverse the verdict. For our interest in the past is exclusively in what we can know of it; and what we can know of it, apart from the narrow grasp of our personal memories, coincides with the records which we interpret it as having left.

This is only another illustration of the fact that Peirce's theory of meaning is not a semantic but a practical theory. He does not seek to analyse a proposition by finding other propositions which are logically equivalent to it. The question he asks is: What does the proposition mean to me? where 'meaning' has the sense of 'purport'. What difference will it make, in terms of my experience, if I accept the proposition or not? And the only rational answer which the question allows for, when it is put in this form, is that if I accept the proposition I expect that I shall be able to make certain observations, either in practice or at least in principle, which I should not expect to be able to make if I rejected it. But since the effect of making these observations is just to confirm me in the belief that the proposition is true, Peirce's theory of meaning dovetails into his theory of truth. And since we have found that his theory of truth resolves itself into a defence of scientific method, it is to the examination of the rest of Peirce's philosophy of science that we now must turn.

CHAPTER THREE

PEIRCE'S PHILOSOPHY OF SCIENCE

A. THE THREE KINDS OF REASONING

'THERE are in science', says Peirce, 'three fundamentally different kinds of reasoning.' These three kinds, which were already distinguished by Aristotle, are Deduction, Induction, and one for which Peirce most frequently uses the term Abduction, though he thinks that Retroduction would be a better name for it and sometimes also calls it Hypothesis. He also admits Analogy, but does not put it on a level with the other three, since he thinks that it combines the characters of Induction and Abduction.[1]

The salient mark of deductive reasoning, in Peirce's view, is that if it is correctly employed it cannot lead from true premisses to a false conclusion. If one or other of the premisses is false, the conclusion may be false, though it need not be; but if the premisses are true, then, so long as the guiding principle of the inference is valid, the conclusion must be true. Deductive reasoning is hypothetical, in the sense that its being bound to lead to a true conclusion is conditional on the truth of the premisses; but given the truth of the premisses, the truth of the conclusion necessarily follows.

In saying that deductive arguments, given the truth of their premisses, necessarily lead to true conclusions, Peirce does not wish to imply that they are infallible. All reasoning, in his view, is fallible inasmuch as we can never have an absolute guarantee that the guiding principles on which we are relying will not subsequently be found to be fallacious: we have seen that he takes this to the point of maintaining that it is not entirely beyond question even that two and two make four. So long, however, as

we have no positive reason for thinking that our logical principles
are fallacious, we are entitled to hold that the reasoning which
they sustain is necessary; and what makes it necessary is that it is
not exposed to empirical refutation. As Peirce puts it, 'the necessity of such reasoning consists in this, that not only does the
conclusion happen to be true of a predeterminate universe, but
will be true, so long as the premisses are true, howsoever the
universe may subsequently turn out to be determined'.[1] What I
take to be the same point is now more commonly put by saying
that a necessary proposition is one that remains true in every
possible universe. This is because its truth is dependent not on
any matter of fact which might have been otherwise but merely
on the interpretation of the signs by which it is expressed.

Peirce holds that all necessary, and consequently all deductive
reasoning is 'of the nature of mathematical reasoning', and that
'mathematical reasoning is diagrammatic'.[2] He claims that this
is no less true of algebra than of geometry, and he devises an
elaborate system of graphs which are intended to show that it is
equally true of symbolic logic. There is a sense, therefore, in
which all deductive reasoning requires the exercise of intuition.
When we scrutinize a particular diagram, or pass from one
diagram to another, we just have to see that the relations which
these instances exemplify hold universally. Though such intuitions
are fallible, they yield only to their like. 'There is no more satisfactory way of assuring ourselves of anything than the mathematical way of assuring ourselves of mathematical theorems'.[3]
It follows too, since all deductive reasoning is mathematical, that
logic depends on mathematics, not mathematics on logic.
'Mathematical reasoning derives no warrant from logic. It needs
no warrant. It is evident in itself. It does not relate to any matter
of fact, but merely to whether one supposition excludes another.
Since we ourselves create these suppositions, we are competent
to answer them.'[4] And again: 'Mathematical reasoning holds.
Why should it not? It relates only to the creations of the mind,
concerning which there is no obstacle to our learning whatever
is true of them.'[5] This accounts for his saying, in a passage which

[1] IV 431.   [2] V 147-8.   [3] II 192.   [4] II 191.   [5] II 192.

I have already quoted, that when logical principles of inference are considered as assertions, they will be found to be quite empty.[1] They are empty just in the sense that they stake no claim on any matter of fact.

There is, however, a sense in which assertions of this type, though protected from matters of fact, are still controlled by them. Mathematics, considered here as including formal logic, is not just a piece of fantasy which we can elaborate in any manner that we please. Even if it can be compared to a game for which we devise the rules, the existence of the rules restricts our freedom: if we break them, the game is nullified. It might be said that this means no more than that we have decided to play a different game; the fact remains that we have to adhere to *some* rules, if we are to play any game at all. Moreover, in this case, the rules are not arbitrary; their selection depends upon the fact that we need to make use of mathematics. We employ deductive reasoning to extend our knowledge, inasmuch as we learn from it what further commitments we have incurred in taking such and such factual propositions to be true. If any one of the propositions to which we are thereby shown to be committed turns out to be false, we have to conclude either that not all the factual propositions to which we applied our reasoning were true, or that the reasoning itself has been at fault. In the latter case, we shall probably discover that we have inadvertently transgressed the rules; but it is also possible that the rules themselves are inadequate. It is because matters of fact can show the rules of deductive reasoning to be, if not incorrect, at least unserviceable, that mathematics can be said to be controlled by them.

Admittedly, this control is flexible. The facts will never leave us with no other option but to alter the rules: they cannot even bring us to the point where we are bound to conclude that our reasoning has been invalid. If a deductive argument has led us from what appear to be true premisses to a false conclusion, it cannot be denied that something is amiss: and for the most part Peirce allows, as we have seen, that the fault may lie in the guiding principle of the inference. There is, however, one passage

[1] See above, p. 19.

in which he takes a different view. In an essay with the curious title 'Some Consequences of Four Incapacities', which appeared in the *Journal of Speculative Philosophy* in 1869, he put forward the implausible thesis that it was possible 'to reduce all mental action to the formulae of valid inference', and noted that the existence of fallacious reasoning can be raised as an objection. His answer is that no reasoning need ever be regarded as fallacious. The inferences which fail to lead from true premisses to true conclusions can belong, he maintains, to only four classes, namely: '1. Those whose premisses are false; 2. Those which have some little force, though only a little; 3. Those which result from confusion of one proposition with another; 4. Those which result from the indistinct apprehension, wrong application, or falsity, of a rule of inference.'[1] In the first of these cases, a false conclusion may result without there being any fallacy in the reasoning. In the second case, the rule of inference has only to be treated as a premiss in order to yield 'a legitimate probable argument'. In the case where two propositions are confused, it must be because the reasoner finds some resemblance between them. If we suppose him to be assuming that because they are equivalent in some respects, they are equivalent in all, he can be held to be making 'a hypothetic inference, which though it may be weak, and though its conclusion happens to be false, belongs to the type of valid inference'.[2] Finally, if we have no other recourse but to say that the reasoner has adopted a wrong rule of inference, we can treat this rule of inference as a false premiss, and so conclude that the falsity of the conclusion is due to the falsity of a premiss rather than to a fallacy in the reasoning. By these means the thesis that the formulae of valid inference are always adhered to can be safeguarded from the facts which seem to refute it.

But while this defence is characteristically ingenious, it is surely a case of misplaced ingenuity. The most that it can be held to prove is that a fallacious argument can always be remodelled in such a way that the fallacy disappears. This is different, however, from saying that the fallacy was not committed. If someone who accepts the proposition that all A's are B's and that X is a B deduces from these premises that X is an A, it can be pleaded in his defence that since the premiss that all A's are B's lends some probability to the supposition that any given B is an A, his conclusion, though not entailed by his premisses, is not unsupported by them; they give it some chance of being true. But this was not the way in which he argued. His belief was not that, given the premisses, the conclusion stood some chance of being true, but that it could not fail to be true: he simply succumbed to the well-known fallacy of the undistributed middle term. Again, to say that his argument would have been valid if it had started from the premiss that all and only A's are B's is not to say that this is what he really meant; he may very well not have considered the proposition that only A's are B's, and if he had considered it, he might have rejected it. Moreover, in the case where the fallacy is due to the adoption of an invalid logical principle as a rule of inference, it does not seem open to Peirce to treat this rule as a false premiss. For since he holds, as we have seen, that logical principles are altogether empty when considered as assertions, it is only *qua* rules of inference that they can be false. The balance of argument would seem, therefore, to be in favour of Peirce's more usual view that in all cases in which deductive reasoning leads from true premisses to a false conclusion, it is to be counted as invalid.

Deductive inference is contrasted by Peirce with probable or factual inference, where the premisses support the conclusion without entailing it. The reason why this weaker type of inference is said to be probable is that the conclusion is made probable by the premisses. It is not that the conclusion itself expresses a judgement of probability. On the contrary, in the case where the conclusion does express a judgement of probability, it is normally represented by Peirce as the outcome not of probable but of deductive inference.

He is able to do this because he limits judgements of probability to assessments of relative frequency. 'Probability', he says, 'applies to the question whether a specified kind of event will occur when certain pre-determined conditions are fulfilled; and it is the ratio of the number of times in the long run in which that

specified result would follow upon the fulfilment of those conditions to the total number of times in which those conditions were
fulfilled in the course of experience'.[1] In other passages, he defines
the probability of B, given A, in terms of the proportion of cases
of A which are also cases of B, or in terms of the proportion of
cases in which an argument from A to B would lead to a true result.

There are various points to be noted here. In the first place, this
account of probability makes it relative to evidence The value
which a judgement of probability assigns to an event depends upon
the data on which this judgement is based: the probability which
an event has in relation to one set of conditions may not be the
same as its probability in relation to another. Nevertheless Peirce
thinks that we can 'speak of the chance of an event absolutely,
meaning by that the chance of the combination of all arguments in
reference to it which exist for us in the given state of our knowledge'.[2] But even in this 'absolute' sense, the chance of an event
is still relative. Peirce thinks it nonsensical to credit an event with
any inherent probability.

The next point to note is that the probability that an event will
occur, under certain conditions, is identified with the frequency
with which events of that kind would, under those conditions,
occur *in the long run*. Peirce says that this talk of the long run
'essentially refers to a course of experience, or at least of real
events; because mere possibilities are not capable of being
counted'.[3] It is rather surprising, therefore, that he speaks of the
frequency with which the event *would* occur rather than the
frequency with which it *will* occur. The explanation may be that
he is thinking of these frequencies as derivable from statistical
laws, and of these laws as entailing unfulfilled conditionals. He
would then be left with the question how such laws could be
established: but this is a problem that is going to arise in any case
in which the sequence of events of type A, by reference to which
the frequency of events of type B is to be determined, has not
already been exhausted.

A special difficulty arises when the A series is infinite, since the
proportion of B's among its members will then be indeterminate,

[1] V 169.   [2] II 676.   [3] V 169.

except in certain special cases. Peirce's solution of this difficulty is to stipulate that 'when we say that a certain ratio will have a certain value "in the long run", we refer to the *probability-limit* of an endless series of fractional values, that is, to the only possible value from o to ∞, inclusive, about which the values of the endless succession will never cease to oscillate: so that, no matter what place in the succession you may choose, there will follow both values above the probability-limit and values below it, while if V be any *other* possible value from o to ∞ but *not* the probability-limit, there will be some place in the succession beyond which all the values of the succession will agree, either in all being greater than V, or else in all being less'.[1] This idea of identifying probability with limiting frequency has been taken up by subsequent writers, though not exactly in the same form. Usually the limit is defined as the one and only ratio from which the frequency does not subsequently deviate by more than any arbitrarily small amount. The awkward problem, on any version of the theory, is to show that such a limit exists.

Leaving aside for the moment the question how any statistical generalizations are to be established, let us suppose that we are in a position to employ them as premisses in arguments. We can then develop a logic of probability which, in Peirce's words, 'is related to ordinary syllogistics as the quantitative to the qualitative branch of the same science'.[2] Corresponding to the necessary syllogism, we have the probable syllogism which, as Peirce expounds it, takes three different forms. There is first what he calls *Simple Probable Deduction*: 'The proportion R of the M's are P's; S is an M; it follows, with probability R, that S is a P'. Secondly, *Complex Probable Deduction*: 'Among all sets of n M's the proportion q consist each of m P's and of $n-m$ not P's; S'S'' S''', etc., form a set of n objects drawn at random from among the M's; hence the probability is q that among S' S'' S''', etc. there are m P's and $n-m$ not P's'. Thirdly, *Statistical Deduction*: 'The proportion R of the M's are P's; S' S'' S''', etc. are a *numerous* set, taken at random from among the M's; hence, *probably* and *approximately*, the proportion R of the S's are P's'.[3]

[1] II 758.   [2] II 696.   [3] II 695–700.

On Peirce's interpretation of probability, there is no doubt that all three syllogisms are valid. It may not be clear, however, from the way in which the last two of them are formulated that the probability which figures in their conclusions is a probability of the second order. In each case it is a question of the proportion of sets of a given magnitude within which a certain character is distributed in a given proportion. In the example of Complex Probable Deduction, since this information is explicitly given in the premisses, the conclusion follows automatically; for to say that there is a probability q that the property P is distributed among the members of the sub-set S in the ratio of m to n is just equivalent to saying that P is distributed in that ratio in a proportion q of all the sub-sets of the same magnitude as S. There is no need even to stipulate that the members of S be selected at random, that is, 'according to a method which will, in the long run, present any instance as often as any other';[1] for since the probability that any given character is distributed among the members of S in such and such a proportion is not dependent on the special composition of S but only on the proportion in which the character is distributed throughout all the sub-classes of that size, the way in which the members of S are selected is immaterial: whether the selection be random or biassed, the value of q will be the same.

The example of Statistical Deduction is less straightforward, since it depends on the tacit assumption of the Law of Large Numbers, which ensures that provided that the samples are sufficiently large the vast majority of all possible samples of a given size will approximately match the total population from which they are drawn with respect to the distribution of any given character; the larger the sample the greater will be the proportion for which this approximation holds. This law is mathematically demonstrable and it is easy to see that Peirce's formula of Statistical Deduction follows immediately from it. Here again, there is no need for him to stipulate that the S's be selected at random. Since the probability that P is distributed among them in approximately the same proportion as it is in the

[1] II 269.

parent population depends only on their number and is, indeed, the same with respect to any sample of an equal size, it can make no difference to its value how they are selected. Whatever their composition, whether all of them have P or none, and whether we know this or not, there is the same probability that the proportion of them which have P is approximately equal to R.

This sounds paradoxical until it is realized that to talk of the probability, in this sense, that some character is distributed in such and such a proportion among the members of a given set, is not to say anything specifically about the members of the set in question, but only to refer to the distribution of the character throughout a class of sets to which this one belongs. This point is often overlooked in discussions of the frequency theory, and seems in this instance to have been overlooked by Peirce himself. For the only reason that he could have, either in this case or in that of Complex Probable Deduction, for making the proviso that the S's are to be selected at random, would be to increase the chance that they constituted a fair sample; he must be looking for some assurance that the frequency with which the character under investigation appears among them matches the frequency with which it appears among the population from which they are selected. But so long as this chance is measured, not by the composition of the sub-class S, but only by its size, the postulate of random selection is entirely otiose. I suspect that the reason why Peirce introduced it here was that he was muddling up two different questions; the question of the probable distribution of P among the members of S, and the still higher order question whether S is likely to be deviant in this respect; that is, whether it is probable that the actual distribution of P among the S's matches its probable distribution. For the only interesting sense that can be given to this second question, so long as we adhere to the frequency theory of probability, is to relate it to a method of selection. It must be construed as asking what proportion of the samples of the same size as S are deviant with respect to the distribution of P, given that they are selected in such and such a fashion; and then, if the condition is that the method of selection be random, it will follow that the proportion which are deviant under this condition is the same as the proportion of deviant samples among all possible samples of the given size. It is to be noted that we are still not concerned with the character of the S's as such, but only with the distribution of a property throughout a wider class to which we assign them; but this is a cardinal feature of the frequency theory. If we try to make a statement of probability about an individual case, it has to be interpreted as a statement about a class.

This comes out even more clearly when we consider Simple Probable Deduction. As Peirce sets it out, this would appear to be a method of assigning probability to an individual case. From the premisses that a proportion R of the M's have the property P, and that the individual S is an M, we are to deduce that there is a probability R that S has P. So, to borrow a well known example, we might argue that given that the vast majority of Swedes are Protestants and that Petersen is a Swede, there is a high probability that Petersen is a Protestant. But now suppose that we learn that Petersen has made a pilgrimage to Lourdes and we know that the vast majority of those who make pilgrimages to Lourdes are Roman Catholics; we are then equally justified in inferring that there is a high probability that Petersen is a Roman Catholic and so not a Protestant; and no doubt we could find other statistics about the members of classes to which Petersen belonged from which we could as validly infer that there was a high probability that he was an atheist or a Hindu. It looks therefore as if the use of Simple Probable Deduction leads to contradiction. In fact, there is no contradiction because none of the conclusions means what it appears to say. What they do mean is just that Petersen is a member of this and that and the other class, and that such properties as that of being a Protestant or a Roman Catholic are distributed in these several classes in such and such different ways. But the contradiction is avoided at the expense of our interest in the individual; he is only an item in a set of statistics: the probability that he has whatever property is in question does not relate to him any more than to anyone else who happens to be a member of the class to which we are referring it; and, as we have just seen, its value might very well be different if we chose to refer it to a different class of which he also happens to be a member. This alone would incapacitate the method of Simple Probable Deduction from being employed to authorize conclusions about particular cases: but the fact, which Peirce does not seem wholly to have realized, is that the method is not designed for any such employment. The conclusion of its argument is simply a restatement of the premises.

A probable syllogism, then, is a deductive form of inference which issues in a statement of probability. The inference is valid but, as we have just seen, trivial. It is not to be confused with a probable inference, of which the defining characteristic is that the premisses support but do not entail the conclusion. Not only is one a species of necessary reasoning and the other not, but their conclusions are bound to take different forms. A probable inference has a statement of probability not for its conclusion but for its guiding principle. So we may employ the statement that it is highly probable that any Swede is a Protestant to authorize a probable inference from the premiss that Petersen is a Swede to the conclusion, not that Petersen is very probably a Protestant, for that would be a necessary inference, but simply that Petersen is a Protestant. But then the trouble is, as we have seen, that we may be able to find an equally strong statement of probability, which will authorize a probable inference from some other fact about Petersen to the conclusion that he is not a Protestant. This does not show that a probable inference of this sort is altogether illegitimate. It can be urged in its favour that if it is in fact the case that most A's are B's, then in making the inference from 'X is an A' to 'X is a B' with respect to every A, we are bound to be right more often than we are wrong. It does show, however, that we have to be circumspect in applying this form of argument to particular cases. We can try to escape from the position of having equal reason to infer both p and not p by insisting on equating the chances of particular events with what Peirce calls their absolute probability: that is, in forming our probable arguments, we have to take account of all the relevant evidence at our disposal. This means that in cases where an individual X belongs to two different classes K' and K", in each of which there is a different distribution of the character C, and there is an ascertained frequency of the incidence of C in the class which is the product of these two, then in estimating the chance that X possesses C, we are to rely on this frequency rather than on that which obtains with respect to C in either K' or K''. But, apart from the problem of justifying this procedure it will not always be serviceable. There will be many cases in which different parts of the available evidence points in different directions and we have no formula for resolving this conflict so as to be left with only a single guiding principle of inference.

For our present purposes, the main thing to be noted about probable inference, in this sense of the term, is that it adds a further measure of uncertainty to that which attends the conclusions of all reasoning about matters of fact. What makes it especially fallible is just that its conclusions do not follow from their premisses. But even in the case where a conclusion does follow from its premisses, the security which it derives from the argument cannot be greater than that of the premisses themselves. And if the conclusion is factual, at least one of the premisses must also be factual. In that case, even though the inference may be necessary, the conclusion itself will not be. It may be reached by valid deduction, but this cannot be the whole of its provenance. For by deductive reasoning alone we cannot arrive at any matter of fact. Outside the sphere of pure mathematics, deduction only operates on premisses which are furnished to us, on the basis of our experience, by another form of reasoning.

This other form of reasoning, through which we come by our empirical premisses, is in Peirce's view not induction, but abduction. 'Induction', he says, 'is the experimental testing of a theory. The only thing that [it] accomplishes is to determine the value of a quantity. It sets out with a theory and it measures the degree of concordance of that theory with fact.' No more than deduction can it 'originate any idea whatever. All the ideas of science come to it by the way of Abduction, [which] consists in studying facts and devising a theory to explain them.'[1]

This is the sort of passage that I had in mind when I said that Peirce's account of scientific procedure anticipated that of

[1] V 145.

Professor Popper.[1] Another quotation may serve to show how close the parallel is. Peirce raises the question how we are to proceed to the construction of a hypothesis and remarks that the only way to discover the principles on which anything ought to be constructed is to consider what is to be done with it afterwards. 'That which is to be done with the hypothesis', he continues, 'is to trace out its consequences by deduction, to compare them with the results of experiment by induction, and to discard the hypothesis, and try another, as soon as the first has been refuted; as it presumably will be. How long it will be before we light upon the hypothesis which shall resist all tests we cannot tell: but we hope we shall do so, at last.'[2]

Peirce agrees also with Popper in rejecting the suggestion that the more probable hypotheses are the ones that we should favour. Indeed, on his view, if the hypothesis takes the form of a scientific law, the question of its probability does not arise. For to say of a hypothesis of this type that it was probable to such and such a degree would be to say that it held good in such and such a proportion of possible universes. But this is a quantity which we have no means of determining, and even if we had a means of determining it, the answer would be of little interest to us. We are interested not in the range of logical possibilities that might have been fulfilled if the universe had been differently constituted, but rather in what is actually likely to happen, our universe being constituted as it is. Peirce does, however, think that we can speak of such hypotheses as being more or less probable, in a derivative sense. He suggests that we might equate their probability with the limiting value of the frequency with which hypotheses of a similar character remain unfalsified. But apart from the difficulty of finding this limiting value, there is also the problem of deciding when different hypotheses are to count as being similar. If we require no more than that they have the form of universal generalizations, then any foolish generalization that anyone has ever believed in will have to be included in the total of those that have been falsified, and what we shall be measuring will be little more than the extent of human credulity. If we confine our reference

---

[1] See K. Popper, *The Logic of Scientific Discovery* (1956).   [2] VII 220.

class to scientific hypotheses which have been reached by what we regard as a reliable method, then we have no need to concern ourselves with the probability of a hypothesis, even in this derivative sense, in order to decide whether to adopt it; for we must already know whether it is the sort of hypothesis that ought to be adopted, before its probability can even begin to be assessed.

But even if its probability is not among them, there are quite definite considerations which, in Peirce's view, should govern our choice of a hypothesis. 'In the first place', he says, 'it must be capable of being subjected to experimental testing. It must consist of experiential consequences with only so much logical cement as is needed to render them rational.' This is an essential condition and the only one that an hypothesis is strictly required to satisfy in order to be admissible; however, not every hypothesis that is admissible is worthy to be adopted. So, 'in the second place, the hypothesis must be such that it will explain the surprising facts we have before us, which it is the whole motive of our enquiry to rationalize. This explanation may consist in making the observed facts natural chance results, as the kinetic theory of gases explains facts; or it may render the facts necessary, and in the latter case as explicitly asserting them or as a ground for a mathematical demonstration of their truth.'[1]

The third consideration which is said to be quite as necessary as the others, 'in view of the fact that the true hypothesis is only one out of innumerable possible false ones, in view, too, of the enormous expensiveness of experimentation in money, time, energy, and thought, is the consideration of economy.'[2] With his love for trichotomies Peirce brings this in its turn under three headings, which he entitles Caution, Breadth and Incomplexity. Caution is needed to ensure that we get the maximum return from the questions which we put to nature. As in the game of twenty questions, the technique is to elicit answers which will most greatly narrow down the area in which the solution must lie. 'The secret of the business lies in the caution which breaks a hypothesis up into its smallest logical components, and only risks one of them at a time.'[3] Correlative to caution is breadth. 'For

[1] VII 220.   [2] Ibid.   [3] Ibid.

when we break the hypothesis into elementary parts, we may, and should, inquire how far the same explanation accounts for the same phenomenon when it appears in other subjects.' Thus the kinetic theory of gases became important when, following on the discovery of the conservation of energy, it was found that it not only explained Boyle's law but also 'would account, in a remarkably satisfactory way, for non-conservative phenomena'.[1] Finally, we shall prefer simpler to more complex hypotheses, because they are easier to emend if it is found that they do not fit the facts. Peirce uses the analogy of a billiards player who makes his stroke in such a way as to leave the balls in a good position for continuing the break.

An example of abductive reasoning to which Peirce frequently refers is that which led Kepler to the discovery of the orbit of Mars. John Stuart Mill had denied that there was any reasoning to speak of in Kepler's procedure, on the ground that it amounted to no more than a description of the facts. Peirce points out that we have only to look at Kepler's own account of his procedure in his book *De Motibus Stellae Martis* to see that Mill is here quite mistaken. What Kepler started with was the record of a large number of observations of the apparent positions of Mars at different times. So far as these data went, they fitted the Ptolemaic system very nearly as well as the Copernican. But Kepler thought that there might be more to the Copernican system than a more elegant and economical description of the appearances. It suggested to him that the sun might have something to do with causing the planets to move in their orbits, and in pursuing this suggestion he was seeking not merely a description of the facts but an explanation of them: he was looking for a theory, in terms of which they would be shown to be necessary. So, having remarked that the apsides of the orbits of the Earth and Mars are not parallel, he formed the hypothesis that they intersected in the sun; and from this he inferred that the proper times for taking the observations to determine Mars's orbit were those at which it appeared just opposite the sun, a practice which had not previously been followed. This gave him a theory of the movements of Mars

[1] VII 221.

which satisfied the longitudes in all the oppositions which had been observed by Tycho Brahe and himself, but one which did not satisfy the latitudes and did not at all square with the observations of the position of Mars when it was far from opposition. This conflict of the theory with the appearances did not, however, lead Kepler to discard it. Instead he modified it first by giving up the theory of the equant which was a legacy from the Ptolemaic system, in favour of the equable description of the areas, and then by postulating a compression of the orbit in order to account for the fact that at ninety degrees from its apsides the planet appeared to move faster than the theory allowed for. In this way he finally arrived at a theory which exactly fitted the observations.

This example is instructive in two different ways. It shows that the inductivist model of scientific theories as mere generalizations of observed facts may be inadequate even with respect to theories which remain at the observational level: at the very least, the observations have to be selected: we need some hypothesis to tell us what to try to observe and under what conditions. But it also shows that if we take the view that the testing of theories consists in an endeavour to refute them, we must remember that the refutation of a theory is not an end in itself, but rather a means to obtain a better theory. It may sometimes, therefore, be right to hold on to a theory even when the appearances are against it; a modification may be all that is needed for the conflict to be removed.

But if, to echo Kant, induction without abduction is blind, abduction without induction is empty. It is only in so far as they are tested by experiment that our hypotheses can lay any claim to truth. The process of induction primarily consists in calculating what observations should be made under the relevant conditions if the given hypothesis is true, in seeing that the conditions are fulfilled, and then if the observations turn out as expected, in regarding the hypothesis as having been confirmed. Since the support which such favourable instances are thought to give the hypothesis would not be trustworthy unless they were typical, induction is also a form of argument in which it is assumed that what is true of certain members of a class, selected from it at random, is true of all its members.

This process of generalizing from the character of a sample to the character of the collection from which the sample is drawn has most commonly been taken as the pattern of inductive reasoning, but in fact it is a form of argument which easily lends itself to misuse. If we look hard enough for similarities in any set of instances we shall almost certainly find them, but it would usually be very unsafe to assume that these similarities extended to other members of the class. Peirce illustrates this amusingly by taking from a biographical dictionary the names of the first five poets listed, and noting what was common to the ages at which they died. He found that in the case of each age of death, the difference between the two digits, divided by three, left a remainder of one, and that two other generalizations of the same type were also satisfied. He was not, however, in the least tempted to infer that these generalizations would equally apply to the ages at which all other poets died.[1]

But why should this not be as good an inductive inference of its type as any other? The reason is not just that the sample is very small, but rather, in Peirce's view, that the character in which the instances agree was not 'predesignated'. Except in the case where 'a large number of samples of a class are found to have some very striking character in common'[2] sampling from a class is significant only if the character for which we are sampling has been decided on beforehand, which is as much as to say that the sampling must be undertaken as a means of testing some hypothesis. This does not mean that we are to hold fast to any fanciful hypothesis that happens to fit a limited set of data. The hypothesis that the predesignated character is distributed in a constant ratio among the members of the class which we are sampling must be one that appears reasonable in the light of our whole experience, special account being taken of the extent to which similar hypotheses have been successful in the past.

Both the choice of hypotheses, then, and their confirmation are subject to methodological rules; but if these directions are

[1] II 738.   [2] II 740.

followed, the practice of scientific method cannot fail, in Peirce's opinion, eventually to lead to the discovery of the truth. On the face of it, this is a stronger claim than most philosophers of science would be willing to endorse. The prevailing view is that although we are bound to rely upon our past experience as a guide to the future, it has been demonstrated once for all by Hume that no procedure of the kind can offer us any assurance of success. It is held indeed that it is a mistake even to look for a justification of induction, since there is nothing in which such a justification could consist. Yet Peirce actually defines induction, in some places, as a method which if it is persisted in, 'will in the long run yield the truth, or an indefinite approximation to the truth, in regard to every question'.[1] Let us now examine the reasons which he gives for supposing that this definition can be satisfied.

B. THE JUSTIFICATION OF INDUCTION

The argument on which Peirce relies to show that the method of induction, as he conceives it, is bound to be successful in the long run, is one that has been taken up in more recent times by exponents of the frequency theory such as Reichenbach. It depends essentially on the fact that induction, on this view of it, is a self-correcting process. Among the many versions of the argument which appear throughout Peirce's works, the clearest and most succinct is to be found in an unpublished paper on the Division of Signs which was written about 1903. I shall quote the passage in full and then consider whether the argument really achieves what Peirce and its later advocates have claimed for it.

'An induction', says Peirce, 'is either a *Pooh-pooh Argument*, or an *Experimental Verification of a general Prediction*, or an Argument from a *Random Sample*. A Pooh-pooh Argument is a method which consists in denying that a general kind of event ever will occur on the ground that it never has occurred. Its justification is that if it be persistently applied on every occasion, it must

[1] II 269.

ultimately be corrected in case it should be wrong, and thus will ultimately reach the true conclusion. A verification of a general prediction is a method which consists in finding or making the conditions of the prediction and in concluding that it will be verified about as often as it is experimentally found to be verified. Its justification is that if the Prediction does not tend in the long run to be verified in any approximately determinate proportion of cases, experiment must, in the long run, ascertain this; while if the Prediction will, in the long run, be verified in any determinate, or approximately determinate, proportion of cases, experiment must, in the long run, approximately ascertain what that proportion is. An Argument from a Random Sample is a method of ascertaining what proportion of the members of a finite class possess a predesignate, or virtually predesignate, quality, by selecting instances from the class according to a method which will, in the long run, present any instance as often as any other, and concluding that the ratio found for such a sample will hold in the long run. Its justification is evident.'[1]

Let us take each of these cases in turn. What Peirce calls a Pooh-pooh argument is simply the expression of a resolve to hold on to a universal generalization, so long as it has not met with a counter-example. The assumption is that if a counter-example exists we are bound eventually to find it. When that happens, we select a fresh hypothesis, which fits both the old and the new evidence, and proceed as before. In this way, if there is a generalization, in the field in question, to which there is no counter-example, we shall sooner or later come upon it.

There are two objections to this argument. In the first place, the assumption that if a counter-example to our generalization exists, we are bound to find it, is not true unless we are able to go through all the instances: but however long the run, even if it is infinitely long, it is surely possible that some instance will go undetected. This is, however, open to the pragmatic rejoinder that instances which remain for ever undetected are of no significance. So long as no counter-example ever in fact presents itself, the predictions which we make in accordance with the hypothesis

[1] II 269.

will not be falsified, and this is all that concerns us. For our purposes a true hypothesis is one that we shall never have any occasion to reject.

The second objection is more serious. As Peirce himself acknowledges, whenever a hypothesis has been falsified we have a very wide, perhaps an infinite, choice of hypotheses with which to replace it. This choice may be limited by our principles of economy; but though we may be well advised to try out the simplest hypothesis that fits the facts, we can never have a guarantee that the true hypothesis is not more complex. If, indeed, we were confined to a universe of discourse, in which there were only a finite number of predicates, then in principle we could try out every combination of every predicate with the negation of every other, so that if there were any laws to the effect that everything that has P has Q, since this is equivalent to denying the combination of P and not Q, we should eventually come upon them. But for scientific purposes this is a very poor universe of discourse. If we have one which is rich enough to permit the expression of functional laws, where the function ranges over all real, or all rational, or even only all cardinal numbers, there will be an infinite number of candidates from which to pick the true hypotheses. In that case the assurance that we are bound to get the right answers if only we go on long enough is practically nullified by the admission that what is meant here by 'long enough' may be an infinite stretch of time.

Against this it may be said that the duration of scientific enquiry is almost certainly finite: and Peirce's method does ensure that at whatever time it comes to an end, the hypotheses which are then accepted will be in accordance with the facts: or, if it be objected that the ascertainment of the facts is itself to some extent an inductive process, the method does at least ensure that there will be a perfect accordance between the surviving hypotheses and what are then believed to be the facts. But this is trivial. There is no question but that we can adjust our theories to the evidence *ex post facto*. If there is to be any point in talking of a justification of inductive methods, it must be shown that they are guaranteed to work predictively; and this the argument fails to achieve. Even if it be granted that by adhering consistently to the Pooh-pooh method we are bound to reach the truth in an infinite time, it will not follow that the method works predictively; for the time at which our predictions attain the promised security may always lie ahead.

Much the same considerations apply to the other two methods. I take it that what is involved in the Experimental Verification of a general Prediction is that we are required to forecast, with respect to a possibly infinite series of events, what proportion of the members of the series possess a given character. Then either the series tends to a limiting frequency with respect to this character, or it does not. In either case we shall eventually discover the right answer, but again if the series is infinite we cannot be sure of getting to the truth in anything less than an infinite time. Otherwise all that we can say is either that a limit has not yet been reached, or that a limit has been reached from which there has not as yet been any significant deviation. Of course if scientific inquiry comes to an end, which means that pragmatically the series becomes finite, the calculation of the frequency which has been attained gives us the correct answer. But once again this is trivial.

The third method differs from the second in that the reference class is finite and that all its members are open to selection at one and the same time. The question then is whether the frequency with which some character is distributed among the members of a random sample is approximately the same as that with which it is distributed throughout the class as a whole. The answer is that it must be, provided that the sample is sufficiently large. For, as has already been remarked, the Law of Large Numbers ensures that the proportion of large samples which are deviant with respect to the distribution among the members of any given character is vanishingly small. We may have the misfortune to begin by selecting only deviant samples, but if we persist this error is bound to be corrected, so long as we are employing a method of selection which in the long run presents any instance as often as any other, since the overwhelming majority of samples of that size are true. But the difficulty here is to ensure that our method of selection is random, in the sense defined. How do we know that it will, in the long run, present any instance as often as any other? Only, it would seem, by ascertaining that it actually does so, which means that we must in fact be presented with every member of the class. But if we are going to run through all the members of the class, the whole process of sampling becomes unnecessary. We obtain our answer without risking any inference at all, just by exhausting all the instances. Even if we run through no more than a large majority of the instances, we may be sure that the frequency with which the character we are investigating is distributed among them is not very far removed from the frequency with which it is distributed throughout the parent class, simply because whatever may be true of the remaining instances they are comparatively too few to make any appreciable difference to the final result. But this assurance is of no interest to us. It tells us no more than we know already. We are still not in a position to make any extrapolative inferences, except on the assumption that we have hit upon a fair method of sampling; and this is an assumption which we have found no means to justify except by acquiring so much information as to remove any need for the inference which it supports. We might try to justify it inductively, on the ground that similar methods have served us well in the past; but then we should be turning in a circle, since the force of such inductive arguments is just what is in question.

The upshot of this is that if there are any laws, whether statistical or causal, which govern the object of our investigation, it is indeed true that we are bound to find them, or at least find some approximation to them, in the long run; but the qualification 'in the long run' robs this conclusion of all its value. It means that if the reference class is finite, we have to examine all, or nearly all its members; if it is infinite we are sure of getting the right answer only in an infinite time. In neither case have we any security at all for our predictions. It would seem, therefore, that Peirce's arguments do not substantiate his claims.

Perhaps, however, a weaker claim can be substantiated. Let us confine ourselves, for the sake of simplicity, to the case of universal generalizations, and let it be admitted that there is no guarantee that we shall hit upon the right hypotheses in anything short of an infinite time. Nevertheless, we may have good fortune. In certain fields, at least, we may have to discard only a relatively small number of hypotheses before discovering the right one. We shall not know for sure that it is the right one, but the predictions which we make in accordance with it will not in fact be falsified; and this is all that we require. Then the justification of induction is that if we do have this good fortune, it enables us to capitalize on it, and that there is no other method which could possibly serve us any better. Even if it is not an absolutely fool-proof policy, it is the best that we can have.

This claim has in fact been made by modern exponents of Peirce's argument. In order to assess it, we have now to consider what other methods there could be. If induction may be characterized, broadly, as the policy of trusting hypotheses so long as our experience confirms them, there appear to be only two alternatives to it. One would be to adopt what might be called a counter-inductive policy, that is, to assume that the hypotheses which will hold good in the future are those which have not held good in the past: the other would be to adopt a policy which took no account of past experience at all.

A counter-inductive policy is not very easy to formulate; indeed it has often been said to be impossible. The model on which I have thought it could be based is that of the Monte Carlo fallacy at roulette. It has seemed to me that it might be possible to generalize the attitude of those gamblers who believe that the longer has been the run of either colour, the greater is the chance that a number of the other colour will come up on the next occasion. This is a fallacy in the theory of probability, but it is a policy that can be consistently followed. There is, however, a difficulty in applying the model to cases where there are more than two alternatives, and above all to cases where the number of alternatives is indeterminate. We are told what we are to bet against, but not what we are to bet on. Suppose, for example, that an exponent of this policy decided that since the Newtonian law of attraction had had an extremely long run, it was due to break down at the very next instant. What should he expect to happen instead? That bodies should cease to attract each other at all, or that they should start attracting each other in accordance with the inverse cube of the distance between them, or the direct square, or what? Perhaps the direct square. He could adopt the rule that all quantitative functions which had hitherto held good were to give way to their reciprocals. But even then he will be allowing the attraction to continue to depend upon distance: he will be assuming also that bodies will continue to exist. Or let us take an example of a different kind. Hitherto men have been born of women. Our counter-inductivist must wager that this will not continue, but how else should he expect them to come into the world? Can he credit them, indeed, with any future in the world at all, since for any men to continue to exist is to perpetuate an association of characters which has already had a pretty long run? One too easily forgets, when one starts playing this sort of game, how many assumptions of continuity are already built into the language in which we formulate the rules.

A thoroughgoing counter-inductivist would have to assume not only that any pair of characters which had hitherto been found in combination would cease to be so, but also that any pair of characters which have not hitherto been combined would combine in the future. But this means that the world, as he pictures it, is one in which there are no universal laws. For every universal statement of the form 'All A is B' is equivalent to a negative existential statement, which denies the combination of A with not B. Then since, according to the counter-inductivist, if A has not combined with not B in the past, it must do so in the future, he is bound to hold that every such universal statement is false. Neither can he admit statistical laws, since he is committed to holding that if a constant proportion of A's have been B's over a certain period of time, this proportion is bound to deviate in the future. What his principles require is that every possible combination of characters, both positive and negative, occurs just once and never again. This would be a world without repetition, and therefore the most disorderly world imaginable; but as Peirce himself remarks of what he calls a thoroughly chance-world, 'Certainly nothing could be imagined more systematic'.[1] If we hit upon the principle which governed it, then, provided that the number of predicates in our universe of discourse was finite, we should be able to predict the composition of every event; the only uncertainty would be with regard to the order in which they were going to occur: we should be able to predict even that the world would come to an end when every possible combination of characters had been exhausted. Only, of course, there would not be any 'we' to do the predicting, or any method of keeping the records which would enable the predictions to be made.

I conclude, therefore, that the notion of *our* pursuing a thoroughgoing counter-inductivist policy is incoherent. It need not, however, be a case of all or nothing. It may still be possible for us to be counter-inductivists in some quite considerable degree. There will have to be enough constancy in the world for there to be predictors, not necessarily persons with exactly the same sorts of characteristics as we now have, but intelligent beings of some kind, and enough constancy for them to be able to keep reliable records of their observations: and there will have to be a fairly stable group of things to serve as subjects for the counter-inductive hypotheses. Then to the extent to which it was possible to divide predicates of the same family into pairs of polar opposites, the method could be put to work. The division of predicates might in many cases appear rather arbitrary, but that would not matter. So, if black and white were taken as a pair of opposing predicates, and all the X's which had so far been observed had been black, we should expect the next one to be white. As we have seen, this policy could not be completely generalized but it could on the face of it be made to extend over quite a large area of our experience.

Suppose now that these conditions are satisfied and that we adopt the policy in a given domain. So long as it is unsuccessful, we know how to proceed. Each time that our expectation that the next instance will differ from its predecessors is disappointed, we become more confident that the tide will turn at the next opportunity. But suppose that the policy succeeds. Suppose that

[1] VI 401.

the tide does turn. What do we do then? Well, to pursue the gambling analogy, we might go on betting that the next X will be white until the number of instances of either colour is equal, and thenceforward bet against whatever colour is ahead. When they are equal we pick one or other at random. Such a method would be workable and it is conceivable that it would yield more successful predictions, in a given domain, than the inductive method of expecting the pattern of the past to be repeated in the future.

But even though the counter-inductivist were to succeed in this way, his very success would ruin him. For no sooner had his policy been established as successful than the inductivist would take it over. If, in our example, it were in fact the case that the number of white and black X's constantly returned to equality, in the way described, we should have a hypothesis which was inductively extrapolable, and one that the method of sampling would easily bring to light. The counter-inductivist might indeed try to escape from the grasp of induction by applying his policy to policies themselves. His principle would be to vary a policy in some radical way as soon as it proved successful. But this device would not preserve his independence. For if the policy of varying policies were successful, it would in its turn fall into the inductivist's grasp.

This shows that even in a limited domain the method of induction is superior, in the sense that any success which its rival enjoys eventually accrues to it also, whereas the converse does not hold. It does not follow, however, that it is always the more profitable method to follow. In our example, it would in fact be more profitable to be a counter-inductivist, provided that one did not take it to the point of abandoning one's counter-inductive policy as soon as it began to be successful. For, in the case which we have imagined, the counter-inductivist would get to the right answer more quickly. He would be having a run of successes, while the inductivist was having a run of failures, until the pattern became sufficiently clear for the inductivist to take over, after which their predictions would be equally successful. But though some counter-inductive policies could get quicker results, induction must be surer. The reason why it must be surer is that any successful *policy* must become an inductive policy, since in order to be successful it must correspond to some pattern in the events with which it deals; and the pattern must be projectible if the policy is to continue to succeed.

But now what of the second alternative to induction? Is it not logically possible that we should fare better by taking no account of the past at all? Once again this could work only in a limited field. If one were to take no account of the past, one would not be in a position to formulate any predictions. There has at least to be the tacit assumption that certain characters will continue to be found in combination; otherwise we should not be able to identify the individuals, or the class, to which our predictions are to apply. But beyond this it is conceivable that, rather than relying on induction, in Peirce's sense of the term, we should do better to trust to guess-work or to inspiration, which might or might not be backed by the authority of divine voices, or stimulated by looking into crystal balls. This is akin to Peirce's third method of fixing belief, the method of accepting whatever seems 'agreeable to reason', except that reason does not enter into it. Let us call it the crystal-gazing method, without necessarily implying that crystals are actually used. Now there is no logical contradiction in supposing that this method pays off every time. Whatever is in fact going to happen, the crystal-gazer predicts.

But again the inductivist takes over. It comes to his notice that whenever the crystal-gazer predicts that such and such an event will occur, the event does occur at the time predicted, and this gives him a good inductive reason for taking the crystal-gazer as his guide. There will, however, once more be a time lag, before the crystal-gazer's credit is inductively established, and this makes it possible to construct a case in which the inductivist could be frustrated. Suppose that there was a company of crystal-gazers, whose familiars gave them different instructions with respect to any given future event. And suppose that crystal-gazer A were always right and the others wrong. The inductivist would catch on to this, and would make it his policy to follow A. But no sooner had he done so than the inspiration would forsake A and light upon B, only to forsake B in turn when the inductivist had started to follow him in place of A. There is no question here of a logical trick. I am not making it a sufficient condition for an event not to occur that the inductivist predicts that it will occur. It is just that when any of the crystal-gazers has had a run of successful predictions which is impressive enough for the inductivist to follow him, the run comes to a stop. Now if this happened in a systematic way, if, for example, once the inspiration had left A, it did not light on him again until it had hit on all the others, and if it stayed with anyone on whom it hit until at least a certain number of successful predictions had been made by him, the inductivist could catch on to the pattern of its operation. It is, however, conceivable that it should move around in a way that he could not predict, not indeed in a way that was unpredictable in principle, since however it operated it would have to adhere to *some* pattern, but in a way that he could not reasonably be expected to detect.

In that case, if the events which the crystal-gazers severally predicted were very startling, if they were out of the course of nature as it has so far been revealed to us, the inductivist would not fare at all well in this domain. And if one of the crystal-gazers had an exceptionally long run of successes before the inductivist caught on to him, he might on the whole do better. But still not very much better. For *ex hypothesi* he too is going to be wrong more often than he is right, namely on all the occasions when the inspiration is with one of the other crystal-gazers and not with him.

At this point one might think of bringing in a second-order crystal-gazer whose familiar told him when and to which of the first-order crystal-gazers the inspiration was about to turn. But this would serve no purpose. For either he will be taken over by the inductivist, or we must enrol him in a similar company of second-order crystal-gazers, and the same story is repeated. We may conclude, therefore, that in situations in which the method of induction would meet with no success, no other method would succeed much better. Even in the examples which are constructed to favour them, the advantages which are enjoyed by its rivals are in the one case temporary and in the other slight.

This justification of induction, so far as it goes, depends upon the fact that if any method of forming hypotheses, including even the unmethodical method of trusting to one's own or some one else's hunches, yields successful predictions, it must be projectible. It would not be a successful method if it did not follow a pattern which corresponded to the pattern of the events with which it dealt. It is indeed no more than a matter of good fortune that the pattern is not too complex for us to be able to detect, but it can still be said that the pursuit of inductive method offers us the surest hope of success, if success is within our grasp at all.

All the same this does not take us very far. It would be quite a satisfactory result if there were a determinate method of induction, in Peirce's sense, but unfortunately there is not. As we have seen, there is never just one projectible hypothesis which will account for a given set of facts. We have to make a choice, perhaps among an infinite number which are alike in being in accord with past observations but yield incompatible results with respect to some or all further instances. It is often assumed that the problem of induction would be solved if only we could find some guarantee that the future would resemble the past; but this is not so. The question is not so much whether the future will resemble the past, since if the world is to be describable at all it must resemble it in some way or other, but how it will resemble it. And here the simple injuction to pursue inductive methods does not help us, since each of the competing hypotheses between which we have to choose will be equally justified in terms of past experience. The observance of Peirce's rules of economy in the selection of hypotheses will indeed save us labour, but does not assure us of success. The assurance which we do have is that we are bound to get the right answer, or approximately the right answer, if we pursue our enquiries long enough. This is perhaps a sufficient encouragement to continue, if any encouragement were needed, but it is still not a very solid guarantee: for, as we have seen, it is consistent with our failing to get the right answer, in any finite period of time.

C. THE FACTOR OF CHANCE

Although, for the reason that I have just given, I do not think that Peirce's vindication of induction has the value that he attaches to it, his treatment of the problem is very much more sophisticated than that which is to be found even in most modern textbooks of logic. He does not make the mistake, which was made by John Stuart Mill, and in a different way also by Hume and by Kant, of supposing that inductive reasoning can be cast in the form of syllogism with the Uniformity of Nature as its major premiss. Apart from other objections, he sees that the syllogism would be invalid, since the principle of the Uniformity of Nature is much too general in its scope to be able to serve as the guiding principle of any such specific inferences as those which derive the properties of a collection from the properties of a sample. The proof of this is that, if the syllogism were valid, any counter-example to a universal hypothesis, which had not previously been violated, would destroy the Uniformity of Nature.

But apart from its being an unnecessary and ineffective assumption for the purpose of justifying inductive reasoning, have we any good reason to think that the principle of the Uniformity of Nature is true? If, indeed, it is interpreted as stating no more than that every event can be subsumed under some generalization or other, it is certainly true, but also trivial. This requirement is so weak that it would be met, as we have seen, even in a universe in which there was no repetition. On the other hand, if the requirement is that every natural occurrence be governed in every detail by laws of manageable simplicity, then it is by no means obvious that it is satisfied, and it is in fact Peirce's view that it is not.

Peirce holds the reign of law to be limited because he thinks that an element of pure chance, or spontaneity, is operative in the world. In his more metaphysical moments, he somehow equates this with a mysterious factor to which he gives the name of evolutionary love. Leaving aside the metaphysics, the points which he chiefly wishes to make, in bringing forward his concept of chance, are first that the process of evolution is such that we constantly meet with new developments which cannot be causally explained in terms of what has gone before, secondly, that in some domains at least the laws which obtain are irreducibly statistical and thirdly, that even where causal laws do prevail, there is a degree of looseness in the way in which they fit the facts; there are variations, such as a scattering of numerical values, among the instances which are regarded as conforming to them, and these variations are due to chance.

In support of the first of these contentions, Peirce argues that if we consider any science 'which deals with the course of time', we can hardly fail to remark that 'everywhere the main fact is growth and increasing complexity'.[1] This increase in complexity cannot be explained in terms of mechanical laws, for 'mechanical law can never produce diversification, . . . anybody can see that mechanical law out of like antecedents can only produce like consequents'.[2] This is illustrated by the fact that mechanical laws are reversible in their operation: if the world were wholly governed by them, the past would be no less determined by the future than the future by the past. A mechanical system is indifferent to time, in the sense that if we had complete knowledge of the state of the system at any one instant, we could calculate its state at any other. But the world, as it progressively reveals itself to us, is not a system of this kind. 'The ordinary view', says Peirce, by which he means the deterministic view, 'has to admit the inexhaustible multitudinous variety of the world, has to admit that its mechanical law cannot account for this in the least, that variety can spring only from spontaneity, and yet denies without any evidence or reason the existence of this spontaneity, or else shoves it back to the beginning of time and supposes it dead ever since.'[3] Against this, Peirce thinks it more logical to regard 'pure spontaneity' as a persisting character of the universe, 'producing infinitesimal departures from law continually, and great ones with infinite infrequency'.[4] He maintains, indeed, that the laws of nature themselves may not be immutable. They are the products of evolution and are presumably, therefore, also subject to it.[5]

[1] VI 58.   [2] I 174.   [3] VI 59.   [4] Ibid.   [5] See VII 514.

That some laws are irreducibly statistical is a view which is strongly favoured by modern developments in microscopic physics. Indeed, the prevailing opinion is that this applies to the most fundamental laws of nature. When Peirce maintained it, this view was not nearly so orthodox as it has since become: he was writing before the advent of the quantum theory. Nevertheless he thought himself justified in speaking of the 'principle of explaining a general phenomenon by the statistical regularities that exist among irregularities'.[1] The illustration on which he chiefly relies is that of the kinetic theory of gases where 'the general properties of gases are explained by supposing that the molecules are moving about in every direction in the most diverse possible ways': the regularity which the theory brings to light is 'the resultant effect of a whole class of irregularities'.[2] Of course it is open to the determinist to maintain in such a case that if only we had more knowledge we should find that the phenomena which displayed these apparent irregularities were in fact subject to causal laws. He cannot, however, prove that this must be so: and in default of any such proof, there seems to be no good reason why we should not allow ourselves to take the view that the phenomena are governed only by statistical laws, if we find it more in accordance with the existing evidence.

That even in those domains in which we do believe that causal laws prevail, the laws fit the facts only loosely is again a contention for which Peirce claims scientific support. 'Those observations', he says, 'which are generally adduced in favour of mechanical causation simply prove that there is an element of regularity in nature, and have no bearing whatever upon the question of whether such regularity is exact and universal or not. Nay, in regard to this *exactitude*, all observation is directly *opposed* to it; and the most that can be said is that a good deal of this observation can be explained away. Try to verify any law of nature, and you will find that the more precise your observations, the more certain they will be to show irregular departures from the law. We are accustomed to ascribe these, and I do not say wrongly, to errors of observation; yet we cannot actually account for such

[1] I 157.   [2] Ibid.

errors in any antecedently probable way. Trace their causes back far enough and you will be forced to admit they are always due to arbitrary determination, or chance.'[1] In other words, our ascription of the deviations to 'errors of observation' is a way of pretending that the rule of law is more stringent than it is actually found to be. In general, Peirce thinks, 'we enormously exaggerate the part that law plays in the Universe'.[2] Even when people claim that 'every event is determined by causes according to law' they do not really mean more than that every event is a member of some causal chain; the concurrence of events in different causal chains does not come under any general law. 'That is merely what we call a coincidence.'[3]

'We are brought, then,' Peirce concludes, 'to this: conformity to law exists only within a limited range of events and even there is not perfect, for an element of pure spontaneity or lawless originality mingles, or at least must be supposed to mingle, with law everywhere. Moreover, conformity with law is a fact requiring to be explained; and since law in general cannot be explained by any law in particular, the explanation must consist in showing how law is developed out of pure chance, irregularity, and indeterminancy.'[4]

What are we to make of these arguments? They are not very easy to evaluate. One of the main difficulties is that it is not clear how much weight should be attached to Peirce's use of the word 'mechanical'. If he is merely contending that the theory of classical mechanics is not adequate to account for all the variety of phenomena that the world progressively reveals, he is plainly right. It does not follow, however, that we are bound to attribute this variety to an element of pure spontaneity. It can still be maintained that there are laws of some kind to which the phenomena are entirely subject, and even that these laws are all derivable from the laws of physics, given that the laws of physics themselves need not be exclusively 'mechanical'. If it were shown that biology could be reduced to chemistry and chemistry to physics, it would not be absurd to maintain that the properties and distribution of the atoms of which the world was initially constituted fore-

[1] VI 46.   [2] I 406.   [3] Ibid.   [4] I 407.

shadowed all the variety that it was destined to exhibit. This would not rule out the factor of chance, since it leaves open the possibility that the laws of physics are basically statistical, but while there may be strong considerations which favour this possibility, it is not pre-eminently supported by the fact that the world exhibits a great deal of variety, or by the fact that it increases in complexity.

It is indeed true that if conformity with law, to the extent that it occurs, were something which itself stood in need of explanation, we should have no serious alternative but to try to show how law has developed out of chance. For, as Peirce truly says, law in general cannot be explained by any law in particular. But might not the correct answer be that the existence of law in general does not call for explanation? After all, it is a necessary fact that any world of which it makes sense to talk at all displays some sort of order; we have seen this to be true even in the extreme case of a world in which no combination of characters is ever repeated. The question is, then, whether the pattern of events is such that they can be brought under generalizations of a manageable kind, which not only fit the facts exactly but are simple enough for the use of scientific method to bring them to light, or whether the pattern is so tortuous that generalizations with any approach to exactitude can only be constructed *ex post facto*. To the extent that the hypotheses which are suggested to us by our past and present observations cannot be successfully projected into the future, and to the extent that even hypotheses which are projectible may not fully determine the facts, we may choose, as Peirce does, to speak of there being limits to the reign of law and consequently of there being an area which is given over to the government of chance. In this sense, the subjection of events to law becomes a matter of degree, and any degree of lawfulness is logically conceivable.

Antecedently to experience, there can be no more and no less reason to expect any set of phenomena to be highly regular, in the sense that they fall under generalizations which both fit them exactly and can be successfully projected, than to expect them to be highly irregular, in the sense that we can have no reasonable

hope of being able to subsume them under any generalizations
of this sort. But in that case conformity to law in general does not
require any more explanation than lack of conformity. It just is
the case that the events exhibit the degree of regularity that they
do. There would indeed be something to explain if the growth
of law out of chance were the historical process that Peirce takes
it to have been: we might then at least look for some lawlike
account of the way in which this development had taken place,
though, as in the case of Peirce's own suggestion that 'all things
have a tendency to take habits'[1] there is a danger that the explanation would come to little more than a restatement of the facts.
But even if such an account could be given, it is hard to see how
it could establish the temporal priority of chance. It would appear,
rather, that if the whole process is lawlike, an element of law must
have been present from the start.

There is a similar difficulty in Peirce's suggestion that the laws
of nature are themselves subject to a process of evolution. In any
case in which there was empirical evidence that the phenomena
within a given range were obeying a different law from that to
which they had previously appeared to be subject, the change
could always be put down to a difference in the conditions. The
two laws, obtaining under different conditions, might then both be
regarded as special cases of a more general law which was operative
throughout. The fact that there could always be this alternative
explanation does not put Peirce's suggestion out of court, but it
does show that it is not forced upon us either by any evidence
that we already have or by any that we are likely to obtain. As
Professor Nagel remarks, in a discussion of this question to which
I am much indebted, 'whether such an assumption will ever be
widely accepted will most likely depend on how effective and
convenient it proves to be in establishing a thoroughly inclusive
and integrated system of knowledge'.[2] It may indeed be said to
be only a question of formulation whether we regard laws as
mutable, or whether we provide for the influence of special
conditions in the operation of immutable laws, but such questions

[1] I 409.
[2] Ernest Nagel, *The Structure of Science* (1961), p. 379.

of formulation can be important, inasmuch as they guide our interpretation of the facts.

So far, our discussion of the claim which Peirce makes for the recognition of Chance as a factor in the world has been inconclusive. We have seen that if the term 'chance' is understood in such a way that an event is attributed to chance in case it is not subject to what I have called a manageable law, then it is not inconceivable that some events are due to chance. On the other hand the general arguments on which Peirce relies to show that there are such events are not decisive. His strongest point is that over the whole range of our experience, strict conformity to law is the exception rather than the rule. That is to say, of the observations that we actually make we are not able to account precisely for more than a small fraction in terms of causal laws. This proportion becomes rather greater if we do not insist upon complete exactitude of detail, but even so there is a very large class of phenomena, especially in the field of human and animal behaviour, which we have not succeeded in bringing under anything stronger than statistical generalizations, of a rough and ready kind. Nevertheless, we cannot rule out the possibility that we should discover these phenomena to be subject to the strictest causal laws, if our enquiries were further pursued. In the domain of microscopic physics, it would indeed appear that so long as the experimental data are interpreted according to the dictates of the prevailing quantum theory, there is no possibility that the laws which govern them will prove to be anything but statistical.[1] It is, however, still the ambition of some physicists to devise a deterministic theory, of a radically different character, which would fit the facts as well or better. It may be thought unlikely that their enterprise will succeed, but so long as any doubt remains upon this point, the determinist can retain at least the hope that the advancement of knowledge will eventually prove him right.

This being so, I think that in his advocacy of the claims of chance Peirce should be taken to be propounding not so much a thesis as a challenge. He is wagering that, however far science

[1] Cf. Nagel, p. 311.

advances, it will never succeed in extending the reign of well-established causal hypotheses so that they are made to cover everything that is observed to happen in every detail. So long as no term is set to the duration of scientific enquiry, this wager can never be strictly won; but there could come a point at which the failure to make good the claims of determinism might lead to a fairly general acceptance of the view that its ideal is unattainable. In the mean time, whether one sides with Peirce on this issue will depend partly on one's assessment of current scientific tendencies, but partly also on one's intellectual temperament. There are those who find it offensive to reason that the universe should not be altogether lawlike but there are others, of whom I think that I am one, to whom the idea that there are absolutely chance events has a romantic appeal. Apart, however, from having this slight prejudice in favour of Peirce's standpoint, I also think it rational to attach some weight to the fact that the current outlook of science rather favours it.

One of the main advantages which Peirce claimed for his position was that by relaxing the bonds of necessity it left room for the freedom of the will. This is a notion that has been very widely shared, but I think that it is mistaken. In the first place, even if it be granted that there are chance events, it has yet to be shown that human actions are among them. But a more serious objection is that even if we had reason to think that some human actions did occur by chance, this is not a conclusion from which the partisans of free-will could reasonably derive any particular satisfaction. The notion of free-will is in many ways obscure, but if anything is clear about it, it is that the attribution of free-will to an agent is supposed to entail that he is responsible for his actions. The reason why the ideal of determinism has been thought to be destructive of free-will is that it has been assumed that if all our actions are causally necessitated, we cannot legitimately be held to be responsible for them. Whether this assumption is justified is a question into which I do not here propose to enter. The only point which I now wish to make is that there is certainly no stronger ground for holding that an agent is responsible for his actions if they are entirely due to chance. From this point of view, there is no more satisfaction in the idea of our being nature's playthings than there is in the idea of our being nature's prisoners. The advocates of free-will would argue that these are not the only alternatives. I think that they are wrong, but I have nothing to add on this subject to what I have already said elsewhere.[1] What concerns us here is that their position receives no support from Peirce's 'tychism'. Whatever reasons there may be for accepting this doctrine, the preservation of the status of free-will is not among them.

[1] See 'Freedom and Necessity' in *Philosophical Essays* (1954) and 'Fatalism' in *The Concept of a Person* (1963).

CHAPTER FOUR

PEIRCE'S CATEGORIES AND HIS THEORY OF SIGNS

A. THE THREE CATEGORIES

1. *Feeling and Perception*

JUST as Peirce distinguishes three fundamentally different kinds of reasoning, so he believes that there are three fundamental categories. He calls them respectively: Firstness, Secondness and Thirdness and refers to them sometimes as Modes of Being and sometimes as Ideas.

As usual, he gives various definitions which differ stylistically rather than in substance. In one of his clearer formulations of the doctrine, he talks of the conceptions of First, Second and Third and explains that 'First is the conception of being or existing independent of anything else; Second is the conception of being relative to, the conception of reaction with, something else; Third is the conception of mediation whereby a first and a second are brought into relation'.[1]

These definitions require elucidation. The first step towards dispelling their obscurity is to remark that Peirce treats Firstness as the domain of what he calls feeling, Secondness as the domain of fact, and Thirdness as the domain of law. In explaining this further we shall also be drawn into his theory of knowledge.

Peirce uses the term 'feeling' to refer to the primary elements of consciousness, including the data which give rise to the judgements of perception on which all our empirical knowledge is ultimately founded. He does not, however, endow these feelings with at all the same characteristics as other philosophers have attributed to the sensory impressions, or sense-data, which they

[1] VI 32.

have represented as the immediate objects of perception. Feelings, for Peirce, are not private entities; they are not even particulars of any kind; they are not located in space, not even in private spaces, nor in time; and so far from the subject's having an infallible knowledge of their properties, his idea of them is only conjectural, and very unlikely to be accurate.

This view is less paradoxical than it sounds. The clue to it is that when Peirce talks of feelings, he is referring to what is given to us prior to all interpretation. Since nothing is observed without being in some way interpreted, feelings themselves are not observed.[1] They are not even introspectible.[2] We can say that they are experienced inasmuch as they supply the raw material out of which we elaborate what we call the evidence of our senses, but we are not aware of them as such; any idea that we may have about their intrinsic character is the outcome of a psychological theory, which cannot be directly tested.

It is indeed precisely because they belong to the category of Firstness that feelings cannot be the *objects* of consciousness. For, if they were the objects of consciousness, they would have to be identified, which would imply that they were compared with and distinguished from other things; and they would have to be located in time, which would also imply that they were brought into relation with things other than themselves. Indeed, since nothing exists in the isolation demanded by the category of Firstness, it follows that feelings have no actuality. This does not mean that they are unreal, or fictitious, but rather that they are situated at too primitive a level for existence to be ascribable to them. As members of the category of Firstness they have only the being of 'pure qualitative possibility'.

There is a strong echo here of Kant. Peirce's primitive elements of consciousness are akin to Kant's things in themselves, in that they are not open to our inspection, but are merely postulated, on the ground that there must be something out of which we construct the objects and events of which we can have knowledge. But, whatever may have led Peirce to take this view, it is hardly consistent with his pragmatism. Since one of his principles is that

[1] See I 253.   [2] See I 310.

'we have no conception of the absolutely incognizable'[1] he presumably did not think of feelings as being quite so inaccessible
to our understanding as the Kantian things in themselves. He
seems to have thought that we could form hypotheses about their
nature, on the basis of the experiences which we were conscious
of having; that we could, as it were, obtain from the manufactured
article some indication of the material of which it was made. It is
not, however, easy to see how these hypotheses could be even
indirectly tested.

If our feelings as such are inaccessible to introspection, then, as
Peirce says, it would be 'the most chimerical of undertakings' to
try to discover any logical relation between even our judgements
of perception and 'the first impressions of sense'. 'Practically, the
knowledge with which I have to content myself, and have to
call "the evidence of my senses", instead of being in truth the
evidence of the senses, is only a sort of stenographic report of that
evidence, possibly erroneous. In place of the *percept*, which,
although not the first impression of sense, is a construction with
which my will had nothing to do and may, therefore, properly
be called the "evidence of my senses", the only thing I carry away
with me is the *perceptual facts*, or the intellect's description of the
evidence of the senses, made by my endeavour.'[2]

These perceptual facts are primitive, so far as anything can be.
They are not the objects of what modern sense-datum theorists,
like Moore and Russell, have called 'direct acquaintance', since
Peirce denies that any such faculty exists. The 'intellect's description of the evidence of the senses' is not infallible and probably
not even true. But however unfaithful the perceptual facts may
be to the actual percepts, they are all that we have to go by. If
we decide that we have been mistaken in acknowledging some
perceptual fact, the reason can only be that it does not fit in with
our interpretation of other perceptual facts which we refuse to
relinquish: it is only for the reason that it does fit in with what we
regard as other perceptual facts that we can be confirmed in our
belief that it was genuine. The perceptual facts are primitive, then,
in the sense that we cannot go behind them. They are not strictly

[1] V 265.   [2] II 141.

forced upon us, in the way that percepts themselves are, because they are the product of a process of reflection which could conceivably be inhibited or take a different course. However, given our intellectual habits, it is usually as though not only the percepts but the perceptual facts are forced upon us. We do not feel at liberty to avoid acknowledging them. And it is because they have this special status that they serve as the touchstone for the whole body of our factual beliefs.

This qualified admission of a form of direct knowledge, which occurs in Peirce's later writings, is a little at variance with the views that he expressed in the two famous early papers, entitled 'Questions Concerning Certain Faculties Claimed for Man' and 'Some Consequences of Four Incapacities', which he published in the *Journal of Speculative Philosophy* in 1868. Of the incapacities in question I have already mentioned the inability to have any conception of the absolutely incognizable: the other three faculties that we are said to lack are the power of thinking without signs, the power of Introspection, in the sense that 'all knowledge of the internal world is derived by hypothetical reasoning from our knowledge of external facts' and the power of Intuition.[1] And here our lack of the power of intuition is taken to imply not only that all our beliefs are fallible but that none of them arises directly out of our observation of the facts. The thesis is that every cognition of an object is determined by a previous cognition of the same object,[2] so that every judgement of perception has another judgement, as it were, standing between it and the state of affairs which it purports to record.

This thesis is not very easy to understand and still less easy to accept. Apart from the difficulty of seeing what such an infinite series of 'cognitions' could possibly consist in, it is open to the obvious objection that whatever may be true of events in general, a series which consists of the judgements made by a particular person with reference to one particular object must surely have a first term. Peirce notes this objection and tries to meet it by invoking the Achilles paradox. The reason why the series has no first term is that it is continuous. It has a beginning in time, in

[1] V 265.   [2] See V 213.

the sense that there are events which precede any term in the series, but there is no term in the series which precedes all the others. In the same way, though Achilles has a starting point from which he tries to overtake the tortoise, there is no distance that he travels from it before he travels any other: however short we take this initial distance to be, in order to traverse it he must already have traversed a shorter distance still. Peirce tries to show that the case of his series of cognitions is analogous by introducing the simile of an inverted triangle which is partly dipped in water. The apex of the triangle represents the object of the cognitions. The cognitions themselves are represented by the lines made by the surface of the water across the triangle, the earlier cognitions corresponding to the lower lines. Then, since any line must be separated by a finite distance from the apex, there is no lowest line.[1]

But while this is an effective illustration, it is a bad analogy. It is true that a process which lasts for any length of time has infinitely many phases, in the sense that any stretch of it can be infinitely subdivided, but this is not to say that it consists of an infinite number of processes of the same kind as itself. The mere fact, which Peirce strangely adduces as an argument in his favour, that cognitions are not instantaneous tells conclusively against him: for if there is a lower limit to the time during which a process of cognition can take place, it follows that, even if it can be represented as having an infinite number of parts, these parts cannot themselves all be cognitions. The fact that the time which it takes is infinitely subdivisible no more implies that the cognition can be so divided than the fact that the distance which Achilles covers in his first step is infinitely subdivisible implies that he thereby takes an infinite number of steps.

It may be of interest to note in passing that Peirce also invokes the principle that a continuous series has no first or last term as a means of accounting for the action of mind on matter. In spite of his believing that mind and matter are not radically different, or even necessarily exclusive of one another,[2] he thinks that it may be the case that 'mind acts *immediately* only on mind and matter

[1] See V 262.   [2] See above, p. 68.

immediately only on matter'.[1] But from this he maintains that it does not follow that 'mind cannot act on matter, and matter on mind, without any *tertium quid*'.[1] The causal relation does not have to be mediated because the antecedent may consist of a continuous series of events with no last term and the consequent may consist of a continuous series of events with no first term. When two such series of objects are causally related the position is that 'any member of either class is *immediately* in this relation only to a member of the same class, while yet every member of one of the classes may be in this same relation to every member of the other class'.[3] So the idea is that when, for example, I experience a sensation as the result of the excitation of my brain, the mental event is not the immediate effect of the physical event, even though there is no other event that stands causally in between them. Since the physical event is divisible into a series of physical events with no last term, each physical constituent of the causal chain will have another physical constituent as its immediate successor, and since the mental event is divisible into a series of events with no first term, each mental constituent of the chain will have another mental constituent as its immediate predecessor. But apart from the dubious propriety of treating every event, whether physical or mental, as an infinite series, merely on the ground that it lasts for some continuous period of time, it does not appear in this instance that the device achieves its object. For if there is any difficulty in seeing how mind and matter can immediately act upon one another, there will be the same difficulty in seeing how the infinite series which constitutes the event in the brain can stand as a whole in a direct causal relation to the infinite series which constitutes the sensation.

To return to judgements of perception, I think that the most we can concede to Peirce is that they are always the outcome of some unconscious process of reflection. This may be held to follow from the fact that every such judgement is an interpretation of the data, rather than a simple act of intuition, in Peirce's sense of the term. This is not to say, however, that these processes of reflection themselves consist in making even a finite, let alone an

[1] IV 611.   [2] Ibid.   [3] IV 628.

infinite number of judgements of perception. It is not clear to me, indeed, what interest Peirce has in putting forward this curious doctrine. If, as he says, he is merely pursuing his campaign against intuition, then it would be enough for him to show that all perceptual judgements are fallible. Since this follows from his view that they are all predictive, the point for which he should be arguing is that they all have consequents rather than that they all have antecedents.

In regard to the objects of perception, Peirce holds a position which is very similar to that of Kant. Like Kant he wishes to reconcile the view that our concepts do not apply to anything beyond the limits of possible experience with a denial of subjective idealism. 'Nothing can be more completely false', he says, 'than that we can experience only our own ideas.'[1] On the contrary 'we have direct experience of things in themselves'.[2] But then these things in themselves turn out to be composed of percepts. 'I see an inkstand on the table: that is a percept. Moving my head, I get a different percept of the inkstand. It coalesces with the other. What I call the inkstand is a generalized percept, a quasi-inference from percepts, perhaps I might say a composite-photograph of percepts.'[3] And what is more 'these percepts are undoubtedly purely psychical, altogether of the nature of thought'.[4]

There might seem to be some inconsistency here. To talk of things in themselves is to talk of things which exist independently of our perceiving them or thinking about them. How then is it possible that these things should consist of percepts, if percepts are purely psychical? The answer is that when Peirce characterizes anything as psychical, or as being of the nature of thought, he may mean no more than that it is an object of experience: he certainly does not wish to imply that it is dependent for its existence on being perceived or thought about by any particular person on any particular occasion. In the passage where he speaks of the inkstand as a generalized percept, he goes on to insist that, without in the least ceasing to be a purely psychical product, it is nevertheless a real and external thing. What makes it external is

[1] VI 95.   [2] Ibid.   [3] VIII 144.   [4] Ibid.

that it 'appears there in spite of me. If I turn away my eyes, other witnesses will tell me that it still remains. If we all leave the room and dismiss the matter from our thoughts, still a photographic camera would show the inkstand still there, with the same roundness, polish and transparency, and with the same opaque liquid within.'[1] It is in terms of this agreement among different observers that Peirce distinguishes external objects from merely subjective experiences. His theory is that for the child who is beginning to learn the use of language, everything is external. The child treats his own emotions and desires as properties of the objects which evoke them. If, for example, he wants to move the table, what he judges is that the table requires to be moved. He finds, however, that unlike many of his other judgements, these judgements are not as a rule corroborated by other people. So having previously assigned the same status to all appearances, he comes to distinguish between those which are confirmed by testimony and those which are contradicted by it. The result is that 'he adds to the conception of appearance as the actualization of fact, the conception of it as something *private* and valid only for one body'.[2]

I do not know how accurate this is as an account of infantile psychology, but I think that it points the way to the correct analysis of the distinction which we commonly make between public objects of perception and private experiences. There is nothing in the character of our experiences, considered in themselves, to mark them off respectively as perceptions of public external objects, sensory illusions or subjective feelings. A purely solitary being, if he were able to acquire any concepts at all, would, I think, have the means of arriving at a distinction between transient and persistent objects. Roughly speaking, the persistent objects would be constructed out of those of his experiences that he could subject to manageable laws, the transient objects would be supplied by the residue of experience which he was unable to fit into the dominant pattern. It would, however, be only when he managed to identify certain persistent objects as other observers that he could find any application for the distinction between the

[1] Ibid.   [2] V 234.

constituents of a public world and his own, or other people's, private mental states. Again very roughly, it is when there is reason to believe that the experiences of different observers correspond, both qualitatively and in respect to their setting, that they are held to be perceiving the identical public object, while it is the lack of any reason to believe in this habitual correspondence between one's own mental images or dreams or feelings and those of other people that causes them to be characterized as private.[1] The distinction is further sophisticated to the point where experiences as a class are taken to be private, in contrast to the public objects which they may be experiences of, but this does not prevent its being fundamentally a distinction between experiences, as Peirce correctly sees.

There is a significant difference here between Peirce's approach and that of the classical empiricists. The question for Locke and his followers was whether we could justifiably arrive at a belief in external objects on the basis of private and momentary sense-experiences. For Peirce, as we have just seen, it is the other way round: the data are presented to us as external, and the problem is to explain how some of them come to be characterized as merely subjective feelings. Thus he speaks of 'that sense of externality, of the presence of a non-ego, which accompanies perception generally and helps to distinguish it from dreaming'.[2] It is to be noted that this sense of externality does not imply a judgement that the objects to which it attaches are external. For to make such a judgement one needs to be self-conscious, since to judge that an object is external is to judge that it exists independently of oneself. But if such judgements accompanied even our earliest perceptions it would follow that self-consciousness was primitive, which Peirce in the pursuit of his campaign against any form of alleged intuitive knowledge unhesitatingly denies. He does not explain in any detail how he thinks that self-consciousness arises, but he appears to hold that it is dependent on one's acquiring the concept of what he calls the 'central body';

[1] These points are taken up again in the last section of this book, in connection with William James's Radical Empiricism. See pp. 325-7.
[2] I 332.

and while he believes that this concept is one of the earliest that children acquire, he does not take their possession of it to be a pre-condition of their perceiving anything else. The position is rather that the child's conception of himself as the central body and his conception of bodies external to himself develop *pari passu*. The sense of externality which accompanies his perceptions is a sense of resistance, a feeling of coming up against something which calls for an answering effort. It is a relation of opposition which makes itself felt before its terms are identified. The child then comes to conceive of himself and of the world outside himself as antagonists in this tug of war.

2. Facts and Laws

This duplicity of the Ego and the non-Ego is used by Peirce to introduce the category of Secondness. 'We become aware of ourself in becoming aware of the not-self. The waking state is a consciousness of reaction: and as the consciousness *itself* is two sided, so it has also two varieties: namely, action, where our modification of other things is more prominent than their reaction on us, and perception, where their effect on us is over-whelmingly greater than our effect on them. And this notion, of being such as other things makes us, is such a prominent part of our life that we conceive other things also to exist by virtue of their reactions against each other. The idea of Other, of *not*, becomes a very pivot of thought. To this element I give the name of Secondness.'[1]

Peirce speaks of this element as the element of struggle and explains that what he means by struggle is 'mutual action between two things regardless of any sort of third or medium, and in particular regardless of any law of action'.[2] It does not appear, however, that the action has to be mutual. For example, Peirce thinks that memory results from the direct action of the past upon the future, while holding that 'the future only acts upon the past through the medium of thirds'.[3] Other instances which he gives of direct action are the operations of the human will and,

[1] I 324.   [2] I 322.   [3] I 325. See above, p. 29.

more unexpectedly, the mechanical attraction between material particles. Peirce allows that it would not surprise him 'if somebody were to suggest that perhaps the idea of a law is essential to the idea of one thing acting upon another': nevertheless he thinks that his opponent must admit that 'no law of nature makes a stone fall, or a Leyden jar to discharge, or a steam engine to work'.[1]

His position here is difficult to understand. He admits that dynamic action, as exemplified in the attraction of one particle by another, is governed by law, and he admits that the attraction operates 'through continuous Time and Space, both of which are of triadic constitution'.[2] He admits even that the dyadic action between the particles 'is not the whole action; and that the whole action is, in a way, triadic',[3] and so dependent upon law. Nevertheless he still takes the case of the action to be dyadic. 'In the law, per se, there is no physical force nor other compulsion. It is nothing but a formula, a maxim.'[4] So too, the function of Time and Space is merely to 'weld together instantaneous impulses' which are in some way prior to the arrangement of the particles in time and space and their subjection to law; and the action of these impulses is direct.

This view was developed by Peirce in the last decade of his life, when the metaphysical strain in his work was becoming more pronounced, and he makes no attempt to reconcile it with his pragmatism. I cannot see, indeed, how they could be reconciled. Not only is there no possible way of verifying the existence of these physical forces, in the literal sense which is here in question, but the postulation of them serves no purpose. It explains nothing that is not already explained by the laws of mechanics. Peirce does not say why he has given up his earlier pragmatic view that mechanical forces are to be identified with the accelerations which they are said to cause,[5] but there is at least an indication that he is moved by a very dubious argument that the particles must have some sort of kinship with reason in order to be capable of obeying rational laws. He therefore credits them with a kind of Leibnizian appetitiveness. This is in line with the general tenor of Peirce's metaphysics, into which I do not propose to

[1] I 323.   [2] VI 330.   [3] Ibid.   [4] Ibid.   [5] See above, pp. 54–5.

enter further, since it represents rather the choice of a world picture than a set of philosophical theses which could be attacked or defended by rational argument. The only feature which it shares with Peirce's pragmatism, and that at a very different level, is its dynamical flavour.

It is consistent with this dynamical approach that Peirce holds existence to be dyadic. He thinks that what is required for anything to exist is just that it be in an active relation with something else. The obvious objection to this is that two things cannot enter into any real relation with each other unless they already exist, from which it follows that their existence cannot just consist in their being mutually related. At this point, however, it must be recalled that the things to which existence is ascribed are constructed out of elements which belong to the category of Firstness, and that the members of this category have only 'the being of pure qualitative possibility'. This might be taken to mean that they are universals, in which case they would require to be instantiated in order to constitute existent things; and then, since this would imply that Peirce was dispensing with ultimate particulars, it would be necessary for him to hold that the instantiation of these universals consisted in their entering into relations of compresence with other universals. I do not, however, believe that this is the correct assessment of his view. He does speak of the First category as the category of quality, and he does treat qualities as universals; but when he casts them in the role of primitive elements he treats them not exactly as particulars, since they are not yet capable of that sort of identification, but at least as if they were already on the way to being particularized. The reason why he credits them only with the being of pure qualitative possibility is not so much that they are abstract but rather, as we have seen, that in order to develop into particulars they stand in need of interpretation. The ground for saying that existence was relational would then be that the elements needed to be ordered into a system for it to make sense to ascribe existence to them. I think that this view is tenable, but it is difficult to reconcile with Peirce's statement that existence is dyadic. Not only, if we are dealing with our actual world and not merely with some fanciful creation, will the system have to be spatio-temporal and therefore, in Peirce's view, triadic, but any form of system belongs to the category of thirdness. Peirce attempts to get round this difficulty by distinguishing between the way in which existence is produced and the condition of its being realized. The existence of an object in a spatio-temporal universe 'consists in being a second to any object in such a universe taken as first'. 'It is not', Peirce continues, 'time and space which produce this character. It is rather this character which for its realization calls for something like time and space.'[1] I must say that I find this distinction very tenuous. It is perhaps to be understood as an echo of Kant: but even on Kantian principles, I do not see how one could separate the 'character' of existence from its spatio-temporal realization.

As we have already remarked, Secondness for Peirce is essentially the domain of fact. This does not mean, however, that everything that one would ordinarily call a fact is assigned by him to this category. There is, indeed, a common and proper usage of the term 'fact', according to which one states a fact of some kind whenever one makes a true statement. In this sense, one can speak of there being negative or general or conditional facts. There are occasions on which Peirce adopts this liberal usage, but when he speaks of facts as belonging to the category of Secondness, his use of the term is much narrower. What he then means by a fact is some absolutely determinate state of affairs, which is either contingent in the sense of being 'accidently actual', or else 'involves an unconditional necessity, that is, force without law or reason, *brute* force'.[2] If one takes what I believe to be the correct view that there can be no force without law, then one will have to deny that there are any facts of this second class. Peirce remarks that those who do not accept his tychism may deny that there are any facts of the first class either, but argues, I think rightly, that even if all events are subject to causal laws, this does not affect their contingency, in the sense which is here in question. The laws may explain why the events occur as they do, but before the explanation can operate the events must be there to be explained; and their being there is just something that

[1] I 433.   [2] I 427.

happens to be so. The facts are accidental in the sense that they are not necessary in themselves; they may be said to have necessity bestowed on them by the laws, but the laws themselves have no other basis than the facts.

In conformity with his view that the category of Secondness embodies the element of struggle, Peirce depicts the facts as engaged in a kind of struggle for existence. They obtrude themselves upon us, either directly or through their effects; they resist our wills: and because they have these relations to ourselves, we are led to conceive of them as taking action against one another. I can see no reason to accept this last conclusion even as a piece of psychology, but it is anyhow of no consequence except for Peirce's metaphysics. What is important for his theory of knowledge is the obduracy of facts in relation to ourselves.

The 'bruteness' of these ultimate facts consists not only in their self-sufficiency, and their imposing themselves upon us, but also in their particularity; if they had an element of generality, they would belong not to the second but to the third category, the category of law. It is not altogether plain to me how this last requirement is to be construed. If it were taken literally, it would imply that facts could not be brought under concepts, since all concepts are general in the sense that there is no limit, in principle, to the number of instances which could fall under them. However, I think it is sufficiently clear that Peirce does not intend the exclusion of generality to be understood in this sense. I think that the sense of generality which he had in mind is that in which a concept is said to be more general according as it is less determinate. Here the criterion of determinacy is the degree to which there can be qualitative differences among the instances which fall under a concept in the respect in which they do fall under it. Thus, the concept of colour is highly indeterminate, since there are a great many different ways in which something can be coloured: the concept of red is more determinate since there are not so many ways in which something can be red: the concept of scarlet is more determinate still. Indeterminacy in this sense is not to be confused with vagueness. What makes a concept vague is not the qualitative range of the instances which can fall under it, but the degree to which the range lacks sharp external boundaries; the measure of a concept's vagueness is the number of instances in which it is neither correct nor incorrect to say that it applies. Thus the concept of colour, though indeterminate, is not vague; the concept of baldness is vague, but not especially indeterminate. Peirce does not make this distinction in these terms, but since he insists that the law of excluded middle applies to every feature of a fact, it is clear that the exclusion of generality is intended to cover vagueness, in my sense, as well as indeterminacy. Accordingly, if anything is to be a statement of ultimate fact the predicates which it contains must be absolutely specific, in the sense that the instances to which they apply are qualitatively indistinguishable from one another in the relevant respect, and they must be absolutely precise, in the sense that there is no possible instance with regard to which there can be any legitimate uncertainty whether the predicate applies to it or not.

These are stringent conditions and it is doubtful whether they can be satisfied. There may indeed be qualities, for example shades of colour, which do not appear to us to vary in any of their instances, but we can never be sure that if our perception became keener, perhaps with the help of finer optical instruments, we should not be able to detect variations which now escape us. Neither is this the only source of doubt. It might be thought that if a concept were entirely determinate, it must follow that it was also entirely precise; for if the instances which fall under it are qualitatively indistinguishable, in the relevant respect, then any instance which does not fall under it must, in that respect, be qualitatively distinct from all those which do: and in that case how could one ever be uncertain whether an instance fell under it or not? It is, however, a well-known psychological fact that with regard to some sensible quality there may be three instances A, B and C, which are such that the observer is not able to detect any difference between A and B or between B and C but is able to detect a difference between A and C. This is sufficient for him to conclude that, in respect of this quality, C does not fall under the same wholly determinate concept as A. But what about B? It cannot belong to each of two mutually exclusive classes. Yet there is equally good reason for assigning it to either of them. It may be conjectured that, with greater powers of discrimination, the observer would be able, in respect of the quality in question, to distinguish B both from A and C, and so to bring it under a third determinate concept, but we cannot be sure that this will ever happen; and even if it did happen, there would remain the possibility of coming upon a further instance B' which stood in the same relation to A and B as B previously stood to A and C. We can, therefore, have no guarantee that any of our qualitative concepts has attained complete precision. This does not mean that we have to give up the law of excluded middle but only that we must always be prepared to meet with doubtful cases; so that the question whether a given concept applies to them or not, has to be settled, if at all, by a more or less arbitrary decision.

This may be thought to be a fairly minor obstacle to Peirce's search for ultimate facts. If vagueness and indeterminacy cannot be entirely eliminated, they can at least be so reduced as to be of little practical account. There is, however, a much more serious difficulty which it seems to me that Peirce is not in a position to meet without a radical alteration in his theory of knowledge. The difficulty is that since the facts are supposed to press themselves, as it were physically, upon us, they must be given to us in sense-experience. Not only that, but if they are to remain within the category of Secondness, they can only consist in the presence or compresence of sensory qualities; anything more ambitious would bring in an unauthorized element of generality. But Peirce's own view, as we have seen, is that one never is presented with such pure percepts. It is not necessary, perhaps, that the perceptual facts, with which he thinks that we are bound to start, should be expressed by the attribution of perceptible properties to physical objects; but it is necessary at least that the data be organized into some sort of spatio-temporal system. It follows, then, that the primitive facts are not given to us in sense-perception: at best they are distilled from more complex situations by a process of reflective analysis.

This means that the element of law is present from the start. I do not think that Peirce would have wanted to object to this conclusion, though he seems occasionally to have overlooked it when he was concentrating on the other categories. It must, indeed, have been clear to him that he was not in a position to object to it, since Thirdness, which is the category of law, is also taken by him to be the category of thought. But evidently some thought is required for the apprehension of any fact, however nearly 'brute' the fact may be.

Not only does Peirce assign law and thought to the same category, but he is disposed even to identify them. Thus, in an unpublished manuscript which his editors date *circa* 1896, he says that 'the third category of elements of phenomena consists of what we call laws when we contemplate them from the outside only, but which when we see both sides of the shield we call thoughts'.[1] Thoughts, he goes on to say, are neither qualities nor facts: not qualities, because they have a temporal history, whereas qualities are eternal, and because they must have reasons, whereas it is absurd to ask for a reason why a quality is as it is: not facts, because thoughts, unlike facts, are general; they are general both in being communicable and 'in referring to all possible things, and not merely to those which happen to exist'.[2] Peirce adds that he has 'no objection to saying that a law is a general fact, provided it be understood that the general has an admixture of potentiality in it, so that no congeries of actions here and now can ever make a general fact. As *general*, the law, or general fact, concerns the potential world of quality, while as *fact*, it concerns the actual world of actuality'.[3]

There is a good deal that is puzzling here. As I understand it, the reason why Peirce identifies laws with thoughts is not that he is going back on his scholastic realism, but that he wishes to contrast the abstractness of law with the concreteness of fact. He does not wish to deny that laws are objectively valid, in the sense that the facts really do conform to them, and I take this to be the point that he is emphasizing when he speaks of them as general facts. At the same time he holds that these general facts are not just collections of particular facts, but rather the outcome of the way in which particular facts are organized by us. This does not

[1] I 420.   [2] Ibid.   [3] Ibid.

prevent him, as we have seen, from maintaining that 'general principles are really operative in nature',[1] but then, as we have also seen, he combines this with the metaphysical view that 'all realities are . . . of purely mental composition'.[2] There might, indeed, seem to be a difficulty in reconciling the identity of laws and thoughts with the admission that thoughts have a temporal history, since it is most commonly held that laws are independent of time: but here it must be recalled that Peirce does not share this opinion. We have already discussed his belief that laws develop out of chance and are subject to the temporal process of evolution.[3]

Conversely, the reason why Peirce identifies thoughts with laws is that he denies us any power of thinking without signs: and from this he infers that our thoughts must consist in the application of the general rules on which our signs depend for their significance. This would not, however, justify his saying that thoughts are general in that they refer to all possible things, if this were intended to be true of every thought. It is feasible to construe universal generalizations of law as referring to all possible things, but it would be very strange to take their case as typical; there are many other types of propositions whose range is much more limited. Even if we were to accept Peirce's pragmatic view that the 'ultimate intellectual purport'[4] of every thought consists in an open set of conditionals, it would still be true, in most cases, that the possible situations to which those conditionals referred, though indefinite in number, were limited in their range; not every possible situation would be relevant. It may be, however, that Peirce meant to assert no more than that it was characteristic of thought, as opposed to fact, that it embraced the possible as well as the actual: and further that no possible situation was beyond the range of thought. If he did mean no more than this, I can see no ground for taking issue with him.

It still remains to be explained why Peirce conceived of thought as essentially involving a triadic relation. The short answer is that it is because he equated thinking with the use of signs, and

---

[1] See above, p. 63.   [2] See above, p. 68.   [3] See above, pp. 106–9.
[4] See above, p. 64.

regarded every sign as necessarily triadic. But this in its turn requires elucidation. To obtain it, we shall have to make an attempt to clarify at least the main features of his theory of signs.

B. THE INTERPRETATION OF SIGNS

'A sign, or *representamen*, is something which stands to somebody for something in some respect or capacity. It addresses somebody, that is, creates in the mind of that person an equivalent sign or perhaps a more developed sign. That sign which it creates I call the *interpretant* of the first sign. The sign stands for something, its *object*. It stands for that, not in all respects, but in reference to a sort of idea, which I have sometimes called the *ground* of the representamen.'[1]

In this passage, which succinctly introduces the main features of Peirce's theory of signs, the word 'representamen' is used as though it were merely a technical equivalent for 'sign'. Elsewhere, however, Peirce explains that this equivalence depends upon the truth of his theory. He uses the word 'sign' to cover 'anything which conveys any definite notion of an object in any way'[2] and defines a representamen as being whatever his analysis of what is essential to a sign applies to. His expression of this definition is that 'a REPRESENTAMEN is a subject of a triadic relation TO a second, called its OBJECT, FOR a third, called its INTERPRETANT, this triadic relation being such that the REPRESENTAMEN determines its interpretant to stand in the same triadic relation to the same object for some interpretant'.[3]

I shall do what I can to make this a little more clear. I take the main point to be that nothing is a sign in itself: for anything to be a sign it is necessary that it be understood to be one. This applies not only to verbal signs, to which a meaning is given by convention, but also to images, maps, diagrams and portraits, and even to natural signs, such as instinctive cries or gestures, or clouds presaging rain, or instruments like barometers and weathercocks.

[1] II 228.   [2] I 540.   [3] I 541.

There is, indeed, a sense in which a cry expresses pleasure or pain, or a barometer shows a rise in atmospheric pressure, whether or not it is so interpreted. The reason why these are counted as natural signs is that they stand in constant empirical relations to the things which they signify, and that these relations obtain independently of our being aware of them. Nevertheless, Peirce would argue, the mere fact that phenomena of different sorts habitually go together is not sufficient to make one a sign of the other. It becomes a sign only for someone who has formed the hypothesis that the phenomena are connected in a lawlike manner, and relies on the connection as a principle of inference. The inference need not be conscious, but it must at least be exemplified in the behaviour of the person who is treating one of the phenomena as a sign of its associate.

Images are akin to natural signs, in that their significance is commonly founded on a natural rather than a merely conventional relation. In the standard case, the image is a more or less faithful replica of that which it is taken to signify. They differ from natural signs, however, in that there need not be any constant factual conjunction between the replica and its supposed original; it is not even requisite that the original should actually exist. There is therefore no question but that they become signs only through being so interpreted. The existence of a likeness is not sufficient by itself to set up any relation of significance. A pair of objects may be as like as two peas, without there being any thought of one's referring to the other; and conversely, the resemblance between an image and what it is taken to signify need not be very close: not all portraits are photographic; not all maps are drawn to scale; memory images are often only very sketchy representatives of the past events to which they are understood to refer. In short, it is not the fidelity of an image to what it copies that turns it into a sign. What makes it a sign, if it is one, is that it comes under a convention in terms of which resemblance is treated as a method of representation. Consider a pair of identical twins, and a portrait of one of them. So far as mere resemblance goes, the twins are more like one another than the portrait is like either of them. If it is only in the case of the portrait that the existence of the likeness constitutes a sign, it is because it is only in this case that it is so interpreted. If the portrait is a portrait of only one of the twins, though it equally resembles both, it is because this is an instance in which another convention comes into play. In interpreting an image of this sort we have to consider not so much what it actually resembles as what it was intended to resemble by the person who produced it as a sign. In fact, the only thing that saves images from being wholly conventional signs is that the choice of this method of representation is based on a natural tendency to associate like with like.

It may be the existence of this tendency that has caused so many people to fall into the mistake of treating images as signs in their own right. Thus, even so acute a philosopher as Hume thought it sufficient to characterize a memory image as being less vivid than the impression which it copied, ignoring the fact that no merely qualitative feature of the image could conceivably indicate that it referred beyond itself. But the mistake has been most prevalent among the advocates of the correspondence theory of truth, with their assumption that true propositions mirror facts. Quite apart from the obvious objection that except in some primitive forms of language the signs by which propositions are expressed are not pictorial and that there is no good reason why they should be, the theory shows a misunderstanding even of the models on which it is based. The fidelity of a drawing or a map does not consist only in its bearing a structural resemblance to the state of affairs which it delineates. It consists in its representing this state of affairs to be what it in fact is. The resemblance comes into account only because it serves in these special cases as the method of representation. Considered as a proposition, a map asserts that certain spatial relations obtain between a set of places which it names. The assertion is true if the places in question are in fact so related. The map is understood to make this assertion because it is interpreted as exhibiting a model of these relations, but the assertion could equally well have been made by means of a method of representation which was not pictorial. Its truth, if it is true, depends upon its content and upon the facts, not upon the means by which it is expressed.

This being so, the choice between pictorial and verbal signs is purely one of convenience. Verbal language is more flexible and more far-ranging: it permits the expression of finer shades of meaning. Pictorial language is sometimes more concise and for certain purposes more perspicuous. It is partly also a matter of temperament. At one extreme there are those whose powers of memory and imagination are exercised by giving verbal descriptions rather than by forming mental images; at the other, those who require even abstract reasoning to be cast in a diagrammatic mould. Peirce himself belonged decidedly to the latter class. Not only did he devise a graphic model to which he insisted that all deductive arguments must conform, but, as we shall see, he held the quite mistaken view that pictorial signs have to intervene if words are to be understood as applying to empirical facts. It is strange that he fell into this mistake, having seen that pictorial signs, no less than verbal signs, need to be interpreted.

I conclude, then, that Peirce is right to maintain that every sign requires interpretation. The next step is to try to show in what this interpretation consists. Peirce gives several answers to this question, of various degrees of complexity. The simplest of them, implied in the quotations with which I introduced his theory, is that the interpretant of a sign is a thought which is itself a sign. It is not necessary that this thought be publicly expressed, nor need it be equivalent, as a sign, to the sign which it interprets. It may be a development of it in any of the kind of ways in which one thought leads to another. It must, however, refer to the same object and stand in the same relation to it.

There are various difficulties in this account, apart from the problem, which we shall come to in a moment, of determining what is the object of a sign. Peirce very often writes as if every sign elicited an interpretant, which was an actual event in someone's mental history: it would, for example, be difficult to put any other construction on the first of the passages which I have quoted. Nevertheless, as he himself admits, it is not possible that every sign should have an actual interpretant. For since this interpretant, being itself a sign, would have its own interpretant, the result would be that every sign would generate an infinite series of signs, all referring to the same object, which, as Peirce says, is absurd. He concludes that 'the relation must therefore consist in a *power* of the representamen to determine *some* interpretant to being a representamen of the same object'.[1] It follows that when he says that the interpretant stands in the same relation to the object as the sign which it interprets, this must be taken as being subject to the proviso that the interpretant actually exists.

Peirce sums this up, in his essay on 'Some Consequences of Four Incapacities', by saying that 'the meaning of a thought is altogether something virtual'. As a psychical event, a 'mere feeling' a thought has no meaning in itself; it owes whatever meaning it has to the possibility of its being interpreted by further thoughts. 'It may be objected', Peirce continues, 'that if no thought has any meaning, all thought is without meaning. But this is a fallacy similar to saying that, if in no one of the successive spaces which a body fills there is room for motion, there is no room for motion throughout the whole. At no one instant in my state of mind is there cognition or representation, but in the relation of my states of mind at different instants there is.'[2]

The trouble with this answer is not only that it is not at all obvious what this relation could be, but that it is hard to see how any relation which merely holds between my mental states could possibly engender a reference to an object which was external to them. The analogy with motion does, however, supply a clue to what Peirce may have had in mind. One of the difficulties which Zeno raised about motion is that when a thing is said to be in movement throughout a given period of time there is no instant within this period at which this movement can occur, since at every such instant the thing must be static, in the sense that there is just one position that it then occupies: to which the answer is that if the thing moves continuously from place p_1 to p_2 during a time t_1 to t_2, its motion consists in the fact that at any two different times between t_1 and t_2 it occupies different places between p_1 and p_2; its getting from one place to another is simply resolved into its being at intermediate places at intermediate times. Similarly, Peirce appears to have held, while no individual

[1] I 542.　　　　　[2] V 289.

sign refers beyond itself since, however complex it may be, it just has the qualities that it has, it acquires significance just through being linked with other signs; its having a reference to such and such an object simply consists in the fact that it figures or at least is capable of figuring in a series of signs of such and such a sort. So, for example, a visual memory-image, considered in itself, is just a pattern of shapes and possibly colours, seen in the mind's eye; it refers to a past event only in so far as it is associated with another sign, for instance a verbal description of the event in question: this sign in its turn, considered in itself, is only a series of noises, uttered or imagined, or a series of marks on paper; it owes its meaning to the fact that it can itself be explicated by further utterances or images which stand at least potentially in the same relation to yet other signs: the series of actual signs must be finite and may in fact be very short, but there is no limit in theory to the possibility of its further development. It is their membership of the series that gives the individual signs their meaning, rather than any special meaningful relation in which they stand to one another.

Some support for this view may be found in a consideration of the way in which we actually do determine that someone has understood a sign. One common method is to question him. We ask him to mention an equivalent sign, in the same or another language, or to make some further comment on the object or the state of affairs to which he takes it to refer: if his answers to such questions seem to us coherent, we conclude that he attaches some meaning to the sign: if they seem to us appropriate we conclude that he attaches the same meaning to it as we do ourselves. But what makes his answers seem coherent or appropriate is just that they join together to form a recognized pattern. Though every one of the answers can then be said to be meaningful, not one of them is meaningful in its own right; each of them acquires its meaning through its association with the rest.

Even so, it may be objected, the original difficulty remains. It is still not clear how the mere accumulation of signs which are meaningless in themselves can endow them all with meaning. The creation of motion out of rest is not a fair analogy, since the point here is that the same object is located at different places at successive instants; no motion would result from the piling up of a number of static objects at the same place. In the same way, a single piece of gibberish does not turn into sense even if enough pieces of gibberish are added to it to make a volume.

I think that this objection is well-founded. Although I am very much in sympathy with Peirce's attempt to give an account of the use of signs which does not at some point rely upon the introduction of 'signifying' as an unanalysed relation, and although I agree that if this aim is to be fulfilled it will have to be shown that a sign can acquire meaning through its connection with other factors which are also not intrinsically meaningful, I do not believe that these other factors can merely consist in the provision of further signs, at least if these are limited to words or images, considered simply as noises or shapes. Something more will be needed to serve as a criterion for distinguishing meaningful from meaningless utterances, and it seems clear that the only source from which it can come is the behaviour of the person who is employing the noises or shapes in question as signs. We have to take account not only of what further things he is disposed to say but also of what he is disposed to do.

Since this conclusion is very much in line with the general tenor of Peirce's pragmatism, it is surprising that he tends to disregard it in developing his theory of signs. It cannot be said, however, that he overlooks it entirely. In the unpublished *Survey of Pragmaticism*[1] which he wrote towards the end of his life, he distinguishes between the emotional interpretant of a sign, which is the feeling produced by it, the logical interpretant which applies only to 'intellectual concepts and the like' and appears to be equated with their connotations, or in the case of propositional signs, with their predicates, and the ultimate interpretant which is a habit of action, or rather the occurrence or the reinforcement of what Peirce calls a 'habit-change'. Since these changes of habit do not themselves require logical interpretants, they bring the sequence to an end; it is for this reason that they are said to be ultimate. The particular actions in which the habit is manifested are called the energetic interpretants of the sign.

[1] V 464-96.

Unfortunately, Peirce makes no attempt to work this theory out in detail. The only example which he develops at any length is one in which the interpreter is trying to find the solution to a problem in applied mathematics, and his changes of habit consist in his adopting different methods of approach. But since the energetic interpretants which these habits furnish are themselves operations with signs, the example stops where it should begin. What needs to be shown is that a sign can acquire meaning through the fact that its production fits into a certain pattern of behaviour: this behaviour may include the production of other signs, or the disposition to produce them, but, as we have just seen, it is essential that it should also consist in acting or being disposed to act in certain ways. That a child pronounces a word in the presence of the object to which it is conventionally applied is not sufficient to show that he understands the use of the word. There has to be evidence that he means the word to refer to the object and this is provided by his actions; for instance, by his simultaneously handling the object in some appropriate way, or by his carrying out some instruction concerning it, which is conveyed to him by the use of the word. Such actions may themselves invoke the occurrence of further signs, at least in the form of thoughts, but again these signs will not have any meaning in themselves; they will acquire their meaning from their association with other signs and with other actions. Accordingly, if the series is not to continue indefinitely, the actions which close it, the energetic interpretants of the signs, must, in the final analysis, figure simply as physical movements. They gain their significance from the contexts in which they occur and from their results.

I regard it as an open question whether this view is tenable. No one will want to dispute that a clue to what people mean by their words is to be found in the ways in which they act, but the theory which I am imputing to Peirce goes much further than this. It requires us to hold that the meaning which a person attaches to his words is not merely exhibited but constituted by his acts. So, to vindicate the theory, one would have to find a procedure for showing that any statement to the effect that a given person was attaching such and such a meaning to such and such words was

analysable in terms of a statement, or set of statements, to the
effect that he was acting or disposed to act in such and such a
variety of ways. Later on I shall attempt to show in some detail
how this undertaking might be carried out,[1] but I do not claim
to have disposed of all the difficulties with which it meets.

In attributing this theory to Peirce, I have been guided more by
a desire to fit his theory of signs into the general framework of
his pragmatism, as well as to make it philosophically interesting,
than by a strict consideration of what he actually has to say on the
topic of interpretation. I do not mean by this that I have consciously misrepresented him but only that I have built rather
extensively on a slender textual basis. In fact, Peirce appears to
have been less concerned to secure the foundations of his theory
of signs than to ramify its super-structure. Thus, in the draft of a
letter to Lady Welby, which bears the date of December 1908, he
says that it is 'requisite to distinguish the *Immediate Interpretant*,
i.e. the Interpretant represented or signified in the Sign, from the
Dynamic Interpretant, or effect actually produced on the mind by
the Sign; and both of these from the *Normal Interpretant*, or effect
that would be produced on the mind by the Sign after sufficient
development of thought'.[2] In a review of Lady Welby's book
What is Meaning? which he contributed to *The Nation* in 1903, he
again distinguishes between the immediate and dynamical interpretants and adds that 'there is certainly a third kind of Interpretant,
which I call the Final Interpretant, because it is that which
would finally be decided to be the true interpretation if consideration of the matter were carried so far that an ultimate
opinion were reached'.[3] Since neither the normal nor the final
interpretant is described in terms which suggest that it is meant to
be a habit of action, it would seem that they are not identical
with what Peirce previously called the ultimate interpretant. It is
not clear even whether they are meant to be identical with one
another. Neither is it clear to me how far the distinction between
the immediate and the dynamic interpretants coincides with that
which he previously drew between the emotional and logical
interpretants. The emotional interpretant does appear to be

[1] See below, pp. 173-9.			[2] VIII 343.			[3] VIII 184.

pretty much the same as the dynamic, but the logical interpretant appears to combine features of the immediate and the normal. I shall not, however, pursue these questions further, as I do not think that the points of philosophical interest in Peirce's theory of interpretation are seriously affected by the discrepancies in his various formulations of it.

There is much the same difficulty in making a consistent theory out of what Peirce says about the objects of signs. One thing which is reasonably clear is that the object of a sign is to be identified with what the sign denotes, rather than with what it signifies. This is explicitly stated in an unpublished paper, which is dated about 1905. 'The object of a sign is one thing: its meaning is another. Its object is the thing or occasion, however indefinite, to which it is to be applied. Its meaning is the idea which it attaches to that object, whether by way of mere supposition, or as a command or as an assertion.'[1] Even this point is obscured, however, by the fact that in the case of a certain class of signs, namely those which Peirce calls symbols, the object and the meaning coincide. As we shall see, when we come to Peirce's division of signs, the representative character of a symbol 'consists precisely in its being a rule that will determine its interpretant'.[2] Consequently the symbol by which a symbol is interpreted is also its immediate object. This applies to all symbols which have a general meaning, that is, in Peirce's view, to all genuine symbols. He adds, however, that 'there are two kinds of degenerate symbols, the *Singular Symbol* whose Object is an existent individual, and which signifies only such characters as that object may realize; and the *Abstract Symbol*, whose only Object is a character'.[3] So, in his review of Lady Welby's book, Peirce says that a sentence like 'the Sun is blue' has two objects, 'the Sun' and 'blueness'. Since he also says, in this review, that 'the Object of every sign is an Individual, usually an Individual Collection of Individuals',[4] it would appear that he independently agreed with Frege[5] that if one attempts to name a property, or as

---

[1] V 6.   [2] II 292.   [3] II 293.   [4] VIII 181.

[5] Cf. G. Frege, 'On Concept and Object'. Included in Peter Geach and Max Black, *Translations from the Philosophical Writings of Gottlob Frege* (1960).

Frege would say a concept, by using an abstract noun, what one succeeds in naming is an individual. In other words, abstract nouns are assimilated to singular symbols, like proper nouns, and it is for this reason that they are said to be degenerate. A singular symbol is degenerate because its objects are not 'of the nature of a law'. It denotes an individual, but it does not signify any determinate character, whereas a genuine symbol must do both.[1]

Not only must the object of a sign be an individual but it must be an individual which the person who interprets the sign is able to identify. Otherwise the use of the sign would convey no information to him, since he would not know what it referred to. Peirce illustrates this by the following example: 'Two men are standing on the seashore looking out to sea. One of them says to the other, "That vessel there carries no freight at all, but only passengers." Now, if the other, himself, sees no vessel, the first information he derives from the remark has for its Object the part of the sea that he does see, and informs him that a person with sharper eyes than his, or more trained in looking for such things, can see a vessel there; and then, that vessel having been thus introduced to his acquaintance, he is prepared to receive the information about it, that it carries passengers exclusively. But the sentence as a whole has, for the person supposed, no other Object than that with which it finds him already acquainted.'[2]

This suggests that in the case where the object of a sign is not a universal character, with which one may be supposed to be acquainted at all times if one is acquainted with it at all, but an existent particular, it must be one which the interpreter of the sign is actually observing or else one which he remembers from what he has observed in the past. He could only understand a reference to a particular which did not fall into this class if he were able to relate it to one which did. A passage which supports this reading is to be found in the *Survey of Pragmaticism*. Peirce there speaks of the existent object which is represented by a sign as being that which causes it, and says that when an infantry officer issues an order to ground arms, the object which this sign represents is 'the will of the officer that the butts of the muskets be brought down to the ground'.[1] This is not, however, the position which he most commonly takes. In his review of Lady Welby's book, he uses the same example and this time he says that the object of the command is 'the immediately subsequent action of the soldiers so far as it is affected by the molition expressed in the command'.[2] The fact that the subsequent action of the soldiers may not take place does not here seem to trouble him. Even the example of the man looking out to sea is glossed by him in a much more liberal way than one might expect. For he immediately goes on to say that 'the Objects – for a sign may have any number of them – may each be a single known existing thing or a thing believed formerly to have existed or expected to exist, or a collection of such things, or a known quality or relation or fact, which single Object may be a collection, or whole of parts, or it may have some other mode of being, such as some act permitted whose being does not prevent its negation from being equally permitted, or something of a general nature desired, required, or invariably found under certain general circumstances'.[3] It would seem, therefore, that almost anything that can be intelligibly referred to is capable, in Peirce's view, of being the object of a sign. The only restriction which he seems to make in the passage which I have just quoted is that in the case where the object is a particular thing, or a particular state of affairs, the person who interprets the sign must at least believe that there is some likelihood of its existing. But even this restriction is not maintained, for there are other passages[4] where he allows that signs may have for their objects the members of some fictitious universe of discourse.

The fact is that Peirce is making several points, which he does not sufficiently distinguish. To begin with, he wants to treat everything that can be significantly spoken of as a possible object of reference. At the same time, he takes the view that nothing

---

[1] V 473.
[2] VIII 178. 'Molition' is Peirce's word for 'volition minus all desire and purpose, the mere consciousness of exertion of any kind'.
[3] II 232.   [4] E.g. VIII 178.

can be significantly spoken of unless it can be identified, and that nothing can be identified unless it is related to something with which one is already acquainted. This may amount to very little. In the normal way, someone who refers to Hamlet will know that he belongs to the universe of discourse which was created by Shakespeare, and he will be able to identify Shakespeare in the sense that, as the result of what he has heard or read, he will have come to know some individuating facts about him. It may be, however, that he knows no more than that Hamlet is a character in some play, or that Shakespeare was an English poet: and in that case all that is necessary is that his past experience should have furnished him with the means of understanding these descriptions. But if that is all he does know, he can interpret the sign only as making an indefinite reference: all that he can understand by it is that there is something, in the relevant universe of discourse, which answers to the given description. In the normal way, however, when people use proper names, they use them to make definite references, to point, as it were, to the individuals in question, and in that case, Peirce thinks, a further condition must be satisfied. If one is to succeed in making a definite reference, whether by the use of a proper name, or in some other manner, it is necessary that the sign which conveys the reference be interpreted in such a way that the thing to which it refers is related to some feature of one's present situation, if it be only to the time or place at which the act of reference occurs.

Now it seems to me that these different theses all have an influence on what Peirce says about the object of a sign. For the most part, as we have seen, he allows a sign to have whatever object it purports to refer to. In the case of a declarative sentence, the objects, which may, if we please, be treated as forming a single complex, include everything that the sentence would ordinarily be said to be about; so that not only concrete existent particulars, but abstract entities, imaginary entities, and particulars falsely believed or vainly desired to exist are capable of being among them. Occasionally, however, he chooses to limit the possible objects of signs to those objects of acquaintance on which he holds that the identification of other objects depends, and more rarely he becomes stricter still and allows a sign to have no other concrete object but one which comes within the present experience of its interpreter. Though he does not make it clear, it would seem that he must have these restrictions in mind when he speaks of the sign as being caused or determined by its object: for it is hard to see how a sign could be determined by an object which did not exist. It is, however, possible that he means no more here than that the character of the sign is specified by the nature of the object to which it purports to refer.

These ambiguities are not dispelled by the distinction which Peirce draws, in his review of Lady Welby's book and also in a letter to William James, between the 'immediate' and the 'dynamical' object of a sign. The immediate object is the object as cognized, or represented in the sign: the dynamical object is the object 'as it is regardless of any particular aspect of it, the Object in such relations as unlimited and final study would show it to be'.[1] So, in the case of the sentence 'the Sun is blue', the immediate object of the word 'Sun' is something which is 'the occasion of sundry sensations', its dynamical object is that which results from 'our usual interpretation of such sensations in terms of place, of mass etc.': the reference to blueness may be either to the immediate object, which is the quality of the sensation, or the dynamical object, which is the 'existential condition, which causes the emitted light to have short mean wave-length'.[2] One difficulty here is that according to Peirce's definition, the immediate object is not a different object from the dynamical, but the same object differently conceived; but while there is no difficulty in holding that the sun which is the occasion of sensation is the same object as the sun to which we ascribe the property of mass, the two bluenesses are so far from being identical that the choice between them makes a difference to the truth-value of the proposition. To say that the sun is blue is false if the reference is to the quality of a sensation, but true, according to Peirce, if the reference is to the condition which causes the emitted light to have a short wave-length. But what this implies is that the word 'blue' is ambiguous, in the sense that under different interpretations

[1] VIII 183.   [2] Ibid.

it refers to different objects, rather than that it refers to the same object in different aspects.

In the letter to William James, Peirce gives the example of his wife's asking him 'What sort of a day is it?' and his replying 'It is a stormy day'. Here the immediate object of the complex sign which expresses the question is said to be 'the weather at that time'[1], but the immediate object of the sign which expresses the answer is said to be 'the notion of the present weather so far as this is common to her mind and mine'[2]: the dynamical object in the first case is said very surprisingly to be 'the impression which I have presumably derived from peeping between the window-curtains': in the second case, it is said to be 'the *identity* of the actual or Real meteorological conditions at the moment'.[3] No explanation is given for these variations, which seem quite unaccountable. It is also strange to find Peirce saying here that the dynamical object is one 'which, from the nature of things, the Sign *cannot* express, which it can only *indicate*, and leave the interpreter to find out by *collateral experience*'.[4] I take the point to be not that the dynamical object cannot be described, for if Peirce's examples are anything at all to go by, it obviously can be, but that the most that any description of an object can tell us is that there is something, or it may be only one thing, that has such and such a property. If we ask *what* it is that has this property, a further description will tell us that it is the same thing as has such and such another property. But then it may seem that the subject of these attributes is eluding us. This is merely a consequence of the fact that all description is general. If we want to pin down the subject, we have to *show* it, or at least show something to which it is uniquely related. All this is brought out much more clearly by Russell's Theory of Descriptions, but there is a fair amount of evidence that Peirce was thinking along the same lines.

Although, in setting out his general theory, Peirce writes as if he thought that every sign functioned in the same way, in that it designated some object for some interpretant, he does in fact realize that this cannot be so. It is not just that different species

[1] VIII 314.   [2] Ibid.   [3] Ibid.   [4] Ibid.

of signs have different sorts of objects, but that there are some signs which, even if they can be said to have objects, at any rate do not denote them. An obvious example is the class of what Peirce called *Copulants*, signs like the English words 'if – then' '– is –' ' – causes –' '– would be –' which, as Peirce puts it, 'neither describe nor denote their Objects, but merely express the logical relations of these latter to something otherwise referred to'.[1] Another such class is the class of what he calls *Selectives*, signs like the English words 'any' or 'some' which do not denote objects but give 'directions for finding'[2] them.

To avoid having to regard these auxiliary signs as exceptions to his general rule, Peirce is inclined to treat them not as signs in their own right but as parts of signs. The signs of which they are parts are sentences and a sentence, which has now to be treated as a single complex sign, can either be said to have for its object the state of affairs which it is understood to represent, or else whatever objects are denoted by its parts. This is of course subject to all the qualifications and refinements that we have already noted.

In the case of sentences that are used to express propositions, there is a further complication. Propositions are classified by Peirce as a species of what he calls *Dicisigns*, it being the characteristic mark of a dicisign that it is 'either true or false, but does not directly furnish reasons for being so'.[3] From this it follows, in Peirce's view, that 'a Dicisign must profess to refer or relate to something as having a real being independently of the representation of it as such and further that this reference or relation must not be shown as rational, but must appear as a blind Secondness'.[4] That is to say, the dicisign is interpreted as having a 'real existential relation' to its object. But if this existential relation is an object of the interpretant it must also be an object of the dicisign, since 'the interpretant of a sign can represent no other Object than that of the sign itself'. Consequently in addition to its 'primary object', which Peirce here identifies not with the whole state of affairs which the proposition represents, but rather with what logicians have called its subject or subjects, a proposition also

---

[1] VIII 350.   [2] VIII 171. See below, p. 155.   [3] II 310.   [4] Ibid.

A.O.P.

has a 'secondary object', which is the complex consisting of the primary object in its relation to the proposition itself. At this point Peirce very properly recoils from the conclusion that every proposition denotes a complex which includes itself, but still maintains that it must contain a part which is represented as being both part of its object and part of its interpretant.

This reasoning is very difficult to follow. It is not at all clear why the dicisign should be obliged to stand in a real existential relation to its object. Any such relation would have, presumably, to be causal, but while there may be good grounds for holding that the utterance of sentences which are used to express true judgements of memory or perception must be causally related to the states of affairs to which these judgements refer, I can see no warrant for extending this requirement to propositional signs in general. The cases of false propositions, or even true propositions which refer to future events, raise obvious difficulties. Of course, if the object of the sign is identified with the cause of its utterance, the conclusion follows analytically, but this interpretation will not serve the argument, since it then will not follow that the object, in this sense, is also something to which the proposition relates.

The consequences which Peirce derives from this argument are easier to understand, although it remains unclear how they are supposed to follow from it. He concludes that every propositional sign must contain two parts, one representing the subject of the proposition and the other the predicate. The subject must be represented as existing independently of being represented, and the predicate must be a 'Firstness (or quality or essence)'[1] which is attributed to the subject. Further, the expression which designates the subject must stand in some causal relation to it, and the expression which designates the predicate must be in some way pictorial. The reason for this last requirement is that for an expression to be interpreted as designating a predicate, it must, in Peirce's view, be taken to be part of the object of the propositional sign of which it is a constituent, and he thinks that only a pictorial sign can satisfy this condition. I confess that I can neither follow

[1] II 312.

this reasoning nor accept the conclusion to which it leads. Nor am I convinced that every proposition must be susceptible of the division between subject and predicate. I shall, however, return to these questions when I attempt to give a general evaluation of his theory.

C. THE DIVISIONS OF SIGNS

1. Types and Tokens

Peirce's love of classification, and his addiction to three-fold divisions are given full rein in his account of the varieties of signs. In an unpublished fragment, which his editors tentatively assign to the year 1897, he obtains ten classes of signs from a process of division by three trichotomies; but in one of his letters to Lady Welby, which was written in 1908, the number of trichotomies is increased to ten and the consequent number of classes to sixty-six. The more complicated version depends upon the use of distinctions such as that between the immediate and dynamical objects of a sign, or that between its immediate, dynamical and normal interpretants, of which I have admitted that I fail to see the point: and I shall therefore not attempt to unravel its complexities. I shall concern myself only with the original set of three trichotomies and even in their case shall concentrate the discussion on a few points which seem to me of special interest.

The first division of signs is said to proceed 'according as the sign itself is a mere quality, is an actual existent, or is a general law'; the second, 'according as the relation of the sign to its object consists in the sign's having some character in itself, or in some existential relation to that object, or in its relation to an interpretant'; and the third, 'according as its Interpretant represents it as a sign of possibility or as a sign of fact or a sign of reason'.[1]

Peirce goes on to distinguish the signs which fall into the different compartments of the first division as Qualisigns, Sinsigns

[1] II 243.

and Legisigns. Elsewhere he uses the term 'token' in place of 'sinsign' and 'type' in place of 'legisign', and it is in this form that the distinction has gained currency.

A qualisign is defined as 'a quality which is a sign', a sinsign or token as 'an actual existent thing or event which is a sign', and a legisign or type as 'a law that is a sign'. Though a quality cannot actually function as a sign unless it is instantiated, its being a sign is supposed to depend solely on its own nature. A token owes its significance either to its exemplifying one or more qualisigns or to its being an instance of a type. What Peirce mostly has in mind when he speaks of 'a law that is a sign' is the existence of some linguistic convention. So, in the sense in which each occurrence of the word 'the' on this page is an occurrence of the same conventional sign, all conventional signs are legisigns. The individual inscriptions of the word are sinsigns or tokens of the legisign or type. Peirce also refers to individual inscriptions or utterances of a word as replicas of it.[1]

The first comment which I have to make on this is that I do not think that there can be such things as qualisigns. The very reason that there is for holding that every sign must have an interpretant is a conclusive reason for denying that anything can be a sign simply in virtue of its nature. What Peirce seems to have thought is that qualities were natural signs of anything that they resembled. So an image would signify in virtue of its appearance, whereas, in general, words would owe their meaning only to convention. But, as I have already remarked, the choice of resemblance as a method of representation is itself a convention; the most that can be said in favour of Peirce's view is that it is a convention which arises out of a natural tendency to associate like with like.

With regard to the distinction between types and tokens, the main problem is to specify the relations which have to obtain between different tokens for them to be replicas of the same types. It is clear that even in the case of two spoken, or two written tokens, something more is required than a relation of physical resemblance; in view of the differences that there are in pro-

[1] II 244-6.

nunciation and in handwriting, it must very often happen that two spoken or written tokens of the same type resemble each other less than one or other of them resembles some token of a different type. This difficulty can be overcome to some extent by taking into account the positions which the tokens occupy in relation to other tokens which are produced on the same occasions; whether it can be fully overcome is a question to which I do not know the answer. If it turns out that a foolproof definition of a type cannot be constructed out of purely structural materials, it will be necessary to refer to the type in order to identify the token: that is to say, the notion of a type will have to be taken as primitive, and that of a token defined in terms of it, rather than the other way around. This would not necessarily involve the admission of abstract entities, since it might be that the employment or interpretation of a given token as a replica of such and such a type could eventually be analysed in terms of the behaviour of the person for whom it served as a sign.

2. Icons, Indices and Symbols

The most interesting and, as Peirce himself says, the most fundamental of his divisions of signs is the second trichotomy; the division into Icons, Indices and Symbols. An icon, like a qualisign, falls under the category of Firstness. It is said to be 'a sign which refers to the Object that it denotes merely by virtue of characters of its own, and which it possesses just the same, whether any such Object actually exists or not'.[1] The existence of the object is, however, necessary for the icon actually to function as a sign. So 'anything whatever, be it quality, existent individual, or law, is an Icon of anything, in so far as it is like that thing and used as a sign of it'.[2]

An index is defined as 'a sign which refers to the Object that it denotes by virtue of being really affected by that Object'.[3] Though it owes its power of reference to its qualities, it lacks the independence to be a qualisign. In any case, what makes it a sign is not its resemblance to its object but its causal dependence on it.

[1] II 247.   [2] Ibid.   [3] II 248.

Finally, a symbol is said to be 'a sign which refers to the Object that it denotes by virtue of a law, usually an association of general ideas, which operates to cause the Symbol to be interpreted as referring to that Object'.[1] This means that symbols are legisigns, operating through the tokens which are their instances. Peirce takes this to imply that the object to which a symbol refers must also be 'of a general nature' and argues that since what is general has its being only in its instances there must be 'existent instances of what the Symbol denotes', adding, however, that 'we must here understand by "existent", existent in the possibly imaginary universe to which the symbol refers'.[2] In a later unpublished paper, he identifies 'the complete object' of a symbol with its meaning and says that 'a *genuine* symbol is a symbol that has a general meaning'.[3] Since he also says that a symbol must denote an individual and signify a character, it looks as if he is equating genuine symbols with propositions. This is confirmed by his going on to say that 'a *Symbol* is a sign naturally fit to declare that the set of objects which is denoted by whatever set of Indices may be in certain ways attached to it is represented by an icon associated with it'.[4] It tallies also with his remarking that 'there are two kinds of degenerate symbols, the *Singular Symbol* whose Object is an existent individual, and which signifies only such characters as that individual may realize; and the *Abstract Symbol*, whose only Object is a character'.[5]

There is much here that calls for elucidation. To begin with, since the category of Firstness to which icons are assigned is the category only of possibilities, no actual sign is an icon. An actual sign may, however, be called iconic so long as its method of representing its object is mainly that of similarity. For signs of this sort Peirce coins the term 'hypoicon'. Inevitably, he divides hypoicons into three classes: images, which represent their objects by resemblance of quality; diagrams, which represent relations between parts of their object by similar relations between their own elements, and metaphors, which are strangely alleged to 'represent the representative character of a representamen by

---

[1] II 449.   [2] Ibid.   [3] II 293.   [4] II 295.   [5] II 293.

representing a parallelism in something else'.[1] A more straight-forward account of metaphor would be that it drew a parallel between different objects, rather than a parallel between object and sign; but then it would not belong in this classification, and Peirce would have been hard put to complete his triad.

Even if we disregard metaphors, the conditions which a sign must satisfy in order to be iconic are not very strict. Thus, a diagram does not have to bear any sensory resemblance to its object: it is enough that there should be some likeness between the relations of their respective parts. Brackets are icons and so, more surprisingly, are algebraical formulae. The justification for their inclusion is that 'a great distinguishing property of the icon is that by the direct observation of it other truths concerning its object can be discovered than those which suffice to determine its constitution'.[2] Evidently, paintings, or at any rate represen-tational paintings, are hypoicons but photographs, in spite of their greater fidelity to their objects, are not. The reason why they are not is that they are produced under conditions which make it physically necessary for them to resemble their objects, and this puts them into the category of indices. Icons may operate by contrast as well as by likeness. For instance, a drunken man who is exhibited as an object lesson is said to act as an icon of tem-perance. In general, we may be said to have an icon, or rather a hypoicon, whenever we are presented with a picture which tells a story without the need of any captions. But this criterion is not precise, and, as the example of photographs shows, the dividing line between iconic and indexical signs is not always easy to draw. A distinguishing mark of an iconic sign is that when it occurs within a proposition it signifies the predicate. I take the reason for this to be that pictures without captions do not in themselves refer to anything; even if they are interpreted as signs, the infor-mation which they convey is just that there is something, not further identified, which more or less closely resembles them; and, strictly speaking, even to convey this information they need to be supplied with a subject in the form of an existential quantifier.

What I find most surprising is Peirce's contention that 'the

[1] II 277.   [2] II 279.

only way of directly communicating an idea is by means of an icon'. Since he also holds that the use of an icon is needed to establish any indirect method of communication, he is led to the startling conclusion that 'every assertion must contain an icon or set of icons, or else must contain signs whose meaning is only explicable by icons'.[1] I shall return to this question later on.

Peirce also holds that 'no matter of fact can be stated without the use of some sign serving as an index'.[2] His reason for saying this is brought out most clearly in an extract from an unpublished and undated set of 'Notes on Topical Geometry'. He there divides indices into two main classes, according as they 'merely stand for things or individual quasi-things with which the inter-preting mind is already acquainted' or are 'used to ascertain facts'.[3] The first and most important of these classes consists of what he calls 'designations'. Their function is to 'force the attention to the thing intended' and they are the indices which are 'absolutely indispensable both to communication and thought' since 'no assertion has any meaning unless there is some designation to show whether the universe of reality or what universe of fiction is referred to'.[4]

The inclusion of designations as one of the main classes of indices is not very easy to reconcile with the requirement that indices be really affected by their object, and in fact Peirce virtu-ally abandons it. He still maintains that 'an *index* represents an object by virtue of its connection with it', but goes on to say that 'it makes no difference whether the connection is natural, or artificial, or merely mental'.[5] This puts such a weak construction on the requirement that the only reason that there would appear to be for Peirce's maintaining it is that he is bent on preserving his triadic scheme by bringing indices, at least nominally, into the category of Secondness.

The other main class of indices consists of those that he calls 'reagents'. Primarily, these cover the cases where one thing becomes the sign of another through being connected with it by some natural law or tendency. So a man's rolling gait is a probable

---

[1] II 278.   [2] II 305.   [3] VIII 368 (editorial footnote).
[4] Ibid.   [5] Ibid.

indication that he is a sailor, a low barometer is an index of rain, a weathercock is an index of the direction of the wind. Examples of this kind explain why Peirce says of reagents that they may be used to ascertain facts. They also lead him at one point into the apparent inconsistency of saying that an index would not lose its character as a sign if it had no interpretant. The example which he gives is that of a piece of mould with a bullet-hole in it serving as a sign of a shot, the argument being that the effect of the shot exists whether or not anyone has the wit to discover its cause.[1] There seems, however, to be no good reason why, even in this sort of case, he should depart from his general rule that nothing counts as a sign unless it is so interpreted; and in fact he remarks elsewhere that 'a reagent can indicate nothing unless the mind is already acquainted with its connection with the phenomenon it indicates'.[2]

Both these main classes of indices incorporate a wide range of cases. Thus, reagents comprise not only such obvious examples as we have given, but also signs of latitude and longitude, clocks and sundials, road signs and street cries, laughter and tears. A meter-rod is an index of this type, rather than an icon, because it is modelled on the standard meter-rod in Paris. So an expression like 'two miles and a half' is said to be a description of a reagent, because it refers to the information which would be obtained by laying down a measuring rod, equal in length to some standard yardstick, so many times on end between one point and another.[3] A cry for help since 'it is not only intended to force upon the mind the knowledge that help is wanted, but also to force the will to accord to it' is 'a reagent used rhetorically'.[4] The same is true of a military word of command, or the ringing of a bell or a knock on the door. A gesture may be a designation if it serves merely to call attention to its author, but it too is a reagent if, as is commonly the case, it also serves to indicate his state of mind.

The most straightforward examples of designations among verbal signs are demonstratives like the English words 'this' and 'that', personal pronouns, and spatio-temporal indices like 'here'

[1] II 304. [2] VIII 368 (editorial footnote). [3] Ibid. [4] Ibid.

and 'now'. These words do not so much force as direct the hearer's attention. They show him where to look for what is being talked about.

Demonstratives of this kind occur covertly in another set of signs, the function of which is to locate an event by linking it with the present context. Words like 'near' and 'far', 'past' and 'future' are obvious examples. So are more precise specifications of distance like 'in the next room', 'five miles away', 'yesterday', 'tomorrow', 'two hours ago'. It may be noted that most of these expressions have the peculiarity of being indexical in two ways, combining designations with descriptions of reagents. Tenses also come in here, since they serve to locate the events which are being referred to by indicating whether they are contemporary with or earlier or later than the utterance of the sentence in which the tense is used.

Relative pronouns are counted as designations on the ground that they call attention to the words that have gone before. Peirce says of them, however, in one passage, that they are not genuine indices because they are not individuals. He there ranks them with proper names, personal pronouns, and the letters attached to diagrams as Subindices or Hyposemes.[1] I suppose that what he has in mind here is that these signs owe their significance to a convention which operates at the level of the type, rather than to a connection which they establish with their objects by being employed as tokens. It must be for this reason that he says that they are not individuals. But the same is true of most of his other examples, including the words 'this' and 'that' which he treats as genuine indices. We may, therefore, ignore this particular refinement.

The inclusion of proper names and of personal pronouns, at any rate in some of their standard uses, may be queried on other grounds. When they are used in the presence of the objects to which they refer, they may indeed function as demonstratives, but proper names and third person pronouns are more frequently used to refer to objects which are not present and then it is arguable that they do the work of descriptions. It is true that they

[1] II 284.

are not equivalent to descriptions, but in most, if not in all cases, it is only by associating them with descriptions that one can come to understand their reference. This is certainly true in all cases in which the name is used to refer to an object which one has not oneself observed. Peirce sometimes speaks of proper names as having a real connection with the objects which they denote, but it is hard to see how this can be justified except in the cases, like that of street signs, where the name is actually affixed to its bearer. Perhaps he means no more than that their demonstrative use is primary. This is borne out by his saying, in the course of a discussion of subjects and predicates, that a proper name is a genuine index only when one meets with it for the first time. It is then, he says, 'existentially connected with some percept or other equivalent individual knowledge of the individual it names'. But 'the next time one meets with it, one regards it as an Icon of that Index. The habitual acquaintance with it having been acquired, it becomes a Symbol whose Interpretant represents it as an Icon of an Index of the Individual named.'[1]

This seems to me a tenable view, except that when proper names have reached the stage of becoming symbols I find it more plausible to say that they do duty for descriptions than that they are, as it were, shadows of demonstratives; even so, there is a case for saying that they mimic demonstratives, though this is rather a matter of their being credited with uniqueness of reference than of their looking back to any actual indices of the individuals which they name. If they do altogether cease to be indices, it will be necessary, on Peirce's principles, to find other indices to replace them in the instances where they appear to stand for the subject of the proposition. This can most easily be achieved by the use of the existential quantifier.

Quantifiers are identified by Peirce with selective pronouns, the most important of which are 'universal selectives' like the English words 'any' 'every' 'all' 'none' 'whichever' 'whoever' and 'particular selectives' like the words 'some' 'something' 'somebody' 'a certain' 'one'.[2] These have developed into the universal and existential quantifiers of modern logic. They are classed as

[1] II 329.   [2] II 289.

designations because they are held to indicate that the assertion applies, in the case of the existential quantifier to just one instance, in the case of the universal quantifier to any instance that one chooses to select 'within limits expressed or understood'.[1] It is a feature also of quantified sentences that the recurrence of the same variable indicates, as it were demonstratively, that the same individual, or the same range of individuals, is being indefinitely referred to.

Another unexpected set of indices, approximating to designations rather than reagents, are 'prepositions and prepositional phrases such as, "on the right (or left) of"'. 'Right and left', says Peirce, 'cannot be distinguished by any general description. Other prepositions signify relations which may, perhaps, be described; but when they refer, as they do oftener than would be supposed, to a situation relative to the observed, or assumed to be experientially known, place and attitude of the speaker relatively to that of the hearer, then the indexical element is the dominant element.'[2] It is made clear in a footnote that the prepositions of which Peirce is thinking are those that denote spatial and temporal relations, and his reason for saying that they are predominantly indexical is that knowledge of the context is usually required to determine the spatial and temporal positions of the objects which they relate.

This brings out the important point that with the exception of quantifiers and relative pronouns, which play only a secondary role in the process of demonstrative identification, designations are token-reflexive. That is to say, their use is determined by the context; what they serve to indicate depends upon the concrete circumstances in which they are produced. This means that in order to understand the sentences in which they occur, a knowledge of the language alone will not be sufficient; one will need also to know such things as the identity of the speaker, his spatial and temporal position, the identity of the hearer, the character of their environment. This follows from the fact that the information which these designations convey is not fully stated, but shown. It has, indeed, been argued that the purpose which is

[1] II 289.   [2] II 290.

served by token-reflexive signs is no more than a purpose of economy;[1] by replacing demonstratives with descriptions, one can make what are effectively the same references without dependence upon context and without the necessity for anything to be shown. Whether this is true or not is a question into which we shall enter when we come to examine Peirce's contention that the use of some sign serving as an index is indispensable for stating any matter of fact.

With regard to symbols, there is an initial difficulty in understanding why they are brought into the triad at all. As we have seen, the kernel of Peirce's conception of a symbol is that it is a sign whose meaning is wholly determined by the rules which govern its use. But surely this is true of all conventional signs? Indeed, Peirce himself admits this, since he remarks that 'all words, sentences, books and other conventional signs are symbols'.[2] How then can he treat symbols, alongside icons and indices, as a special variety of signs? It is true that he always thinks of symbols as legisigns or types, whereas icons are supposed to be qualisigns and indices, though very often treated as types, are officially regarded as tokens. But symbols, like icons, can only operate through tokens, and, natural indices apart, all tokens are symbolic.

The solution of this difficulty may be that although his definition of a symbol covers all conventional signs, Peirce does commonly think of symbols as restricted to propositions or propositional functions. This is borne out by his classification of signs, where it is only as fulfilling these roles that symbols are mentioned. The second division of signs would then become a sort of Hegelian triad, culminating in symbols as a fusion of icons and indices. I think, however, that Peirce is also inclined to overlook the fact that iconic and indexical signs stand as much as any others in need of interpretation, and so tends wrongly to contrast symbols, as governed by conventional rules, with these other varieties of signs which he sometimes falls into the mistake

[1] E.g. W. V. Quine, *Word and Object* (1960), ch. v. Cf. also my essay on 'Names and Descriptions' in *The Concept of a Person*.

[2] II 292.

of treating as though they were, in their different ways, intrinsically significant.

3. Propositions and their Subjects

The third trichotomy is the division of signs into Terms, Propositions and Arguments. A term is sometimes called by Peirce a Rheme, and a proposition a Dicent sign or Dicisign. The definition given of a term, or rheme, is that it 'is a sign which, for its Interpretant, is a sign of qualitative Possibility, that is, is understood as representing such and such a kind of possible Object'.[1] What this is intended to mean may perhaps be inferred from another passage in which Peirce says that 'that which remains of a Proposition after removal of its Subject is a Term (a rhema) called its Predicate'.[2] This leads his editors, no doubt correctly, to equate terms, in Peirce's usage, with propositional functions.

As we have already seen, the account which Peirce gives of propositions is not only very complicated but in some ways very obscure. There are, however, one or two points that come out fairly clearly. The first is that propositions are taken to be symbols, rather than the possible states of affairs which are symbolized. 'A proposition is equivalent to a sentence in the indicative mood.'[3] This might seem hard to reconcile with the rule, to which Peirce strictly adheres, that every proposition is either true or false, if only for the reason that not every sentence in the indicative mood is meaningful. Peirce himself, indeed, goes so far as to count such sentences as meaningless if they fail in their reference. Thus he characterizes the admittedly ludicrous proposition 'Every phoenix, in rising from its ashes, sings "Yankee Doodle" ' as meaningless, apparently on the ground that there are no phoenixes, and goes on to say that 'if "Man is a biped" be allowed to be an explicative proposition, it means nothing unless there be an occasion in which the name "man" may be applied'.[4] His adoption of this unusually strict view of meaning, with the consequent enrichment of the class of meaningless propositions, does not, however, impair his loyalty to the law of excluded middle. His procedure is to count

[1] II 250.   [2] II 95.   [3] II 315.   [4] Ibid.

a proposition as false if it conflicts with experience and otherwise as true. So the proposition about phoenixes singing 'Yankee Doodle' is said to be perfectly true, since we can be sure that it is not in conflict with any experience. He goes even further to the point of saying that ' "Every four-sided triangle is deep-blue", is necessarily true, since it is impossible that any experience should conflict with it'.[1] In short, 'all universals, whether affirmative or negative, are true of the non-existent'[2] and if their protases are contradictory, they are necessarily true. This extension of the domain of true propositions is unconventional, to say the least, but it is pragmatically harmless, since it can never lead to our mistaking falsehood for truth.

It should, however, be added that the criterion of falsehood which Peirce adopts in these logical studies is not entirely consistent with his overall pragmatism. One would expect him to hold that a proposition was false only if it conflicted with experience in the indefinitely long run. Instead, he says here that a proposition is false 'if any proposition could be legitimately deduced from it, without any aid from false propositions, which would conflict with a direct perceptual judgement, could such be had'.[3] The main objection to this definition, at least on his own principles, is that it overlooks the fact that direct perceptual judgements themselves are corrigible.

A second principle to which, as we have already noted, Peirce uniformly adheres is that every proposition has a subject and a predicate. He is not, however, altogether consistent in his usage of these terms. Sometimes he writes as though its subject and predicate were parts of the proposition and therefore signs. Sometimes as though the subject were that to which the indexical part of the proposition refers and the predicate that which is predicated of it. Thus in one passage he speaks of the subject as being among things 'a proper name or other designation of an individual',[4] in another he says 'I term those occasions or objects which are denoted by the indices the *subjects* of the assertion'.[5] Though he perhaps more frequently adopts the usage in which

[1] Ibid.   [2] Ibid. fn.
[3] II 327.   [4] II 357.   [5] II 338.

subjects and predicates are signs, the fact that he is careful to distinguish the grammatical subject of a proposition from its logical subject, and that it is the logical subject that he is concerned with, makes the other and more familiar usage the more appropriate for his purposes.

Peirce's attempts to find a subject and a predicate for every type of proposition are not always felicitous. For instance, in the case of the proposition 'Cain killed Abel' he argues, quite plausibly, that the proposition, with its two subjects 'Cain' and 'Abel', 'may be regarded as primarily relating to the Dyad composed of Cain, as first, and of Abel as second member',[1] and that this pair can be held to constitute a single individual object. But then he goes on to say that the Dyad is 'not primarily the pair' but 'a mental Diagram consisting of two images of two objects, one existentially connected with one member of the pair, the other with the other, the one having attached to it, as representing it, a Symbol whose meaning is "First", and the other a Symbol whose meaning is "Second" '.[2] Once more this is the fallacy of supposing that images are somehow intrinsically significant in a way that verbal signs are not. As we have already remarked and shall have occasion to remark again, the fact is that one can perfectly well understand a proposition without having any mental images of the individual to which it refers. Moreover, even when it is evoked, the image achieves nothing that words cannot; it merely acts as a supplementary sign. In the present example, since Cain and Abel are anyhow fictitious characters, the fanciful pictures that one might succeed in forming of them are particularly superfluous. They are dragged in by Peirce in order to strengthen his claim that names like 'Cain' and 'Abel' are indices, but in fact this procedure only weakens it. From a similar motive he maintains, even less plausibly, that a complex mental diagram is needed for the proper understanding of a universal proposition like 'Every man is the son of two parents'. The case of conditional propositions leads him further astray to the point of saying that the meaning of the proposition 'If it freezes tonight, your roses will be killed' is that 'any replica of the proposition "It will freeze tonight" which may be

[1] II 316.   [2] Ibid.

true, co-exists with a true replica of the proposition "your roses will be killed" '.[1] But, quite apart from the oddity of construing this conditional as a proposition about signs, it is clear that a token of the words 'It will freeze tonight' may be used to assert a truth in all sorts of contexts where there is no occasion to speak of roses at all, and that even if these words are uttered in the relevant context, there is no reason whatever for assuming that the other sentence will invariably accompany them. The most that can be claimed is that if both replicas are in fact uttered, in the appropriate context, they will both be true. But if the replicas are merely possible, they cannot provide the proposition with the subject that Peirce requires.

As Peirce himself shows elsewhere, these unfortunate complications are quite unnecessary. Having taken the step of including quantifiers in the class of indices, he has a straightforward way of making good his general thesis. The sign which denotes the subject of a symbolic proposition may be a gesture, provided that the gesture is intended and understood to have this reference, or it may be a demonstrative expression, or a proper name functioning as a demonstrative, or it may just be implicit in the context. As Peirce puts it, 'if somebody rushes into the room and says "There is a great fire", we know he is talking about the neighbourhood and not about the world of the *Arabian Nights' Entertainments*'.[2] The other possibilities are excellently dealt with by Peirce in the article from which this quotation is taken. He begins here by speaking of the subject as a sign, but the sense of his words can easily be transposed into the other usage.

'When the subject is not a proper name, or other designation of an individual within the experience (proximate or remote) of both speaker and auditor, the place of such designation is taken by a virtual precept stating how the hearer is to proceed in order to find an object to which the proposition is intended to refer. If this process does not involve a regular course of experimentation, all cases may be reduced to two with their complications. These are the two cases: first that in which the auditor is to take any object of a given description, and it is left to him to take any one

[1] Ibid.   [2] II 357.

he likes; and, secondly, the case in which it is stated that a suitable object can be found within a certain range of experience, or among the existent individuals of a certain class. The former gives the *distributed* subject of a *universal* proposition, as 'Any cockatrice lays eggs'. It is not asserted that any cockatrice exists, but only that, if the hearer can find a cockatrice, to that it is intended that the predicate shall be applicable. The other case gives the *undistributed* subject of a *particular* proposition, as 'Some Negro albino is handsome'. This implies that there is at least one Negro albino. Among complications of these cases we may reckon such subjects as that of the proposition, 'Every fixed star but one is too distant to show a true disk', and, 'There are at least two points osculating any given curve'. The subject of a universal proposition may be taken to be, 'Whatever object in the universe be taken': thus the proposition about the cockatrice might be expressed: 'Any object in the universe having been taken, it will either not be a cockatrice or it will lay eggs'. So understood, the subject is not asserted to exist, but it is well known to exist: for the universe must be understood to be familiar to the speaker and hearer, or no communication about it would take place between them: for the universe is known only by experience. The particular proposition may still more naturally be expressed in this way, 'There is something in the universe which is a Negro albino that is handsome'.[1] Peirce goes on to remark that a proposition may have several subjects, in the sense that it may contain a string of quantified variables, and that the meaning of the proposition is affected in certain cases by the order in which the quantifiers occur. As he puts it, 'the order in which the selection of individuals is made is material when the selections are different in distribution'[2]. To assert, for example, that every man now alive has some ancestor is clearly not the same as asserting that someone is the ancestor of every man now alive.

This leaves very little more to be said. The only difficult case that it fails to cover is that of unfulfilled conditionals. Ordinary conditionals present no great problem. If one insists on finding a subject for a proposition like 'If it freezes tonight, your roses will

[1] II 357.   [2] Ibid.

be killed', the best choice would seem to be the place and time to which the proposition is understood to refer. Then what is predicated of this stretch of space-time is that it does not contain a frost without also containing the killing of the roses. But suppose that it does not freeze and that someone says the next morning 'If it had frozen last night, your roses would have been killed'. How is this proposition to be handled? Presumably, the subject remains the same, but what can be taken to be predicated of it? The same as before, with the substitution of 'would not' for 'does not'? But this yields a very strange sort of attribute. Peirce himself says in one place that 'the quantified subject of a hypothetical proposition is a *possibility*, or *possible case*, or *possible state* of *things*'[1] but then he appears to define possibility in a way that excludes the case where the state of things in question is known not to be actual. If we ignore this restriction and transfer the talk of possibility to the predicate, which appears to be the proper place for it, if it can be fitted into this framework at all, we can construe the unfulfilled conditional as predicating of the relevant stretch of space-time that it could not contain the one feature without containing the other; in our example, that it could not contain the frost, without containing the killing of the roses. But apart from the fact that such modal predicates call for further analysis, they will not always do what is here required of them: there may be occasions on which one is willing to assert that if one thing had occurred, another would in fact have occurred, for example, that if such and such a person had stood for such and such an office, he would have been elected, without wishing to imply that no other result would have been possible.

Perhaps, then, the best course would be to recur to Peirce's distinction between questions of fact and questions concerning the arrangement of facts. On this view, the factual content of the unfulfilled conditional, 'if f had occurred then g would have occurred', is simply the non-occurrence of f without g, and it is this that is predicated of the relevant spatio-temporal region. It follows that so long as f does not occur, it is equally true to the facts to assert either that if f had occurred g would have occurred,

[1] II 347.

or that if *f* had occurred *g* would not have occurred. The difference between these assertions must then be taken to consist in the different indications that they give of the way in which the speaker organizes his beliefs. What they indicate is that he has a disposition, grounded on his acceptance of various generalizations, to infer the occurrence of *g* from that of *f*, under conditions of this sort, or alternatively to infer the occurrence of not-*g*. Even if there is no difference of truth and falsehood, so long as *f* does not occur, it can still be said that one of these assertions is more acceptable than the other, according as one or other disposition more generally results in true beliefs. If a theory of this kind is correct, the implication of the present argument would be that the difference between material and subjunctive conditionals does not consist in a difference in their subjects and predicates. This conclusion is anyhow in line with one strand in Peirce's thought.

Apart from a number of historical remarks, the main thing which Peirce has to say concerning the predicate is that it is general. What I take him to mean by this is that the use of a predicative sign carries no implications with regard to the number or identity of the individuals which fall under the predicate. Definite descriptions might appear to provide a counter-example, but in this case one must distinguish between the predicates, which they contain and the assertions, which they imply or presuppose, that these predicates are uniquely satisfied. A possible counter-example, which Peirce considers, is that of a statement of identity like 'Boz was Charles Dickens'. His answer is that in this proposition 'the Subjects are Boz and Charles Dickens and the predicate is "identical with"', identity being in his view a 'general relation'[1]. As it stands, this answer is hardly satisfactory, since if Boz is in fact identical with Charles Dickens, there would appear to be one subject and not two. It is a slight improvement to speak, as Peirce does elsewhere,[2] of identifying the objects of two indices, where these objects are regarded as different aspects of the same things, but this notion of an aspect still needs to be classified. However, the point that 'identical with' is a general concept remains unaffected.

It may be noted that Peirce here excludes the copula from the predicate on the ground of its being 'purely formal, and containing no special matter or complexity'.[1] In another place, however, he speaks of it as 'an inseparable part of the class-name'.[2] Either way, he refuses to treat it as a third term in the proposition, representing its syntax. His decisive objection to this view, which he traces to Abelard, is that 'it is plain that one does not escape the need of a Syntax by regarding the Copula as a third part of the proposition, and it is simpler to say that it is merely the accidental form that Syntax may take'.[3] Nevertheless, in one of his letters to Lady Welby, he includes 'is' in the class of 'Copulants',[4] which he puts into a triad along with nominative signs, here called 'Designations' and predicative signs, here called 'Descriptions'. The sign 'is' is counted among the 'pure copulants' of which Peirce says that they are indispensable, that they cannot be explicated and that they have the property of being 'Continuant'. What he means by their being continuant is illustrated by the example of 'A is red'. This sign, he says, 'can be decomposed so as to separate "is red" into a Copulative and Descriptive, thus: "A possesses the character of redness". But if we attempt to analyse "possesses the character" in like manner, we get "A possesses the character of the possession of the character of Redness"; and so on *ad infinitum*.'[5] What this seems to me to prove, however, is that, given the necessary conventions, the syntax of a proposition is something which it just exhibits, rather than something which needs to be represented by the inclusion in the proposition of any special type of sign.

An Argument, coming last in the trichotomy after terms and propositions, is said to be 'a Sign which, for its Interpretant, is a Sign of law'.[6] The point of this is again to preserve a correspondence with the categories, a term being, as we have seen, a sign of qualitative possibility and a proposition being taken, however obscurely, as a sign of actual existence. I suppose that the justification for treating an argument as a sign of law is that it represents a lawful derivation of one proposition from another. As Peirce

[1] II 343.   [2] II 328.   [3] II 319.   [4] See above, p. 145.
[5] VIII 352.   [6] II 252.

puts it, 'the Interpretant of the Argument represents it as an instance of a general class of Arguments, which class on the whole will always tend to the truth. It is this law, in some shape, which the argument urges: and this 'urging' is the mode of representation proper to Arguments'.[1] We have already dealt at some length with Peirce's account of the different forms that argument may take.

The three trichotomies lead, as I have said, to a division of signs into ten classes, with various subdivisions. These classes are obtained by combining elements of different trichotomies. Thus, a spontaneous cry is given as an example of a Rhematic Indexical Sinsign, a demonstrative pronoun, considered as a type, is a Rhematic Indexical Legisign, a proposition is a Dicent Symbol, and so forth. The whole exercise is somewhat scholastic, and I do not think that any useful purpose would be served, at this stage, by our going through the list in detail.

D. APPRAISAL OF PEIRCE'S THEORY OF SIGNS

The greatest obstacle which we have found to giving a coherent account of Peirce's theory of signs is the obscurity of his notion of the object of a sign. I believe that this obscurity is not, as so often with Peirce, a matter of formulation but that it results, at least in part, from some confusion of thought. His passion for threefold divisions leads him, as we have noted, to credit every sign not only with an object, as well as an interpretant, but also with a ground which 'stands for the object not in all respects, but in reference to a set of ideas'.[2] He says very little about this third factor, though it appears to survive in his later writings under the guise of the dynamical object. I shall argue presently that although it is sometimes possible to distinguish the object to which a sign refers as it is in itself from the object as it is envisaged by

[1] II 253.　　　[2] II 228.

the user of the sign, and both of them from the range of interpretations that can legitimately be put upon the sign, these distinctions are not necessary, or even very helpful, to a theory of meaning. I shall try to show that all that really matters is the process of interpretation.

Before attempting this, however, I want to say something about the other main issue which has emerged from our review of Peirce's theory. This is his contention that if a proposition is to have any factual content, it must contain, explicitly or implicitly, a nominative sign which is indexical and a predicative sign which is iconic. I do not propose to enter further into the question of subjects and predicates but only to consider the thesis that both indexical and iconic signs are indispensable.

With regard to indexical signs, the thesis almost ceases to be controversial through the fact that quantifiers are included among them. The only question which then remains is whether the elimination of singular terms can be carried to the point where quantified variables are replaced by operators, so that we are left with a wholly predicative form of language. Professor Quine has outlined a method by which this might be done,[1] and I see no reason why his undertaking should not be successful. I shall not, however, pursue this question here.

In recent discussions, the question whether indexical signs can be dispensed with has been identified with the question whether language can be totally freed from dependence upon context. In other words, the term 'indexical', at any rate as applied to verbal expressions, has been limited to token-reflexive signs, which, as we have seen, are a sub-class of indices, in Peirce's usage. It is not maintained that a context-free translation can always be found for every proposition in which a token-reflexive sign occurs, but only that the proposition can be adequately paraphrased, the test of an adequate paraphrase being that there is no loss of information. So it can be argued that instead of fixing the spatio-temporal position of the speaker by the use of demonstratives like 'here' and 'now', one can make use of landmarks which are uniquely identified by means of general descrip-

[1] See W. V. Quine, 'Variables Explained Away' in *Selected Logic Papers* (1966).

tions which they alone happen to satisfy, that proper names can be eliminated after the same fashion, that what is indicated by the use of tenses can be made explicit by descriptions identifying the temporal position of the utterance of the sentence and stating how the event in question is temporally related to it. I have gone into this elsewhere,[1] in some detail, and concluded that this programme can be carried out, provided that one is willing to accept the identity of indiscernibles as a necessary truth. Otherwise one will have to maintain that things which satisfy all the same descriptions can still be distinguished demonstratively, or, to put it in old-fashioned terms, that things which have all their properties in common may still differ in substance. For instance, it would be conceivable, on this view, that there should be someone who satisfied every single predicate that I satisfy, including every spatio-temporal description, and yet was different from me simply in being himself and not myself. I confess that I can see no way of deciding which view is correct.

In any case, even if we admit the possibility of doing without token-reflexive signs, the consequences, from Peirce's point of view, will not be very serious. For although a reference to context within the language may not be necessary for the purposes of communication, there will still be occasions, in practice, when we shall need to rely upon the clues which are provided by the actual circumstances in which the communications are produced. The way in which we are told that there is a fire will enable us to decide whether this is intended to be a statement of fact or fiction and, in the case where it is a statement of fact, whether or not the fire is near at hand. It is true that the location of the fire can be given descriptively; it can be said to be such and such a distance away from some standard landmark, or from some prominent feature of the hearer's environment. But still the point of reference has to be recognized: if the hearer is not familiar with it, there has to be a tacit understanding that he is to look for it in the neighbourhood; he is not to worry over the fact that the description which he has been given of it may after all not be unique; that there may be something somewhere else that satisfies

[1] See 'Names and Descriptions' in *The Concept of a Person.*

it. In short, even if the information which is conveyed by any proposition can be completely expressed in purely descriptive terms, the way in which one reacts to the information and so, in Peirce's use, interprets it may still depend upon the directions which are embodied in the context. But then the question whether these directions are inserted into the language or confined to extra-linguistic clues and conventions does not appear to be of major importance.

It would seem then that there is no strong reason to object to Peirce's account of the part played by indexical signs in conveying information about matters of fact. The same cannot, however, be said of his contention that every predicative sign must be iconic, or at any rate such that its meaning is only explicable by icons. I take it that what he had in mind was that the full explanation of the meaning of any predicative sign would involve a demonstration or description of the observable states of affairs which would count as verifying the propositions into which it entered, and that at this stage, at any rate, iconic signs would necessarily come in. The theory would be that in order to understand a proposition which refers to an observable state of affairs, one has to have an image in which this state of affairs is depicted; the proposition is then held to be true or false according as this image corresponds or fails to correspond to the relevant percept. But even if we grant the assumption that, at least in the case of empirical propositions, the meaning of the predicative signs which they contain is ultimately to be rendered in observational terms, the inference that it must therefore be explained by icons is simply invalid. Not only does one constantly succeed in classifying the things that one observes without going through any conscious process of comparing them with images, but even when images do intervene, the part that they play is only auxiliary. The proof that they are not necessary for the purpose of recognizing objects is that, in order to serve this purpose, their properties must themselves be recognized. Then either they are recognized directly, or we are landed with an infinite regress. And if the properties of images can be recognized directly, so can the properties of the objects which the images are supposed to represent.

The only general argument which Peirce advances in support of his thesis is that no other sign but an icon can have its interpretant as its object. The reasoning behind this, so far as I can follow it, is that the predicative part of the proposition is to be understood as representing that the possible state of affairs, which it primarily represents, is related to the subject of the proposition in a way which corresponds to the way in which it is itself related to the indexical part of the proposition. The sense in which it has its interpretant as its object would then be just that part of what it must be understood to assert includes a reference to itself. But, as I have already said, I can see no good reason why propositions should be interpreted in this way, neither can I see why their being so interpreted should be thought to entail that their predicative parts are iconic. We must remember that, as Peirce uses the term, a proposition is just a string of signs. The relations which obtain between its constituents are, therefore, relations of spatial or temporal adjacency. It seems to me absurd to pretend that such relations pictorially correspond to the relations of qualities to the occasions which exemplify them, or even, except in a special set of cases, to the structure of the state of affairs which the proposition represents. We have indeed admitted that propositions can be said to exhibit their syntax, but all that this comes to is that in order to understand a proposition it is necessary not only to know the meaning or the reference of its constituent signs, but also to be able to draw the proper inferences from such things as their stress or their relative positions. But the fact that the use of language presupposes such conventions in no way entails that there is anything of which the syntax of a proposition can be taken to be a mirror.

So far, indeed, am I from accepting Peirce's view that a proposition has a double object that I think that he would have done much better to avoid crediting it with any object at all. This is not to deny that there are objective states of affairs, which render propositions true or false. The point is rather that if we are concerned only with analysing the meaning of a proposition, it is irrelevant whether the state of affairs in question exists or not. For example, if I say that it will rain this afternoon, the truth or falsehood of my assertion depends upon the actual occurrence or non-occurrence of the rain, but the meaning of the proposition remains the same in either case. One may therefore be tempted to identify the objects of propositions with the possible states of affairs which they are intended to symbolize. But apart from the fact that this is quite unilluminating, these possible states of affairs are very dubious entities. Much of the difficulty which we found in making any sense of Peirce's account of the objects of signs was due to his hovering between the admission of possible entities as objects and a variety of attempts to find some actual entities to play the part.

The main objection, however, to Peirce's attempt to explain the meaning of signs in terms of their objects as well as their interpretants is that it involves him in a vicious circle. For, as we have seen, he maintains, correctly, that a sign stands for something only in virtue of being so interpreted. Let O then be the object, in this sense, of a sign S. It follows that there must be a sign S' which interprets S as standing for O, and that it is only because of this interpretation that O comes to be the object of S. But then we cannot say, as Peirce does, that what makes S' the interpretant of S is its being an equivalent sign, in the sense that it stands for the same object, or for some development of the same object. For this implies that S already stands for O, independently of its interpretation by S'.

Peirce tries to escape from this circle by giving the interpretant a twofold object. Not only does S' stand for O, but it also stands for the representation of O by S. But apart from the fact that S and S' then cease to be equivalent, it is not at all easy to see how any one sign can perform this double function, let alone our having to assume that every interpretant does so.

In the face of these difficulties, there are, so far as I can see, three courses that might be followed. The first would be to take 'interpreted by as standing for' as a primitive three-term relation. This would avoid the circularity, since we then should not have to say both that O becomes an object for S through the action of S' and that S' becomes an interpretant of S through having the same object O. The mere fact that S, S' and O were terms, taken in that order, of the primitive relation would be enough to establish them in their respective roles. There would be no need to treat the relation between the original sign and its object as a further object of the interpretant. It is true that the interpretant would itself require to be interpreted, but this would create no special difficulty. There would be an endless series of actual or possible signs $S_1 \ldots S_n$ such that S_1 was interpreted by S_2 as standing for O, S_2 was interpreted by S_3 as standing for O, S_3 was interpreted by S_4 as standing for O and so *ad infinitum*. On this view it would be a necessary and sufficient condition for a sign S to stand for an object O that S be interpreted by an infinite series of signs each of which is interpreted by its immediate successor as standing for O. Alternatively, and perhaps more plausibly, we could take S_2 as interpreting S_1 as standing for O, S_3 as interpreting S_2 as interpreting S_1 as standing for O, S_4 as interpreting S_3 as interpreting S_2 as interpreting S_1 as standing for O, and so on. In that case, the only member of the series to have O for its object would be the first. I say that this version is perhaps the more plausible, because I find it easier to accept the idea of an infinite metalinguistic hierarchy than that of an infinite progression of signs, each of which has the same object. Peirce, in fact, conflates the two versions, and thus greatly adds to the difficulties of his account.

I think that a position of this kind is tenable, but I should prefer not to have to hold it. Not only does it still commit us to a ragbag of possible entities, but by taking the relation of 'being interpreted by to stand for' as primitive, it denies us any analysis of the relation of signs to what they signify. All that it contributes to the theory of meaning is the principle that every sign must have an interpretant, and even the implications of this principle are left obscure.

A second course, with which Peirce shows some sympathy at least in the case of propositions, would be to conceive of the sign as having a natural, as opposed to a merely semantic relation to its object. More specifically, the idea would be to analyse the meaning of a sign in terms of the state of affairs which caused or would cause it to be uttered. Clearly the only conventional signs to which this could apply directly would be propositional signs which referred to something which the speaker currently observed or felt; perhaps also to what he remembered. It might, however, be held that the meaning of other propositions could be shown to depend on their relation to propositions of this class and that the meaning of non-propositional signs could be analysed in terms of their possible occurrence in propositions. There are obvious difficulties in the way of such a programme, but I shall not explore them here, as it seems to me that the theory breaks down even in the instances which are most favourable to it. No doubt, when one uses a propositional sign to refer to an object which one is currently observing, the existence of the object is causally instrumental to the production of the sign, but it certainly does not follow either that in every case in which the sign purports to refer to the object as present, its production is causally dependent on the existence of the object, or that in every case in which it is causally dependent, it is used to refer to the object. On the one hand, the observer may be mistaken or lying, and on the other his perception of the object may elicit a reference not to it but to something which he associates with it. These are simple objections, but they seem to me to be decisive. Of course they do not prove that causality cannot enter into a successful analysis of meaning, but they do show that even in the case of statements of observation, the relations of signifying and being caused by cannot be simply equated.

The third and, to my mind, the most promising course would be to dispense altogether with the object as an element in the analysis of the meaning of a sign, and make the sign's being understood to stand for something entirely a matter of the character of its interpretants and of the relations that obtain between them. If we follow this course, we cannot take any semantic relations like that of 'naming' or 'designating' or 'being interpreted as standing for' as primitive since they all require an object for the sign to signify. Allowing that every sign must be interpreted, though not necessarily by another sign, we have to analyse 'S is interpreted as standing for O' in a way that will both eliminate O as the accusative and avoid the use of these semantic terms in explaining what it is for a sign to be interpreted. This is not an easy and may not be a possible undertaking. I shall, however, give a rough sketch of the way in which I think it might be carried out.

Let us begin with propositional signs. In what follows, I shall use the term 'proposition' not in the way that Peirce uses it as an equivalent to 'propositional sign' but rather in the way it is more commonly used, to designate that which a propositional sign is used to express. This is done purely for convenience of exposition. Since it turns propositions into the objects of propositional signs, they are introduced on the assumption that they can later be eliminated.

Now anyone who uses or interprets a propositional sign on any particular occasion is bound to be adopting what may be called a propositional attitude. In certain cases, as when he is making up a story, or telling a joke, or giving an example, he may not be concerned with the truth or falsehood of the proposition which the sign is understood to express. In the cases where he is concerned with its truth or falsehood, he may simply consider the proposition, or believe it, or disbelieve it, or doubt it, or wonder about it: this list is not intended to be exhaustive. Most commonly his attitude will be one of belief, at any rate on the occasions when the propositional sign is overtly produced. People generally believe what they say, and they also tend to believe what other people tell them.

Let us then take the case in which a person A interprets a propositional sign s as expressing a proposition p which he believes. Then A's belief that p will consist, in this concrete instance, not only in his uttering or assenting to s but also in his being disposed to behave in various characteristic ways: and among these dispositions will be a disposition to utter or assent to a number of other propositional signs. I shall speak of these signs as occurring in the expansion of this instance of A's belief that p. It should be clear from our earlier examination of the pragmatic theory of belief that this is not intended as a definition of what it is for A to believe that p, let alone a definition of what it would be for anyone to hold this belief. It is at most a specimen of a belief that p: it is to be understood as setting out what A's belief actually comes to in this particular instance.

When two or more propositional signs occur in the expansion

of the same instance of a belief, I shall speak of them as being mutually interpretative. It will be clear that the fact that two such signs are mutually interpretative does not entail that they are equivalent. For instance, let s_1 be a sign which is used by A to express the proposition p and let s_2 be a sign, not equivalent to s_1, which is used by A to express the proposition q. Then s_2 may still occur with s_1 in the expansion of A's belief that p, either because A believes that p entails q, or because he believes that the states of affairs which are represented by the two propositions are causally connected, or because he believes that the state of affairs which is represented by q is a manifestation of that which is represented by p, as for example, yawning is a manifestation of boredom or universal suffrage a manifestation of democracy. In order, therefore, to arrive at a criterion of equivalence we have to find a way of ruling out these other possibilities. This can be achieved by stipulating first that s_1 be interchangeable with s_2, in the sense that if either were to enter into the expansion of any of A's beliefs so would the other, and secondly that they would remain interchangeable, in this sense, no matter what other beliefs A were to hold, exception being made, of course, for beliefs which related to the usage of the signs themselves. The point of this second condition is that it would be violated in the case where the fact that s_2 is included with s_1 in the expansion of A's belief that p is due to his also holding a belief in some generalization which connects p with q. So long as these two conditions are satisfied, we can conclude that A interprets these signs as being mutually equivalent.

Following this line of thought, we can now give an account of what it is for a sign to be interpreted as expressing such and such a proposition. We can use the same example of A's believing that p, but also need to introduce a commentator X who may or may not be identical with A. Then it can be said of X that he construes a propositional sign s, in A's usage, as the expression of a proposition p if and only if he takes A's assenting to s as a criterion for A's believing that p, no matter what other beliefs he supposes A to hold, exception again being made for beliefs which relate to the usage of s itself. This does not necessarily yield the conclusion that A in fact uses s to express p, since X may be mistaken in his interpretation of A's usage: for instance, if he knows that s is conventionally used to express p, he may take it for granted that A uses it in this way, though a closer study of A's behaviour would show that he did not. We therefore need to add the proviso that X interprets A's usage correctly and to supply criteria for determining this. In the case where X is identical with A we have no serious problem; the difficulty is rather to give a sense to the hypothesis that A misconstrues his own usage. In the case where they are not identical, a satisfactory criterion would be that A attributes to others the use of s to express p in cases when he believes that their usage coincides with his own.

Since we are entitled to assume that the meaning of a propositional sign remains the same, whether the proposition which it is used to express is believed, disbelieved, doubted or merely considered, there is no need for us to deal separately with these other propositional attitudes. For instance, if A's use of a sign s occurs as part of a pattern of behaviour which furnishes an instance of his doubting whether p, the fact that X is disposed to take A's assenting to s as a criterion for A's believing that p is enough to establish for him the requisite link between s and p, even though A's actual response to s on this occasion is not that of assent. By the same means we can handle sentences in the interrogative and imperative moods, sentences which are used to express promises and so forth. We have only to correlate these sentences, by means of grammatical rules, with sentences which are used assertorically. So in the case where the interrogative, like 'Who killed Cock Robin?', asks for a value to be given to the variable in a propositional function, it can be correlated with the sentence which states that the function is satisfied by something or other, this being the presupposition of the question. In general, the state of affairs the existence of which is presupposed, queried, desiderated, or brought about, as the case may be, by the use of a sentence of the first class can be identified with that in the existence of which the speaker's assent to the corresponding sentence of the second class would, in the appropriate circumstances, be construed as evincing belief.

Since natural signs can always be assimilated to propositional signs by spelling out the information which they are understood to convey, the only cases which remain to be considered are those of the conventional signs which are not propositional. Here again the easiest course to follow will be to correlate them with propositional signs. Thus the meaning of a predicative sign, as used on a given occasion, can be derived from the proposition which the speaker would have been understood to express on that occasion by coupling the predicative sign with an existentially qualified variable. The meaning of a nominative sign can be derived from the proposition which results from its replacing an existentially quantified variable in a propositional sign the predicative part of which has already had its meaning determined. There is no need to credit signs of either of these types with independent objects. If we do insist on speaking of nominative signs as having objects to which they are used to refer, we must remember that our analysis of their meaning goes back to the expression of belief, and that belief is subject to referential opacity. This means that two nominative signs with the same reference cannot necessarily be credited with the same object. They will have the same object only in the case where one can legitimately replace the other in the expansion of the same belief. That this is not true in general is shown by the fact that one may assent to a propositional sign in which a predicate is ascribed to an individual under one description and not assent to a propositional sign in which the same predicate is ascribed to the same individual under another description, owing to one's not having the belief that the individuals which answer to the two descriptions are the same. But in any case, as I have already said, I think it better not to speak of these signs as having any object at all. Anything that we may want to say about their reference can be included in the interpretation of the propositions into which they enter and in comments on the manner in which the propositions turn out to be true or false. For example, we can distinguish between the case in which a proposition is rendered false by the failure of the predicate to apply to the designated individual and that in which it is rendered false, or as Peirce would say, trivially true, by the failure of anything to answer to the designation.

So far, our analysis has related only to the use of a sign by a particular person on a particular occasion. It is, however, easy to see how it can be generalized. To say that a person habitually uses a sign in such and such a fashion is to say that he uses it in this fashion on all or nearly all the occasions on which he uses it at all. To say that a sign s has such and such a standard use in a language L is to say either that it is habitually used in this way by the majority of those who employ the language L, or possibly that this is the way in which certain speakers of L, who are regarded by the others as setting the standard, decree that it should habitually be used. In any case, it is obvious that the only way in which a sign, as a type, can come to have a meaning is through the meaning which is, or should be, given to the tokens in which it is exemplified.

Even if this sketch of an analysis is acceptable, it may still be doubted whether we have succeeded in our aim of dispensing with the objects of signs. It all turns on the question whether we are able to eliminate propositions as the objects of beliefs. The way in which we have attempted to do this is to equate a person's belief in a given proposition with his disposition to behave in certain ways, including his disposition to assent to certain propositional signs; and here it must be made clear that assenting to a propositional sign is not to be identified with accepting the proposition which the sign is understood to express: if it were so identified, our analysis would be circular. It must be taken to imply no more than that the speaker is disposed to utter the sign when the occasion arises, that his utterance of it is not attended by feelings or manifestations of doubt, that he readily acquiesces in its utterance by others and so forth; we have to rely upon the circumstances, and upon other aspects of his behaviour, including his private and public reaction to other signs, for criteria of his sincerity and for a means of distinguishing the cases when his negative reaction to the utterance of the sign, by himself or others, is a manifestation, let us say, of his sense of decorum and not of disbelief. Assenting to a propositional sign, in this sense, must not even be taken as presupposing an understanding of its meaning. The implication is rather that the meaning which the speaker attaches to the sign is determined by the circumstances in which he assents to it.

The fulfilment of our aim is therefore dependent on the behavioural theory of belief. As we have seen, this theory led us into serious difficulties, but we have also found some reason to think that these difficulties can be overcome. I cannot claim, however, to have shown conclusively that this is so and until it is conclusively shown I am afraid that the possibility of giving an account of signs which does not take the question-begging form of simply representing them as terms in a semantic relation must also remain open to doubt.

The account which I have tried to give is certainly not identical with Peirce's, but in its main features it strongly displays his influence. It seems to me, in fact, that his own theory is an unsuccessful blend of two rival strains in his philosophy; the scholasticism which leads to the proliferation of abstract entities and the pragmatism which aims at their removal. Here, as elsewhere, it is the pragmatic strain in Peirce's thinking that I have found the most interesting and the most fruitful to exploit.

WILLIAM JAMES

CHAPTER ONE

INTRODUCTION

ALTHOUGH William James, who lived from 1842 to 1910, was only a slightly younger man than Peirce and almost his contemporary at Harvard, he occupies a distinctly later position in the history of Pragmatism. There was an interval of thirty years between the appearance of Peirce's early pragmatist papers and the publication, under the title of *Pragmatism*, of a series of 'popular lectures on philosophy' by William James, which were mainly responsible for bringing the pragmatist movement for the first time into the foreground of the philosophical scene. One reason for this delay was that James was late in developing into a professional philosopher. He took a medical degree, though he never practised medicine, and entered academic life in 1872 as an instructor in physiology at Harvard, where he remained for the rest of his career, becoming a lecturer in psychology in 1876 and a professor of philosophy in 1880. His reputation was made by his first and major work, *The Principles of Psychology*, which appeared in two large volumes in 1890. This book, which uniquely combines a physiological with a philosophical approach to the traditional problems of psychology, remains a classic, and is probably the best general review of the subject that has yet been written. In its more scientific aspects, it lies outside the range of this study, but I shall have occasion to refer to it for the part that it plays in the development of James's 'Radical Empiricism', which is, as we shall see, his most original and fruitful contribution to philosophical theory.

James published two shorter text books on psychology in the 1890s and his fascinating Gifford Lectures on *The Varieties of Religious Experience*, which were delivered in 1901–2 and published in 1902 are mainly psychological in scope. Apart from an unfinished introduction to philosophy which was published posthumously under the title of *Some Problems of Philosophy*, his philosophical books are all either reprints of lectures or collections of essays. A lecture on 'The Will to Believe', which was published in the *New World* in 1896, gave its title to a collection which came out in the following year. The papers included in it, which are mainly reprints of addresses to philosophical and religious societies, go back in date to 1879, but the earlier ones, apart from some effective criticism of the aberrations of Hegel and of Herbert Spencer, are not of any great technical interest. Pragmatism is barely foreshadowed, and although in the preface James uses the designation of Radical Empiricism to characterize his philosophical standpoint, its central theses are not in fact developed in this book.

James's great period of philosophical activity came in the last six years of his life. His *Essays in Radical Empiricism* were not published until after his death but with one exception, a brief attack on one of the English neo-Hegelians, which goes back to 1884, all the twelve papers which it contains were first published in the years 1904–5. The other posthumous work, *Some Problems in Philosophy*, was begun in the spring of 1909, just two years after the publication of the lectures on *Pragmatism*. In 1909 also he published two other books, *A Pluralistic Universe*, which is a reprint of a course of lectures which he delivered in that year at a Protestant seminary in Oxford, and *The Meaning of Truth*, a collection of fifteen essays of which only two were written before 1904. In the main, these essays are attempts on James's part to elucidate his version of the pragmatic theory of truth and to defend it against the numerous objections which his earlier formulation of it had aroused.

As we shall see, these objections cannot be altogether dismissed, as James himself was inclined to dismiss them, on the ground that they resulted from mere misunderstandings of his view. Both his theory of truth and his theory of radical empiricism, which were closely bound together, are exposed to more serious technical difficulties than he appears to have allowed for. Nevertheless he was right in thinking both that his critics had misunderstood him and that this was his fault as well as theirs. He was a very gifted writer, in a forceful, lucid, manly, open-air style, which is almost the antithesis of that of his younger brother, the novelist Henry James. There are philosophers, such as Hume and Russell, who have written with greater elegance, but no modern philosopher who matches William James in the vividness and range of his imagery or the freshness of his humour. But aiming, as he mostly did, at a wider audience than that of his professional colleagues, he was more concerned to present his opinions in a way that would appeal to the imagination than to fortify them against minute criticism.

Temperamentally also, he was a man who took large views. The very earnestness with which he held his opinions, the importance which he attached to philosophy as a view of life, made him inattentive to questions of technical detail. Not that he was lacking in respect for facts. On the contrary, it was for their lofty indifference to matters of mere empirical fact that he chiefly censured his Hegelian opponents. But feeling that his vision was correct, he was impatient with arguments that seemed to him not to go to the heart of it but merely to turn on niceties of formulation. In the case of his radical empiricism, at least, this attitude was hardly justified: its interest chiefly lies in its being a technical theory, and it is therefore not at all unfair to subject it to minute analysis. On the other hand, James did have reason to complain that, with few exceptions, the opponents of his pragmatism addressed themselves more to the letter than to the spirit of his writings. He characteristically hit off a pettifogging strain in the Oxford philosophical tradition when he said of one of his critics: 'I feel as if Mr. Joseph almost pounced on my words singly, without giving the sentences time to get out of my mouth.'[1]

It must, however, be admitted that James was inclined to make too light of objections or arguments which seemed to him purely formal. He believed that his philosophical theories were true to the facts of common human experience: and he tended to think that purely logical argument, even though it were free from internal fallacy, might still be unsuited to apply to concrete facts. One of his favourite illustrations of this was the attempt of certain

[1] *Essays in Radical Empiricism* (1912), p. 246.

Roman Catholic theologians to refute Darwin's theory of evolution by invoking the principle that the lesser cannot generate the greater. Admittedly, the moral of this example is not that there is any breakdown in the application of formal logic, but rather that one should not pass off as *a priori* principles what are no more than empirical hypotheses, especially if these hypotheses are false. Still the theologians' argument rested on the assumption that their principle was true *a priori*: and James's point was that it was a mistake to try to settle even philosophical questions on purely *a priori* grounds.

James's tendency to look askance at logic becomes easier to understand when it is remembered that the logic with which he was principally confronted was the logic of Hegel. It took a long time for the Hegelian movement to make its way in English-speaking countries against the prevailing empiricist tradition, but by the turn of the century the influence, among others, of Bradley and T. H. Green at Oxford, McTaggart at Cambridge, and James's own colleague Professor Royce at Harvard, had made it into a dominant force. It is against this background that we have to set not only the whole of James's philosophy but also the early work of Russell and Moore. Their counter-attack was so successful that the whole dispute has lost interest for us. The position of these neo-Hegelians seems so palpably untenable that it is hard for us to understand how they could ever have been taken seriously. But to James, in the philosophical climate of his time, they were formidable antagonists: and it is necessary to give at least a brief account of his divergencies from them if his own position is to be fairly understood.

It is characteristic of James that to a large extent the roots of his objection to Hegelianism were emotional and moral. Emotionally he found it stifling. In a well-known passage, which I cannot refrain from quoting because it so perfectly illustrates his style and temper, he speaks of the 'through-and-through universe' as seeming to suffocate him 'with its infallible impeccable all-pervasiveness'. 'Its necessity, with no possibilities; its relations, with no subjects, make me feel as if I had entered into a contract with no reserved rights, or rather as if I had to live in a large seaside boarding-house with no private bed-room in which I might take refuge from the society of the place. I am distinctly aware, moreover, that the old quarrel of sinner and Pharisee has something to do with the matter. Certainly, to my personal knowledge, all Hegelians are not prigs, but I somehow feel as if all prigs ought to end, if developed, by becoming Hegelians. There is a story of two clergymen asked by mistake to conduct the same funeral. One came first and had got no further than "I am the Resurrection and the Life", when the other entered. "*I* am the Resurrection and the Life", cried the latter. The "through and through" philosophy, as it actually exists, reminds many of us of that clergyman. It seems too buttoned-up and white-chokered and clean-shaven a thing to speak for the vast slow-breathing unconscious Kosmos with its dread abysses and its unknown tides.'[1]

'The old quarrel of sinner and Pharisee.' If James is on the side of the sinner it is because the sinner is at least not hypocritical. What he finds morally shocking in Hegelianism is its pretence that pain and evil are not real, or anyhow not real enough to worry about. 'The very presence of ill in the temporal order is the condition of the perfection of the eternal order', was the view of Professor Royce. 'The Absolute', in Bradley's opinion, 'is the richer for every discord and for all the diversity which it embraces.' James quotes with approval the reply of an anarchist writer that what Bradley means by this is that when men commit suicide because they cannot find work to keep their families from starving their deaths 'make the universe richer, and that is philosophy. But while Professors Royce and Bradley and a whole host of guileless thoroughfed thinkers are unveiling Reality and the Absolute and explaining away evil and pain, this is the condition of the only beings known to us anywhere in the universe with a developed consciousness of what the universe is. What these people experience is Reality.'[2] To tell them that their sufferings are all resolved in a higher synthesis is not only cruel but frivolous. It

[1] *Essays in Radical Empiricism*, pp. 276–8.
[2] M. I. Swift, *Human Submission*; quoted by James, *Pragmatism* (1907), p. 30.

is a bland evasion of the problem of evil, which is just as much a stumbling-block to a Neo-Hegelian as to an orthodox Christian. For the Absolute is credited with perfection. If it does away with any personal deity, it is only by supplanting him. It has much the same responsibility, in the sense that its existence is supposed to justify everything that happens.

But James's objections to Hegelianism are also intellectual. He sees quite clearly that if appearances really were contradictory, in the way that the Hegelians claimed, then no amount of higher synthesizing could save them. The contradictions reappear in the synthesis and the Absolute has to be brought in as a *deus ex machina* to conjure away the difficulties which your preposterous logic has created. The needs which are satisfied by the Hegelian dialectic are those of a spectator at a pantomime. 'In the pantomime all common things are represented to happen in impossible ways, people jump down each other's throats, houses turn inside out, old women become young men, everything "passes into its opposite" with inconceivable celerity and skill; and this, so far from producing perplexity, brings rapture to the beholder's mind. And so in the Hegelian logic, relations elsewhere recognized under the insipid name of distinctions (such as that between knower and object, many and one) must first be translated into impossibilities and contradictions, then "transcended" and identified by miracle, ere the proper temper is induced for thoroughly enjoying the spectacle they show.'[1]

James sees also that the central flaw in the Hegelian method lies in its treatment of relations, in the fallacy of supposing that every relation into which a thing enters makes a difference to its identity, so that the existence of any one thing is logically inseparable from the existence of everything else, in the equally fallacious idea that related things just fall apart unless there is something beyond the relation to bind them together, so that a cat cannot look at a king unless some higher entity is looking at them both,[2] and finally in the absurd assumption that anything not explicitly ascribed to a subject is implicitly denied of it.

[1] *The Principles of Psychology*, I (1890) 369 n.
[2] *A Pluralistic Universe* (1909), pp. 61-5.

James refers to this last step as 'the treating of a name as excluding from the fact named what the name's definition fails positively to include' and calls it 'vicious intellectualism'.[1] His own view is that relations other than those which are merely formal, are to be taken at their face value, that is as maintaining genuine factual connections between the terms which they relate, and it is his belief in the power of related terms to preserve their separate identities that makes him declare himself a pluralist. We shall see also that the working out of his radical empiricism very largely depends on the assumption that spatio-temporal relations, no less than their terms, are immediate objects of experience.

Intellectualism is suspect to James because he equates it with the sort of abstract thinking of which he regarded the Hegelian system as the typical fruit. Partly for this reason, and partly also because he came to believe that discursive thought could not do justice to the continuity of our experience, he was led into a form of irrationalism, which avowedly owed much to Bergson and would also have made him sympathetic to the Existentialists. Following Bergson, he came to believe that 'instead of being interpreters of reality, concepts negate the inwardness of reality altogether',[2] and he concluded that philosophy should seek the kind of 'living understanding of the movement of reality, which results from putting oneself in intuitive sympathy with "things in the making" ', and 'not follow science in vainly patching together fragments of its dead results'.[3]

Whether James's own attempt to give a rational account of the world breaks down as seriously as this would suggest is a question which we shall have to examine. But whatever problems it may encounter we shall not be likely to find that the line of 'giving up logic' on the ground that reality in its experienced concreteness 'exceeds, overflows and surrounds it',[4] provides the solution to them. In spite of the respect for hard fact which governs all his philosophizing, I doubt, indeed, if James would have made this concession to irrationalism, if his running fight with the Hegelians had not left him with the mistaken feeling that there was an

[1] Ibid., p. 60. See also *The Meaning of Truth* (1909), p. 249.
[2] *A Pluralistic Universe*, p. 246.   [3] Ibid., pp. 263-4.   [4] Ibid., p. 212.

unbridgeable gulf between the static world of intellectual concepts, in which for all the apparent agitation of their dialectic the Hegelians complacently dwelt, and the dynamic flux of experience in which ordinary men live and move and have their being.

There was, however, another underlying motive. It was a feature of James's moral and intellectual earnestness, perhaps also a legacy from his Swedenborgian father, the elder Henry James, that he was very strongly preoccupied with the question of religious belief. He was not only interested in it as a phenomenon, but also very anxious to persuade himself of its truth. The God in whom he sought to believe was not exactly the God of Christianity. James agreed with John Stuart Mill that a God who was omnipotent and yet permitted all the pain and evil that exist in the world would not be a religious object. The only sort of God whom he could regard as worthy of the name would be one who 'works in an external environment, has limits, and has enemies'.[1] Such a God would be, or possess, a super-human consciousness but he would also be finite, 'either in power or in knowledge, or in both at once'.[2] James needed to believe in something of this kind because he wanted the forces of goodness in the world to have a champion, but he did not deceive himself into thinking that the existence of a being of even such limited superiority could be proved by any of the standard theistic arguments. Logic stood in his way, but if it turned out that the inner nature of reality eluded the grasp of logic, then perhaps he could satisfy his religious yearnings without having to sacrifice his intellectual integrity.

This point is of fundamental importance for the understanding of James's thought, since his desire to make room for religious belief, without either relaxing his intellectual standards or manipulating the evidence, was also one of the principal motives for his pragmatism. In particular, it strongly coloured his interpretation of the pragmatic theory of truth. How this is so we shall now proceed to examine.

<hr>

[1] *A Pluralistic Universe*, p. 124.   [2] Ibid., p. 311.

CHAPTER TWO

THE WILL TO BELIEVE
AND THE
PRAGMATIC THEORY OF TRUTH

A. JAMES'S EMOTIONAL COMMITMENTS

IN a famous passage in the first of his lectures on *Pragmatism*, James declares his opinion that 'the history of philosophy is to a great extent that of a certain clash of human temperaments'.[1] He has in mind a fundamental difference in outlook which he thinks is also exhibited in other fields, such as politics or literature. In philosophy it comes out as the distinction between Rationalists and Empiricists, or as James more picturesquely puts it, between the tender- and the tough-minded. The tender-minded philosopher is not only Rationalistic, going by 'principles', whereas the tough-minded is Empiricist, going by 'facts', but also Intellectualistic while the other is Sensationalistic, Idealistic as opposed to Materialistic, Optimistic as opposed to Pessimistic, Religious as opposed to Irreligious, Free-Willist as opposed to Fatalistic, Monistic while the tough-minded is Pluralistic, and Dogmatical while the tough-minded is Sceptical. Though it is doubtful whether any great philosopher satisfies all the criteria on either side, this is a fair summary of two persistently opposing tendencies in philosophy, going back to the almost wholly tender-minded Plato and the tough-minded Sophists whom Plato sought to discredit. No doubt the models whom James chiefly had in mind were Hegel and his followers on the one side and Hume, James Mill and John Stuart Mill on the other.

Now the interesting fact is that James himself cuts sharply across this classification. In some ways he is markedly tough-

[1] *Pragmatism*, p. 6.

minded; an extreme empiricist, a thorough-going sensationalist who tries to analyse factual knowledge wholly in terms of sense-experience, a good deal of a materialist, at least in his psychology, a convinced pluralist, and if not exactly a sceptic, at any rate not a dogmatist. On the other hand, he is temperamentally optimistic, religious, a believer in free-will, and outside his psychology closer to idealism than materialism. What he wanted, therefore, was to make the best of both worlds. We shall see that in his theory of knowledge, he tried to reconcile idealism and materialism, or rather to show that their division was based upon a false antithesis. For the rest, he sought the advantage of being tough-minded with regard to any question of natural fact, and tender-minded with respect to morals and theology. What attracted him to Pragmatism was that it seemed to him to make this possible.

It was the tender-mindedness that presented the main problem. James had already made an attempt to solve it in the title essay in *The Will to Believe*. He there starts from the premiss that there are significant and important questions, such as the question whether God exists, which cannot be decided on intellectual grounds. It is not just that they cannot be decided with certainty, for nothing is 'indefectibly' certain except 'that the present phenomenon of consciousness exists',[1] but rather that there is no agreed criterion by which the truth of either the positive or the negative answer to them could be determined. In these circumstances it might seem that the proper course would be to suspend judgement. This would be in accordance with the general scientific rule that one should not assent to any proposition, unless the balance of evidence is in its favour. But James does not find this rule acceptable. It is all very well for those to whom the truth or falsehood of the proposition in question is of no more than academic interest. But suppose that the issue is one with which we are vitally concerned; must we still remain neutral? Let us not forget that there are cases 'where a fact cannot come at all unless a preliminary faith exists in its coming'.[2] At the very least, if we are dealing with a religious hypothesis, its truth, if it be true, is not likely to disclose itself to us unless we make the first advances.

[1] *The Will to Believe* (1912), pp. 14–15.   [2] Ibid., p. 25.

But if this is so, then 'one who should shut himself up in snarling logicality and try to make the gods extort his recognition willy-nilly, or not get it at all, might cut himself off forever from his only opportunity of making the gods' acquaintance'.[1] For this reason James declines to accept what he calls the agnostic rules for truth-seeking. It seems to him that 'a rule of thinking which would absolutely prevent me from acknowledging certain kinds of truth, if those kinds of truth were really there, would be an irrational rule'.[2] Moreover, in the religious case, there is no genuine neutrality. To be neutral, with regard to the question of God's existence, is effectively to take the negative side. So far as religious practice goes, there is no essential difference between an agnostic and an atheist.

The same considerations, in James's view, apply to the question of morality. He is concerned here not with the validity of this or that moral judgement, but rather with the question whether there are any moral truths at all. 'Are our moral preferences true or false, or are they only biological phenomena, making things good or bad for *us*, but in themselves indifferent?'[3] Again James takes this to be a question which cannot be decided on purely intellectual grounds. If anyone chooses to be a moral sceptic, there is no logical way of refuting him. But this does not mean that those who feel in their hearts that there are moral truths are not fully entitled to adhere to this belief and conduct their lives in accordance with it.

A point which James barely notices is that if there is any force in his argument it works both ways. It gives exactly the same licence to the atheist as to the theist, to the disbeliever as to the believer in the objectivity of moral values. If James uses it to support the tender-minded standpoint, it is partly no doubt because of the strength of his own inclinations in that direction, but partly also because he sees the cause of religious and moral enthusiasm as the one which the intellect puts on the defensive. He wants to rescue the theist from the logic which forbids him to believe. That this also liberates the atheist to whom the same logic would deny the opposite belief might well seem a small

[1] Ibid., p. 28.　　　[2] Ibid.　　　[3] Ibid., p. 23.

　　　　　　　　　　　　　　　　　　　　　A.O.P.

price to pay for disposing of agnosticism. Given James's premiss that there is no evidence either way, the more common reaction would be to suspend judgement rather than embrace atheism as a matter of faith. But while we may understand James's motives for ruling out agnosticism, we can hardly agree with him that a procedure which would debar us from acknowledging certain true propositions, so long as we had no reason to think them true, is less rational than one which would authorize us to accept either these propositions or their contradictories with an equal lack of reservation. To claim the freedom to believe whatever one chooses may be emotionally satisfying, but I should hardly call it rational.

James's position, then, is dubious, even if we grant him the assumption that these moral and religious questions are not intellectually decidable. But this assumption itself is open to attack. Indeed, so far from its being the case that logic has nothing to say to the question whether there are moral truths, it would seem to be a question that can and must be decided on logical grounds. It is not a matter of speculating whether there are moral blueprints in some Platonic heaven, but rather of analysing the way in which moral judgements operate and so eliciting the criteria by which their validity is to be assessed. With regard to the question of God's existence, the position is less clear because we are not told what in this instance we are to understand by 'God': but certainly before the proposition that any such being exists can even become a candidate for faith, our intellect must first be satisfied that the predicates by which it is defined are neither meaningless nor inconsistent.

The fact is that James's own attitude to his assumption is equivocal. His purpose in maintaining that such questions as that of the existence of God or the objectivity of morals are not decidable on purely intellectual grounds is to ensure that certain propositions which he strongly wishes to believe are not put out of court by *a priori* argument. He is determined to protect them from being summarily disqualified either by scientific positivism or by the Hegelian dialectic. It does not appear, however, that he really wants to hold that these propositions are not susceptible

of evidence. On the contrary, the position towards which he is
moving is that they are subject to experimental tests, but
that these tests are of a special kind. What verifies or falsifies
them is their agreement or disagreement not with our perceptual
but with what may be broadly called our moral experience.

This comes out more clearly in some of the other essays which
appear in the same volume as *The Will to Believe*. Thus in one
early essay called 'The Sentiment of Rationality', he claims that
in answering such a question as 'Is this a moral world?' 'we might
proceed exactly as does the physical philosopher in testing an
hypothesis. He deduces from the hypothesis an experimental
action *x*: this he adds to the facts M already existing. It fits them
if the hypothesis be true; if not, there is discord. The results of
the action corroborate or refute the idea from which it flowed.
So here: the verification of the theory which you may hold as
to the objectively moral character of the world can consist only
in this – that if you proceed to act upon your theory it will be
reversed by nothing that later turns up as your action's fruit. . . .
If this be an objectively moral universe, all acts that I make on
this assumption, all expectations that I ground on it, will tend
more and more completely to interdigitate with the phenomena
already existing. M+ *x* will be in accord; and the more I live, and
the more the fruits of my activity come to light, the more satisfactory the consensus will grow. . . . If, on the other hand, I
rightly assume the universe to be not moral, in what does my
verification consist? It is that by letting moral interests sit lightly
. . . by refusing to take up a tragic attitude, I deal in the long run
most satisfactorily with the facts of life.'[1] James goes on to
explain that although for the sake of simplicity he has written as
if this experiment could be carried out by a single individual, his
view is that the truth or falsehood of propositions of this kind
can only be finally settled by the experience of the entire human
race. The reason which he gives for this is that the scope of the
question is too large to be capable of being decided within the
lifetime of a single individual: a better reason for referring to
the balance of total human experience would have been that the

[1] *The Will to Believe*, p. 105.

question is one over which the verdicts of different individuals might not coincide.

This position is developed along more general lines in another early essay called 'Reflex Action and Theism'. He there maintains that if a 'view of the Universe' fails to win general acceptance, it is because it has one of three defects. 'Either it has dropped out of its net some of our impressions of sense, – what we call the facts of nature, – or it has left the theoretic and defining department with a lot of inconsistencies and unmediated transitions on its hands; or else, finally, it has left some one or more of our fundamental active and emotional powers with no object outside of themselves to react on or to live for.'[1] As I understand it, the implication here is not only that any adequate system of beliefs must satisfy our moral requirements, as well as agreeing with the facts of sensory experience and maintaining logically correct relations between its constituent ideas, but that these three different needs are met by different kinds of propositions, which are severally defined by the functions which they perform. Thus, for James, it is an essential characteristic of religious and moral theories that their role is to satisfy our emotional and practical demands.

B. THE NATURE OF TRUTH

I am all the more confident of this interpretation, as it seems to me to supply the key to the understanding of James's pragmatic theory of truth. He gives various formulations of the theory, which are by no means obviously equivalent; to an unsympathetic critic it might even seem that some of them were mutually inconsistent. Thus, in his lectures on Pragmatism, he asserts successively that 'ideas (which themselves are but parts of our experience) become true just in so far as they help us to get into satisfactory relations with other parts of our experience';[2] that 'a new opinion counts as "true" just in proportion as it gratifies

[1] Ibid., p. 125.   [2] *Pragmatism*, p. 58.

the individual's desire to assimilate the novel in his experience to his beliefs in stock';[1] that 'if theological theories prove to have value for concrete life, they will be true, for pragmatism, in the sense of being good for so much'; and that 'for how much more they are true, will depend entirely on their relations to the other truths that also have to be acknowledged';[2] that 'the true is the name of whatever proves itself to be good in the way of belief, and good, too, for definite, assignable reasons';[3] that 'true ideas are those that we can assimilate, validate, corroborate and verify; false ideas those that we cannot';[4] that 'truth *happens* to an idea', that 'its verity *is* in fact an event, a process; the process namely of its verifying itself, its veri-*fication*; its validity is the process of its valid-*ation*';[5] that we have 'a general stock of *extra* truths, of ideas that shall be true of merely possible situations' and that 'whenever such an extra truth becomes practically relevant to one of our emergencies . . . you can say of it then either that "it is useful because it is true" or that "it is true because it is useful" '; that 'both these phrases mean exactly the same thing, namely that here is an idea that gets fulfilled and can be verified';[6] that ' "the true", to put it very briefly, is only the expedient in the way of our thinking, just as "the right" is only the expedient in the way of our behaving; expedient in almost any fashion and on the whole of course; for what meets expediently all the experiences in sight won't necessarily meet all further experiences equally satisfactorily';[7] and finally that 'the "absolutely" true, meaning what no further experience will ever alter, is that ideal vanishing point towards which we imagine that all our temporary truths will some day converge'.[8]

I have already remarked that not all these statements are easy to reconcile with one another; in several cases they are also hard to reconcile with our ordinary conception of truth. Thus, while no one would dispute that a proposition is discovered to be true by being verified, this is very different from saying that the process of verification makes it true. If it is to be held that the truth of an 'idea' consists in the process of its verification, then

[1] Ibid., p. 63.   [2] Ibid., p. 73.   [3] Ibid., p. 76.   [4] Ibid., p. 201.
[5] Ibid.   [6] Ibid., p. 204.   [7] Ibid., p. 222.   [8] Ibid., pp. 222-3.

it seems inconsistent to allow that some ideas are true of merely possible situations, since *ex hypothesi* these ideas have not been actually verified. If the truth of an idea in any way depends on its referring to an actual or even to a possible situation, it again seems inconsistent to say that a belief is true if and only if it is expedient; for it appears undeniable that a belief might conduce to the advantage of the person who held it even though the situation to which it referred neither was nor could be realized. In general, it is this apparent equation of truth with utility that has been both the most popular and the easiest target for James's critics. While admitting that it is no doubt more profitable, as a general rule, to hold true beliefs than false ones, they have had no difficulty in finding examples both of true beliefs the possession of which is either useless or positively harmful to the person who holds them and of useful beliefs which by any normal standard are not true.[1]

These objections are so obvious that it is hard to understand how James could have remained unmoved by them if he really held the views against which they were directed. He did, indeed, protest that his identification of truth with expediency was never intended to imply that a belief could be true, even though it disaccorded with fact: but what in that case it was intended to imply he did not make clear. Otherwise his rejoinders to his critics mainly took the form of a *tu quoque*. Even if his theory of truth did encounter certain difficulties, what better theory had they to offer in its place?

Here I think that he did himself an injustice. His pragmatic standpoint may be open to criticism, but given this standpoint, and taking into account also his underlying assumptions about the different parts that different types of propositions play in our total system of beliefs, I shall try to show that his statements can reasonably be interpreted in such a way as to yield a consistent and even tenable theory.

The first point to make clear is that James is no more interested than Peirce in arriving at a formal definition of truth. He is

[1] Cf. G. E. Moore, 'Professor James's "Pragmatism"', *Proc. Arist. Soc.* 1907-8, reprinted in his *Philosophical Studies* (1922).

perfectly willing to admit that truth consists in the agreement of an idea, or a belief, or a proposition, with reality. His objection to the definition is not that it is incorrect but that it is uninformative. We must go on to ask what 'agreement with reality' amounts to in concrete terms, what, to use a favourite expression of James's, is its 'cash-value'. How are we to decide, in particular instances, whether a proposition agrees with reality or not? In short James follows Peirce in conducting his enquiry into the nature of truth from the standpoint of the individual thinker who is actually concerned with forming his beliefs. For someone in this position the cash-value of the question 'What is truth?' is 'How can I decide what propositions to accept?'

James's general answer to this question is that a proposition is to be accepted if and only if it works. Here again, as with Peirce, the theory of truth is linked with a theory of meaning. That a proposition is to be accepted or, as James would have preferred to put it, that a belief is to be adhered to, if and only if it works is the consequence of a method of interpreting concepts to which James gives the name of the Pragmatic Rule. 'The pragmatic rule', he explains, 'is that the meaning of a concept may always be found, if not in some sensible particular which it directly designates, then in some particular difference in the course of human experience which its being true will make. Test every concept by the question "What sensible difference to anybody will its truth make?" and you are in the best possible position for understanding what it means and for discussing its importance. If, questioning whether a certain concept be true or false, you can think of absolutely nothing that would practically differ in the two cases, you may assume that the alternative is meaningless and that your concept is no distinct idea. If two concepts lead you to infer the same particular consequence, then you may assume that they embody the same meaning under different names.'[1]

In the second of his lectures on *Pragmatism*, which is entitled 'What Pragmatism Means', James illustrates the workings of this rule by the celebrated anecdote of the man, the squirrel and the tree-trunk. He relates that a number of his friends had fallen into

[1] *Some Problems of Philosophy* (1911), p. 60.

what he calls a metaphysical dispute. They had imagined a tree-trunk with a squirrel clinging to one side of it and a man standing on the opposite side. The man tries to get sight of the squirrel by moving round the tree, but fails because the squirrel also moves so as always to keep the tree-trunk between itself and the man. The question in dispute was whether the man went round the squirrel or not. The ground for saying that he did was that the squirrel was on the tree and the man went round the tree. The ground for saying that he did not was that he never passed the squirrel. When asked to adjudicate, James said that the answer depended on 'what you *practically* mean by "going round" the squirrel. If you mean passing from the north of him to the east, then to the south, then to the west, and then to the north of him again, obviously the man does go round him, for he occupies these successive positions. But if on the contrary you mean being first in front of him, then on the right of him, then behind him, then on his left, and finally in front again, it is quite as obvious that the man fails to go round him, for by the compensating movements the squirrel makes, he keeps his belly turned towards the man all the time, and his back turned away. Make the distinction, and there is no occasion for any further dispute. You are both right and wrong according as you conceive the verb "to go round" in one practical fashion or the other.'[1]

It can hardly be denied, I think, that James gives the right answer to this conundrum. What is more questionable is his taking it as a model for metaphysical disputes. Admittedly such disputes do arise, in many instances, because the different criteria for the application of some concepts yield conflicting results, but I doubt if they ever turn on quite such simple ambiguities as James's story would suggest. He refers to the questions 'Is the world one or many? – fated or free? – material or spiritual?'[2] as instances of unending metaphysical disputes which his pragmatic method could be used to settle; but we shall find that his own treatment of these problems shows that he sees much more in them than a straightforward confusion about the meaning of certain words. Other examples which he gives of the application

[1] *Pragmatism*, p. 44. [2] Ibid., p. 45.

of the pragmatic rule show it as reducing what are often taken to be rather abstruse concepts to very simple terms. For example, 'Substance' is said to mean that 'a definite group of sensations will recur'; 'Infinite' either that 'you are always confronted with a remainder' or that 'you can count as many units in a part as you can in the whole'; 'Necessity' that 'your way is blocked in all directions save one'; 'Cause' that 'you may expect certain sequences'.[1] As so often with James, the simplifications tend to go too far, but the fact that he is given to cashing concepts for less than their full value does not in itself invalidate the method. How far this operationalist line can legitimately be taken is a question which I have already done my best to answer when discussing Peirce's rather more sophisticated version of it.

Though James speaks of the pragmatic method as being 'primarily a method of settling metaphysical disputes that otherwise might be interminable',[2] he in fact makes a much wider use of it. The equation of true beliefs with those that work is intended to apply to beliefs of every kind. What he should have made much clearer than he does is that true beliefs are not treated by him as being all of a pattern. They all work, but they work in different ways. The criteria by which we have to assess a belief which relates to a matter of empirical fact are different from those which apply to a belief which is concerned only with relations between ideas: and these are different again from the criteria which apply to beliefs whose function is to satisfy our moral and emotional requirements. These distinctions are implicit in James's writing, but he does not draw attention to them. In my view, it is his failure to set them out explicitly that has been mainly responsible for the extent to which his position has been misunderstood. In particular, the notion that a belief is to be accounted true if it gives one satisfaction to hold it is applied by him only to beliefs of the third class, and to them only with reservations. It has, however, been almost universally assumed by James's critics that he puts this forward unconditionally as a general criterion of truth.

---

[1] *Some Problems of Philosophy*, p. 62.
[2] *Pragmatism*, p. 45.

1. Truth in Relation to Matters of Fact

To see that this is not so, we have only to consider how he actually deals with the other types of proposition which enter into our total system of beliefs. Most of these propositions relate to empirical matters of fact, and in their case there is no question, for James, of our being entitled to accept anything that suits our purpose. In this domain, the only purpose that counts is that of arriving at beliefs which are in accordance with the facts: and what this means, apart from their having to be mutually consistent, which is indeed required of all our beliefs, is that they must be corroborated by our sense-experiences. How James supposes this to work in detail is a question which we must defer until we come to examine his radical empiricism. The gist of it is that he takes the cash-value of all factual propositions to consist in the sense-experiences which they either record or predict, the predictions being in many cases only conditional. He holds, as Peirce does, that our sense-experiences force certain beliefs upon us, though he takes a rather different view of what these beliefs are. In so far as the beliefs which arise in this way fulfil or disappoint our previous expectations, they sustain or discredit the beliefs which these expectations 'cash'. A new stock of beliefs is thus created, giving rise to further expectations which are fulfilled or disappointed in their turn. These expectations relate not only to what we are able to observe but also to what we are able to do. 'To agree, in the widest sense, with a reality can only mean to be guided either straight up to it or into its surroundings, or to be put into such working touch with it as to handle either it or something connected with it better than if we disagreed.'[1] The second clause is introduced in deference to the view, which James shares with Peirce, that beliefs are to be analysed, at least in part, in terms of propensities to action.

It is his wish to emphasize the dynamic character of this process that leads James to speak of ideas as becoming true only when they are verified. This statement is not, however, to be taken

[1] *Pragmatism*, pp. 212–13.

very strictly. In the first place, the verification need not be direct. As he himself says, in the course of the same lecture, 'the overwhelming majority of our true ideas admit of no direct or face-to-face verification'.[1] Our ideas of past history are an example since 'the stream of time can be remounted only verbally, or verified indirectly by the present prolongations or effects of what the past harboured. Yet if they agree with these verbalities and effects, we can know that our ideas of the past are true.'[2] And not only may the processes of verification be indirect, they may also be only potential. Even in the case of beliefs which can be directly tested, it would be excessively laborious and unprofitable for us never to regard any of them as acceptable until we had actually tested them. On many occasions we are rightly content with circumstantial evidence; we assume, without bothering to check, that what we have found to be true of a number of objects of a certain kind will hold for further instances. In a characteristically happy image, James speaks of truth as living on a credit system. 'Our thoughts and beliefs "pass", so long as nothing challenges them, just as bank-notes pass so long as nobody refuses them. But this all points to direct face-to-face verification somewhere, without which the fabric of truth collapses like a financial system with no cash-basis whatsoever. You accept my verification of one thing. I yours of another. We trade on each other's truth. But beliefs verified concretely by *somebody* are the posts of the whole superstructure.'[3]

I do not see how any serious exception can be taken to this as an account of the way in which our factual beliefs are validated. It may indeed be said, here again, that the account is oversimplified. The verdict of experience is not always straightforward. Something needs to be said about the interplay of theory and observation. As we have seen with Peirce, the purely 'instrumentalist' view of scientific theories, to which James also is committed, meets with considerable difficulties when an attempt is made to work it out in detail. But none of this throws any doubt upon his general principle that our factual beliefs are

[1] Ibid., p. 214.   [2] Ibid.   [3] Ibid., pp. 207–8.

constantly subject to the control of the concrete evidence which sensory experience alone supplies.

What will not be so easily conceded is that any such account of the process of empirical verification can serve as an account of truth. Even those who insist that all genuine factual propositions must be empirically testable will be unlikely to regard the truth of such a proposition as being dependent on its actually passing the relevant tests, or even on our having reason to think that it would pass them. When we verify a proposition we discover it to be true, but we do not confer truth upon it. Its truth or falsehood belongs to it quite independently of our knowledge, because of its relation to the objective facts.

James goes a certain way to meet this objection. He takes the example of the constellation of the 'Great Bear' and admits that it would ordinarily be said that the stars which make up this constellation were seven in number before they were counted, and that their clear resemblance to an animal was always truly there, whether anyone had ever noted the fact or not. But then he goes on to ask what is meant by 'this projection into past eternity of recent human ways of thinking'. Are we to say that these stars were 'explicitly seven, explicitly bear-like, before the human witness came'? His answer is: not explicitly, but implicitly. Not explicitly, because there is no subject here for truth or falsehood until the question of the number and appearance of the stars is actually raised. Implicitly, because once the question is raised, 'the stars themselves dictate the result'. The fact can therefore be said to 'pre-exist virtually' in the sense that if ever the question of its existence were to be raised, it would determine the answer.[1]

This concession will not satisfy those who adhere to what I have called the formal concept of truth, but with them James's disagreement is not really a dispute about the analysis of a concept but rather a fundamental difference in the point of view from which the question is approached. As I tried to show in the similar case of Peirce, there is a sense in which both parties are right, the formalists in maintaining that the question whether a proposition is true and the question whether it is accepted are

[1] *The Meaning of Truth*, pp. 92-3.

logically independent, the pragmatists in maintaining that all that actually concerns us is to find out what propositions are true and that the cash-value of this question is the question what propositions are acceptable. To some extent, therefore, James was fighting an unnecessary battle. It would have cost him nothing to concede to the 'intellectualists' their formal concept of truth, so long as they raised no objections to his account of the process by which truth is actually ascribed to our factual beliefs.

2. A priori *Truths*

When it comes to beliefs which are non-factual in the sense that they are concerned, in Hume's terminology, not with matters of fact but with relations of ideas, James's equation of truth with what we are willing to accept is more in accordance with received opinion. For it is now quite widely held that the truth of necessary propositions is wholly dependent upon the conventions which govern the use of the signs by which they are expressed. James's version of this theory is rather simple and he does not attempt to work it in any detail or to consider the objections which might be raised against it. He speaks of our having 'a rather intricate system of necessary and immutable *ideal truths of comparison*, a system applicable to terms *experienced* in any order of sequence or frequency, or even to terms never experienced or to be experienced, such as the mind's imaginary constructions would be'.[1] These truths record our ways of classifying mental objects: our ideas of 'white', 'grey' and 'black' being what they are, it is 'eternally' true that white differs less from grey than it does from black. Since the relations which are expressed by propositions of this sort are 'perceptibly obvious at a glance', no sense verification of them is necessary: neither can they be confuted by experience, for if in any such instance 'you failed to get the truth concretely, you would say that you had classed your real object wrongly'.[2]

[1] *The Principles of Psychology*, II 646.   [2] *Pragmatism*, pp. 209–10.

The same 'origin and essential nature' is ascribed by James to the truths of formal logic, which are based, in his view, on what he calls the principle of mediate predication or subsumption, the *dictum de omni et nullo*, that 'whatever has an attribute has all the attributes of that attribute', or more briefly that 'whatever is of a kind is of that kind's kind'. Since a broader formulation of this principle is that 'the same can be substituted for the same in any mental operation', James is able to conclude that the 'rational proposition' on which all deductive reasoning is founded is only the result of the mind's function of comparison, so that 'both Systematic Classification and Logic are seen to be incidental results of the mere capacity for discerning difference and likeness'.[1] This applies also to mathematics, divided by James into arithmetic, where we compare numbers, and geometry, where we compare extensive magnitudes. Bearing in mind the way in which he thinks that these formal sciences arise out of our experience he characterizes arithmetic as 'mediate equality of different bundles of attention-strokes' and geometry as 'mediate equality of different ways of carving space'.[2] But while he ascribes an empirical origin to them he does not think that these branches of mathematics, any more than the other formal sciences, have 'anything to say about facts, about what is or is not in the world. Logic does not say whether Socrates, men, mortals or immortals *exist*: arithmetic does not tell us where her 7's, 5's and 12's are to be *found*: geometry affirms not that circles and rectangles are *real*. All that these sciences make us sure of is that *if* those things are anywhere to be found, the eternal verities will obtain of them.'[3]

I believe this position to be basically correct, though it may be doubted whether the distinction between relations of ideas and matters of fact, which is anyhow not easy to define, is quite so clear-cut as James supposed. His own view of this distinction owes something to Kant in that he attributes the necessity of *a priori* propositions to the constitution of the mind. 'Our ready-made ideal framework for all sorts of possible objects follows from the very structure of our thinking. We can no more play fast and loose with these abstract relations than we can do so with our

---

[1] *The Principles of Psychology*, II 650–1.   [2] Ibid., p. 663.   [3] Ibid.

sense-experiences. They coerce us: we must treat them consistently, whether or not we like the results.'[1] But the fact which James strangely overlooked is that we are not coerced; we are not determined to think logically, even though we may fall into error if we fail to do so. His argument, therefore, suffers from the same defect as that of the moralists who condemn certain practices on the ground that they are unnatural. If it proved anything, it would be that we could not think otherwise than in accordance with the rules of logic rather than that we *should* not. But while James may be indebted to Kant for his unsatisfactory explanation of the necessity of *a priori* propositions, he does not take the Kantian view that they necessarily apply even to all phenomenal objects outside the mind or that they legislate for all possible experience. 'They are primarily interesting only as subjective facts. They stand waiting in the mind, forming a beautiful ideal network: and the most we can say is that we *hope* to discover outer realities over which the network may be flung so that the ideal and real may coincide.'[2]

There is at least a show of inconsistency here. James seems to imply that we might discern outer realities which did not fit into the ideal network. But if the network emanates from 'the very structure of our mind', it would seem to follow that the only realities which we could apprehend would be those that did fit into it. One answer to this might be that the structure of our minds is not entirely rigid but is capable of being modified by the course of experience; so that if there were a radical alteration in the character of the realities with which we were confronted, the ideal network would be adapted accordingly. James is, indeed, a believer in innate ideas, to the extent of rejecting the view of the classical empiricists that all the connections among ideas in the mind can be 'interpreted as so many combinations of sense-data',[3] but this is not incompatible with the admission that our regulative principles are themselves conditioned by the experiences which they serve to organize. It could then be conceded to Kant that all possible experience must be capable of being brought under some conceptual system; there would still be no necessity

[1] *Pragmatism*, pp. 210–11.　[2] *The Principles of Psychology*, II 665.　[3] Ibid., p. 620.

for it all to be brought under the particular system which we have fashioned to deal with the experiences that we have actually had.

3. Moral and Aesthetic Judgements

The idea that our reason makes demands on the facts which they are not bound to satisfy comes out most prominently in James's treatment of what he takes to be the two remaining classes of propositions deriving from our mental structure: those which express metaphysical axioms, and those which express moral and aesthetic principles. The sense in which these propositions may be classified as *a priori* is just that they are not empirical generalizations. They are not, however, analytic, as the standard types of *a priori* propositions are: they do not express the mere results of comparing our ideas. Neither does James think that they are necessarily true. In his view, metaphysical axioms, when they are not just barren verbiage, have a fertility simply as ideals. He gives as one example the principle that nothing can happen without a cause. 'We have no definite idea of what we mean by cause, or of what causality consists in. But the principle expresses a demand for *some* deeper sort of inward connection between phenomena than their merely habitual time-sequence seems to us to be. The word "cause" is, in short, an altar to an unknown god; an empty pedestal still marking the place of a hoped-for statue. *Any* really inward belonging-together of the sequent terms, if discovered, would be accepted as what the word cause was meant to stand for.'[1] It is not clear what James thinks would count as an instance of such inward connection, or how he thinks that it could be empirically discovered, but since he goes on to say that the molecular systems of physics meet the demand at least to some extent, his idea may be that we speak of causal connection in cases where we are able to account for the fact that certain sorts of phenomena are regularly correlated, in terms of a theory which

[1] *The Principles of Psychology,* II 671.

does not merely fit the facts but also appears to us to render them intelligible. The metaphysical principle of universal causation would then express our faith in the possibility of subsuming all conjunctions of phenomena under theories of this type. Since this implies that there are other grounds for evaluating theories than their simple efficacy, it may seem to run counter to James's pragmatic view that two theories are equivalent if they have the same empirical consequences. It is, however, open to him to admit that even if two theories are factually equivalent there may be economic, aesthetic, or psychological reasons for giving one of them our preference.

In fact, he does explicitly say that in many cases what pass for metaphysical principles are no more than expressions of aesthetic feeling. 'Nature is simple and invariable: makes no leaps, or makes nothing but leaps: is rationally intelligible; neither increases nor diminishes in quantity; flows from one principle, etc., etc.,– what do all such principles express save our sense of how pleasantly our intellect would feel if it had a Nature of that sort to deal with?'[1] In general, our aesthetic and also our moral judgements are said to express 'inner harmonies and discords between objects of thought'. These harmonies are subjective in the sense that they are not just reflections of external facts, and they may strike different people in different ways. There is, for example, a perpetual conflict in morals between those who go more by instinct, with the tendency to treat each concrete case as *sui generis*, and those who go by reason, in the sense that they judge every individual case in accordance with some abstract principle. But whatever the harmonies, in morals as in metaphysics they are only 'postulates of rationality'. There is no necessity for the facts to conform to them.[2]

In *The Principles of Psychology*, from which I have been quoting, James seems to think that the truth or falsehood of moral and aesthetic judgements is in the end an empirical question. The experience of mankind either will bear out these postulates or it will not. He fails, however, to explain how this is to be determined. It is not at all clear how experience could either verify

[1] Ibid., p. 672.   [2] Ibid., pp. 672–5.

or confute such maxims as that 'the fulfilment of my desire is intrinsically no more imperative than that of anyone else's' or 'what it is reasonable that another should do for me, it is also reasonable that I should do for him',[1] or even more specific rules such as that it is good to be charitable or wrong to take other people's property. If one is determined to find a way in which such propositions can be empirically verified, the only course would seem to be to construe them as empirical propositions: one might, for example, follow the Utilitarians in treating them as propositions about what is or is not conducive to the increase of human happiness.

James is not exactly a Utilitarian, in spite of his saying in one of his popular addresses that 'the essence of good is simply to satisfy demand',[2] but the position at which he arrives in his later work is not very different from theirs. The general principle that beliefs are true if and only if they work is held by him to cover moral and aesthetic beliefs; but in this case what constitutes their working is our being satisfied to hold them. It is made clear, however, that this is not simply a matter of our giving our formal assent to certain moral or aesthetic rules: it is a condition of our genuinely accepting the rules that when the occasions arise we are ready to act upon them. The moral rules which will retain our allegiance will be those that abide the consequences of putting them into practice. No doubt the most important of these consequences is the effect upon human happiness, but there may be principles which we value for their own sakes, independently of their relation to happiness: an example would be the principle of justice. In his optimistic way, James overlooks the fact that people have shown themselves to be satisfied with holding moral beliefs which merely indulge their superstitions or prejudices, or have adhered to rules the general enforcement of which conduces to their own prosperity at the expense of others' misery. The satisfaction of any given man's emotional requirements and the fulfilment of those ideals which a civilized philosopher like William James would deem to be moral are not at all bound to coincide.

[1] Ibid., p. 673.					[2] *The Will to Believe*, p. 201.

It might be thought that James had met this difficulty by stipulating that what determines the truth or falsehood of a moral principle is not the experience of a single individual but that of the entire human race.[1] This is in line with his definition of the absolutely true as 'the ideal vanishing point towards which we imagine that all our temporary truths will some day converge'.[2] But this attempt to secure objectivity is even less effective in the case of moral judgements than it is in that of scientific hypotheses. In the scientific case, as we remarked when discussing Peirce's view, the assumption that the progress of enquiry will lead to an universal and undisturbed agreement is rather an ideal postulate than a serious prediction: nevertheless, it is quite plausible to hold that in putting forward a scientific hypothesis one is predicting that it will be found to be in accord not only with our own future experience but with that of any other accredited observer. On the other hand, it can hardly be maintained, neither is it James's view, that when one subscribes to a moral principle one is predicting that in the course of time it will be found to satisfy not only one's own but everybody else's emotional requirements. No doubt when one puts forward a moral principle one is laying down the law for others besides oneself; whether or not it is the distinctive mark of a moral imperative, as some philosophers have claimed, that its content can be universalized, it certainly does not make any distinction of persons; it requires of any one at all that if he be in such and such a kind of situation he should act in such and such a way. But this does not mean that if other people fail to comply with a moral principle which I hold, or even if they refuse to acknowledge its utility, I am bound to conclude that the principle is false. In asserting its truth, I am not predicting their behaviour: I am not even predicting my own. This is, indeed, a point on which James himself is not altogether clear. He does not deny that one is entitled to hold fast to one's moral principles even if they prove unacceptable to other people; but he does not make their validity altogether independent of one's own future attitude, since he holds that in claiming truth for a moral principle I am implying

[1] See above, pp. 195–6.   [2] Quoted above, p. 197.

that I shall not have occasion to reject it. The fact which he has overlooked is that my attitude may change merely owing to some change in my own character; for example, I may suffer an illness which affects my moral disposition. It might seem that this difficulty could be met by saying that what I must be understood to be predicting is only that no facts will come to light which are such that, if I were now aware of them, I should find that the moral principle in question could not be sustained. But the objection to this is that it rules out the possibility, which James wishes to admit, of one's moral judgements being falsified through one's becoming morally more enlightened. Once again the truth is that James's wish to have the best of both worlds, to maintain his pragmatic standpoint without giving up the concept of moral truth, runs into formal difficulties with which he is not sufficiently concerned. He would have been on safer ground if he had been content to say that the only question which concretely arises for any given person, with regard to the validity of moral judgements, is the question which moral principles he is prepared to uphold and act upon, and that the rational way to deal with this question is to adopt the principles with the operation of which our experience has led us to believe that we will be morally satisfied. The only objection that I can see to this is that the conclusion is rather trivial; but at this level of generality it could hardly be otherwise.

C. THE WILL AND ITS FREEDOM

Though he was evidently a man of strong moral feeling, James does not display much interest in the more specific problems of moral philosophy; the only one which he discusses in any detail is that of the freedom of the will. To understand the terms in which he envisages this problem, it is necessary to know something about his general theory of volition. This is intended to be a psychological theory; its aim is to describe exactly what goes on in the mind when one performs a voluntary act. The first point on which

James insists is that we have to learn by experience what movements it is possible to make and that these lessons must be retained if we are ever to succeed in acting. He rather surprisingly
sets it down as certain that 'whether or no there be anything else
in the mind at the moment when we consciously will a certain
act, a mental conception made up of memory images of these
sensations, defining which special act it is, must be there'.[1] Since
he goes on to refer to these memory images as 'kinaesthetic ideas
of what the act is to be', it may be that he means no more than
that we have to be physically 'set' to perform the act in question,
though if this is all that he does mean his way of putting it is
rather strange. I suspect, however, that he is making the assumption that every voluntary movement has to be preceded by a
shadowy rehearsal, and this is surely a mistake. If the action is
voluntary, there is indeed a sense in which one is bound to know
what one is doing, or what one is about to do: but this knowing
what one is about to do surely does not consist in having a
mental preview of the sensations which might be expected to
result. Certainly my own introspection fails to detect the constant
presence of any such anticipatory images. It may be that I have
not looked for them carefully enough, but I am more inclined
to think that this is one of the rare cases in which James's assessment of the empirical evidence has been vitiated by a mistaken
theory.

However this may be, his theory does not draw him into the
further mistake of supposing that a mental impulse is required
to mediate between the idea of the action to be performed and
the actual performance of it. He goes into this question thoroughly
and concludes, on both theoretical and empirical grounds, that
the 'feelings of innervation' which contemporary psychologists
had cast for this role just do not exist. People suppose that there
has to be some kind of 'will-force' to translate intention into
action because they think of the cases in which an action is con-
templated but is not carried out. But the explanation of these
cases, in James's view, is just that 'they are cases of inhibition by
antagonistic thoughts'. In the normal cases, where there is no

[1] *The Principles of Psychology*, II 492.

such inhibition, 'there is actually no hiatus between the thought-process and the motor discharge. Movement is the natural immediate effect of feeling, irrespective of what the quality of the feeling may be. It is so in reflex action, it is so in emotional expression, it is so in the voluntary life.'[1]

James's belief that 'it is the essence of all consciousness to instigate movement of some sort'[2] makes it easy for him to reject the utilitarian view that pleasure and pain are the only spurs to action. He admits that feelings of pleasure and pain have what he calls an impulsive quality, but argues most convincingly that the idea that they are the only feelings that impel us, and still more the idea that all our purposive actions are undertaken with a view to obtaining future pleasure or avoiding future pain, are simply not in accordance with the facts. Not only do we often, out of weakness or inertia, do things that we know that we shall not enjoy; not only do some people have pathological impulses towards self-torture or self-destruction; but 'all the daily routine of life, our dressing and undressing, the coming and going from our work or carrying through of its various operations, is utterly without mental reference to pleasure and pain, except under rarely realized conditions'.[3] The reason why people accept the utilitarian view is not because they find that it agrees with their experience but because they are deceived by the argument that if an action is voluntary the thought of it must be pleasant to the agent, or else he would not do it. But if this is understood to mean that the thought of what one is going to do is attended by a conscious feeling of pleasure, or by a feeling of lesser pain than that of any alternative action, it is not true in all cases: and even if it were true it would not prove what is required. As other philosophers besides James have pointed out, from the fact that the anticipation, or the initiation, or the performance of an action is pleasant it in no case follows that the action itself consists in the pursuit of pleasure. The argument rests upon a simple confusion between an idea of pleasure and a pleasant idea.

Let it be granted then that our purposes are various. This makes no difference to James's main contention that, in default

---

[1] Ibid., pp. 526–7.   [2] Ibid., p. 551.   [3] Ibid., p. 553.

of inhibition, action always results from the thought of something to be effected, though this thought may not amount to more than the kinaesthetic idea of a future sensation, and that where there is inhibition it is always by another thought. The victory goes to the thought which has, in James's terms, the greatest 'interest' for us at that moment: an explanation which I find hard to distinguish from the tautology that the victory goes to the thought which prevails.

But surely we are not just passive spectators of the contest between our thoughts, like slaves put up for auction. Surely there is some way in which we influence the result, other than by just having the thoughts in question. Does not experience show that it often requires great effort on our part to embark on or adhere to a particular course of action? James does not deny the existence of these efforts but he holds that, in so far as they consist in anything more than our having muscular sensations, they are efforts of attention. 'The essential achievement of the will', he says, 'when it is most "voluntary" is to ATTEND to a difficult object and hold it fast before the mind. The so-doing *is* the *fiat*; and it is a mere physiological incident that when the object is thus attended to, immediate motor consequences should ensue.'[1]

It is because he believes that the power of a thought to move us to action is psychologically only a function of the attention which we pay to it that James comes to speak of the will as a relation between the mind and its ideas. This conclusion sounds paradoxical and lends itself easily to misinterpretation. James is not suggesting that ideas are the only product of our wills: on the contrary, he appears to take the view that our thoughts and feelings are supplied to us by external stimuli and that the only role which the will can play is to pay more or less attention to them. He does hold that the will operates only on ideas, but this is to be seen as a consequence of his denial that there is any psychological force, independent of our thoughts and feelings, which moves us to action. It being taken for granted that there is a psychological process of willing and that it has something to do with causing us to act, and there being no room for it between

[1] Ibid., p. 561.

the thought-process and the motor discharge, there would appear to be no other possibility but to conclude that it operates on the thought-process. It may be said that James ought to have taken the more radical view that 'willing' is not the name of any psychological process at all, but it seems hard to deny that there is some psychological difference between the performance of a purely reflex or purely habitual action and the performance of an action which requires a conscious effort. If we take James to be saying that the difference consists only in the fact that in the second case we concentrate on the end which we are pursuing, or dwell on the alternatives between which we are hesitating, in a way that we do not when the action is reflex or habitual, I think that his conclusion loses its air of paradox and indeed becomes acceptable. The main objection that I can see to this theory is the one that I have already made: that in the case of the large class of voluntary actions which are performed as a matter of routine he exaggerates the extent to which we are explicitly conscious of their intended results.

What place does this account leave for the freedom of the will? It would seem, very little. Our thoughts just come to us. The emotions which may move us to act are physiologically determined. Indeed, James goes further: he adopts the theory, which he attributes also to a Danish psychologist, Professor Lange, that an emotion is nothing more than the feeling of the bodily changes that follow the perception of the fact which excites it. As he whimsically puts it: 'the more rational statement is that we feel sorry because we cry, angry because we strike, afraid because we tremble, and not that we cry, strike or tremble because we are sorry, angry or fearful, as the case may be'.[1] Once more, this is gratuitously paradoxical. It is possible, and indeed quite plausible, to hold that our emotions are causally dependent upon our bodily states, without holding that the bodily states on which they are dependent are those in which they are ordinarily thought to be expressed. A more natural view would be to take the state of our nervous system as being causally responsible both for our feelings and for their physical expressions. It seems to me more doubtful,

[1] Ibid., p. 450.

if only on introspective grounds, whether an emotion just *is* the feeling of a bodily state. James challenges his critics to say what else it could be and asks rhetorically what fear would be without the feeling of quickened heart-beats or visceral stirrings, what rage would be without dilation of the nostrils or clenching of the teeth, what grief would be without its tears, its suffocation of the heart, its pang in the breastbone. He concludes that 'a purely disembodied human emotion is a nonentity'.[1] But even if it is true, as I think it is, that having an emotion of this sort entails having these physical symptoms, it does not follow that they are all that it entails. The point is arguable, though, if introspection is not to be trusted here, I do not know how it is to be decided. What matters in the present context is that even if there is a mental residue to our emotions, there is no reason to think that it is not physiologically determined.

The room, then, which James can find for the exercise of free-will is certainly not extensive. Does it exist at all? He thinks that it may exist, in the degree of attention that we pay to our ideas. It is often true that we should have acted differently if we had exerted a different amount of effort or exerted it in a different direction. The question is whether this is ever possible; whether, as James puts it, we can make more or less of the objects which are presented to us, as we choose, or whether 'whatever object at any time fills our consciousness was from eternity bound to fill it then and there and compel from us the exact effort, neither more nor less, which we bestow upon it'.[2]

For James this is a question of fact, but one which we have no means of resolving. That we often have the feeling that different alternatives are open to us proves nothing, for we have this feeling also in cases of effortless volition, where James thinks that it is merely a delusion. He regards it as certain that a man's effortless volitions are all 'resultants of interests and associations whose strength and sequence are mechanically determined by the structure of that physical mass, his brain' and admits that 'the general continuity of things and the monistic conception of the world may lead one irresistibly to postulate that a little fact like

[1] Ibid., p. 452.   [2] Ibid., p. 571.

effort can form no real exception to the overwhelming reign of deterministic law'.[1] Nevertheless, he insists that it cannot be proved not to be an exception. To show that the amount of effort that was made on a given occasion was the only amount that could possibly have been made in the existing circumstances, one would have to have exact knowledge of the relevant psycho-physical laws as well as the means of measuring the psychic and neural quantities involved. But these conditions are not in fact fulfilled, nor likely to be. James asserts, perhaps rather rashly, that the measurement and reasonings which this method of proof implies 'will surely be forever beyond human reach'.[2]

Assuming then that the question of fact is practically undecid-able, James is able to indulge the will to believe. Since we have no intellectual ground for concluding either that the will is free or that it is not, and since the question is too important, in his view, for us to be able to suspend judgement, we are required to make an emotional choice. As might be expected, James opts for the alternative of freedom, mainly, he says on ethical grounds. To the scientific postulate 'that prediction of all things must be ideally, even if not actually, possible' he prefers the moral postulate that 'what ought to be can be, and that bad acts cannot be fatal, but that good ones must be possible in their stead'.[3] In James's case, however, as in that of Peirce, the value to ethics of his espousal of free-will is very much diminished by his holding, in my opinion rightly, that to the extent that an event is not entirely governed by law, it must occur by chance. He is careful to point out that this does not mean that, in the sphere of human conduct, a man's actions may be entirely unrelated to his motives or his character: free-will operates only on 'the possibles which really tempt a man'; but among these possibilities it may be a matter of chance that he wills to realize one rather than the other. As I have already remarked,[4] this is hardly a vindication of human responsibility: and though there may be some comfort in the thought that bad acts are not fatal, it must be remembered that this works both ways. Chance might have substituted good acts for bad ones, but it might also have substituted bad acts for good.

[1] Ibid., p. 572.   [2] Ibid.   [3] Ibid., p. 573.   [4] See above, pp. 110–11.

Thus the ethical advantage of maintaining a belief in free-will, as James conceives it, is not very great; and in fact I doubt whether his motives for rejecting determinism are mainly ethical. What chiefly moved him, I think, was an emotional dislike for the idea of a universe in which everything was previsible. It had too much resemblance, for his liking, to the 'block-universe' of the Hegelians: indeed, in an early paper on 'The Dilemma of Determinism' he explicitly associates indeterminism with pluralism.[1] Unlike Peirce, however, he makes no attempt to justify his belief in chance by any theoretical argument. He assumes, rather, that if it cannot be proved to operate in the domain of human action, there is no hope of proving that it operates elsewhere. The important question for him is whether its operation can be disproved: to the extent that it cannot be, the scientist's belief in determinism is also an article of faith. It is a faith to which James, as an empirical psychologist, is quite strongly attracted; but his emotional repugnance to it is stronger still.

D. THE PLACE OF RELIGIOUS BELIEF

James's will to believe in the actuality of chance affects the character of his religious beliefs. His main reason for holding them is that the existence of a God would give us ground for optimism: he speaks of 'the craving of our nature for an ultimate peace behind all tempests, for a blue zenith above all clouds'.[2] But if chance is to be operative in the world, then not only must there be a limit to the deity's power, since *ex hypothesi* the events which occur by chance are not under his control, but there must also, in James's view, be a limit to his knowledge. I do not think that this conclusion is strictly necessary, since I can see no formal contradiction in supposing uncaused events to be foreseen, but James includes in his notion of a chance event the requirement that it be what he calls 'ambiguous in its content' and thinks that this requirement would be violated if it were known that the event

---

[1] *The Will to Believe*, pp. 145–83.   [2] Ibid., p. 180.

was going to occur. For the same reason James concludes that the deity must be 'subject to the laws of time': since if he were outside time and so in a position to survey the temporal series as a whole, the occurrence of a chance event would not be uncertain for him.

With a God who is subject to such limitations, the victory of the power that makes for righteousness cannot be guaranteed, but James conceives of him as being strong enough to make his will prevail on the whole, even though he is not in command of every detail. He compares him to an expert chess-player who can be relied upon to win the game against a novice, although he neither dictates nor can foresee every one of his opponent's moves. Again, the analogy is felicitous, but it does lead one to ask what game James believes his deity to be playing. What powers is he supposed to have and in what way is he supposed to exercise them?

The answer to these questions is all the less clear in that James is scornful of the attempts of 'systematic theology' to define the attributes of God. In dealing, he says, with such a word as 'God', if you stop with the definition, 'thinking that to be an intellectual finality, where are you? Stupidly staring at a pretentious sham! "God is Being, underived, outside and above every genus, necessary, one, infinitely perfect, simple, immutable, immeasurable, eternal, intelligent" etc. – wherein is such a definition really instructive? It means less than nothing, in its pompous robe of adjectives. Pragmatism alone can read a positive meaning into it, and for that she turns her back upon the intellectualist point of view altogether. "God's in his heaven, all's right with the world!" *That*'s the real heart of your theology, and for that you need no rationalist definitions.'[1]

It is not surprising that James can find no meaning in the definition which he quotes, but the difficulty which he appears to overlook is that his rejection of what he calls the intellectualist point of view leaves his concept of the deity quite undetermined. The nearest that he comes to determining it is in the concluding

---

[1] *Pragmatism*, pp. 121–2. I have translated the list of God's attributes from the Latin in which James gives it.

chapter of *The Varieties of Religious Experience*, where he speaks rather vaguely of something 'more' which is 'conterminous and continuous' with the higher part of one's consciousness. This 'wider self' is said to be a source of 'saving experience'; it is operative in the universe outside oneself and one is able to keep in 'working touch' with it. The evidence for the existence of this 'transmarginal consciousness' is to be found in people's religious, and especially their mystical, experiences. These experiences do not, however, reveal whether this consciousness is anything more than a projection of our own unconscious states; whether it is even a single entity; what power, if any, it has to affect the course of nature; or by what means and in what manner this power is exercised. Having chosen to call 'the higher part of the universe' by the name of God, James wishes to vindicate 'the instinctive belief of mankind: God is real since he produces real effects'.[1] But the only real effects that he can discern are the feelings of greater energy, security and satisfaction which are obtained by those who believe that they are in contact with God or at least that they are fulfilling his demands.

It is clear that this argument does not take us very far. It is not to be denied that people have religious experiences, that they attach value to them and that very often as the result of their having them their lives are enriched in other ways. What is in dispute is the interpretation of these experiences: whether they have any cognitive import; whether they provide a basis for any legitimate inferences about the origin or nature of the universe. But to these questions James hardly attempts to offer any serious answer. He admits to the 'over-belief' that the world is susceptible of a religious interpretation, and maintains that this is not just a matter of one's choosing to see it in a rosier light: 'the world interpreted religiously is not the materialistic world over again, with an altered expression: it must have, over and above the altered expression, a *natural constitution* different at some point from that which a materialistic world would have'.[2] But apart from his hints about a transmarginal consciousness he does not say what this different constitution of the world would be or

---

[1] *The Varieties of Religious Experience* (1902), p. 517.   [2] Ibid., p. 518.

how its existence would be verified. It is almost as if he thought that the religious composition of the world simply consisted in the fact that people have religious experiences and in the practical effects on their conduct which these experiences produce. Certainly the only ground that he gives for taking 'the hypothesis of God' to be true is that experience has shown that it works satisfactorily:[1] and what he appears to mean by its working satisfactorily is that, by and large, the people who believe in God lead more satisfactory lives. From the pragmatic point of view, the idea that God's in his heaven is not a justification of the claim that all is right with the world but only a more picturesque expression of it.

The result is that James is able to claim truth for the religious hypothesis at the cost of stripping it of its intellectual content. It falls into the category of those propositions with regard to which we are allowed to indulge our will to believe, just because no question of fact arises, or at any rate none that can be rationally decided. It might be objected that if the religious hypothesis is construed pragmatically, it is no more undecidable than any other general hypothesis about human behaviour: there are surely ways of ascertaining whether the belief in God enhances people's lives: it is to be supposed that we can lay down criteria for the statement that all is right with the world, and that it is a plain matter of fact whether these criteria are satisfied. I agree that this is a possible interpretation of James's view, and that if this interpretation were adopted, his religious hypothesis would be empirically testable. But hypotheses which are empirically testable can be falsified, and I doubt if James really regarded his religious hypothesis as being open to falsification by experience. I think that if he had so regarded it he would not have been quite so confident of its truth. After all he had no very strong assurance that human aspirations would in the long run be fulfilled. As I understand him, he treated his religious hypothesis more as the expression of a hope than a prediction: he assumed that however badly things appeared to be going, whatever misery men were suffering and however little their moral demands were met,

[1] *Pragmatism*, p. 299.

they could still cling to the hope that all would be well in the end. This is, indeed, an empirical assumption: it is at least conceivable that things should come to such a pass that even any hope of future well-being would be taken from us. To the extent that they ignore this possibility James's religious beliefs do rest upon an empirical basis. But the maintenance of the empirical basis is a precondition rather than a criterion of their truth. The main point for James is that so long as people are psychologically able to have religious faith, and so long as it gives them emotional satisfaction, the beliefs which are its embodiment may be allowed to pass for true.

Since the common criticism of James's theory of truth is that it allows a proposition to be made true merely by our willing, or finding it useful, to believe it, independently of its accordance with the facts, it is worth repeating that his equation of what is true with what one finds it satisfying to believe applies only to questions of faith or morals, with regard to which there are no ascertainable facts. It may be objected that for him to employ the word 'truth' at all in this sense was very misleading, if not linguistically incorrect; but here we must remember that the question whether any given belief is true is always construed by James pragmatically as the question whether it is to be accepted; and religious and moral beliefs present themselves for acceptance or rejection like the rest. It is just that in their case the criteria by which James wishes to determine whether they are acceptable come down to being purely subjective. Where James may be fairly criticized, I think, is in the extent to which he glosses over the negative consequences of his approach. He hardly makes it clear that he strips his religious hypothesis of all pretension to give any sort of explanation of the world; it is a licence for optimism which is in fact devoid of anything that would ordinarily be counted as religious support.

When it comes to matters of fact, James's theory of truth agrees with that of Peirce. Where they differ is in their interpretation of the empirical propositions to which the theory is applied. The extent of this difference will become clear when we have examined James's doctrine of radical empiricism.

CHAPTER THREE

RADICAL EMPIRICISM

A. THE DATA OF EXPERIENCE

1. Sensation and Perception

IN the preface which James wrote in 1909 for his collection of essays entitled *The Meaning of Truth*, he explains that the reason why he attaches importance to the pragmatic theory of truth is that it lends strong support to the doctrine of radical empiricism; and it is in this doctrine that his interest lies. 'Radical empiricism', he continues, 'consists first of a postulate, next of a statement of fact, and finally of a generalized conclusion.

'The postulate is that the only things that shall be debatable among philosophers shall be things definable in terms drawn from experience. (Things of an unexperienceable nature may exist *ad libitum*, but they form no part of the material for philosophic debate.)

'The statement of fact is that the relations between things, conjunctive as well as disjunctive, are just as much matters of direct particular experience, neither more so nor less so, than the things themselves.

'The generalized conclusion is that therefore the parts of experience hold together from next to next by relations that are themselves parts of experience. The directly apprehended universe needs, in short, no extraneous trans-empirical connective support, but possesses in its own right a concatenated or continuous structure.'[1]

As we have seen, the reason why the pragmatic theory of truth is held to support this doctrine is to be found in James's conception of the way in which our ideas about matters of fact

---

[1] *The Meaning of Truth*, pp. xii–xiii.

'work'. Their function is to lead us from one item of experience to another by a route which is itself a feature of experience, and if they can fulfil this function they are true. Whether they 'correspond' to objects which lie outside our experience is nothing to the purpose. James admits, half ironically, that such objects may exist, but when he says that they are not part of the material for philosophical debate, the implication is that we cannot possibly know anything about them. To try to take account of them would, on pragmatic principles, be not only futile but nonsensical.

What makes this a radical form of empiricism is not the exclusion of anything which is not accessible to our experience but rather the refusal to differentiate between the objects of experience and its parts. It is common ground among empiricists that the only things of which we can have any knowledge are within the grasp of our experience, in the sense that some possible observation would count as perceptual evidence of their existence. Not all empiricists, however, would go so far as to require that every such object be definable in terms which are drawn from our experience, in the narrow sense which James here intends. Many of them would wish to distinguish between the sensations and feelings of which our experience is formed, and the external objects of which it makes us aware. They would allow that we could not have any knowledge of physical objects unless they stood in some discoverable relation to the contents of our experience, but they would not take this to imply that they must be definable in terms of these contents. On the other hand, James not only limits the universe of which we can significantly take account to that which we directly apprehend, but also assumes that anything that we directly apprehend is a part of our experience. This does not prevent him, as we shall see, from admitting the distinction between merely subjective impressions and objectively existing things, or between our states of apprehension and the things which we apprehend, but it does commit him to an attempt to analyse these distinctions in terms of the ways in which different parts of our experience are related to each other. Our experience has to be rich enough to furnish the entire world.

Mind and matter, space and time, appearance and reality, all have to be constituted out of it.

In what, then, does our experience consist? 'The baby', as James puts it in a well-known and characteristic phrase, 'assailed by eyes, ears, nose, skin and entrails at once, feels it all as one great blooming, buzzing confusion.'[1] This confusion is overcome by the exercise of the child's innate powers of association and discrimination. What makes it possible for him to overcome it is the fact that qualitatively different total impressions contain elements which are qualitatively similar. In other words, he detects recurrent features in the flux which is presented to him, and finds that some of them habitually go together. These features are likely to be more complex than the 'simple ideas' or 'sensible qualities' which Locke and Berkeley took as their primitive data, but they play the same role. They furnish the sensory contents on which our perceptual judgements are based.

In James's view, the distinction between sensation and perception is not sharp. The difference between them is a difference of function, rather than a difference of object or content. Perception always entails sensation, and at least in adult life sensation is never unaccompanied by perception. A pure sensation, he says, is an abstraction but 'the nearer the object cognized comes to being a simple quality like "hot", "cold", "red", "noise", "pain", apprehended irrelatively to other things, the more the state of mind approaches pure sensation. The fuller of relatives the object is, on the contrary; the more it is something classed, located, measured, compared, assigned to a function etc. etc.; the more unreservedly do we call the state of mind a perception, and the relatively smaller is the part in it which sensation plays.'[2]

The theory is, then, that our sensations develop into perceptions as a result of our identifying their objects in such a way as to fit them into a larger framework. In characterizing what we perceive we draw on a more elaborate set of concepts than are needed to characterize what we merely sense. As James puts it, sensation yields 'mere *acquaintance* with a fact', whereas perception gives us 'knowledge *about* a fact; and this knowledge admits of

[1] *The Principles of Psychology*, I 488.   [2] Ibid., II 1.

numberless degrees of complication'. But the shift from sensation to perception makes no difference to the status of the fact itself. In both cases 'we perceive the fact as an *immediately present outward reality*'.[1]

This does not mean that no place can be found in the domain of 'outer perception' for the distinction between publicly perceptible objects and merely private sensations: there are criteria by which we can distinguish between veridical perception and illusion or hallucination, or between the events of a dream and those of waking life. It does mean, however, that this is a sophisticated distinction: it is not psychologically primitive. And the same applies, in James's view, to the case of inner perception. He holds that 'all that is experienced is, strictly considered, *objective*'.[2] Only on subsequent reflection does it divide 'into two contrasted parts, one realized as "Self", the other as "not-Self"'.[3] As we shall see, when we come to examine his theory of self-consciousness, he holds that one's awareness of oneself is dependent on one's awareness of one's body; he even goes so far to suggest that psychologically the self, as an object, can be identified with a certain set of bodily feelings. There is, therefore, no question, in his view, of our being confronted with any data which are represented from the outset as being private to ourselves.

Nevertheless we do come to think of ourselves as having private thoughts and feelings; and however difficult this notion of privacy may be to analyse, the belief appears to be empirically justified. Might not the same be true of our sensations? At a more sophisticated level, might we not have good reason to accept the view of those philosophers who have distinguished between the private data of sense and the public objects which we commonly say that we perceive? The philosophers who reject this distinction usually adopt a naïve realist theory of perception. They deny that there are any objects of sensation, other than the physical objects which we directly perceive; and in their view these physical objects are certainly not to be identified with any part of anyone's experience. On the other hand, if we do admit objects of

[1] Ibid., II 2.   [2] Ibid., I 304.   [3] Ibid.

sensation, and think of them, as James does, as being extracted from the flux of experience, then are we not bound to regard them as private? And if they are private objects, how can they be elaborated to form the public objects which we are supposed to perceive?

James's position on this point is not entirely clear. 'In the last analysis', he says, 'we believe that we all know and think about and talk about the same world, because *we believe our* PERCEPTS *are possessed by us in common*.'[1] It would seem, however, that James holds this belief to be false, since he goes on to speak of the hypothesis that 'my feelings' of a book which I am showing to another person resemble his as being 'something of which we can never be sure'; and here the implication is that the two sets of percepts are at any rate not numerically identical. One might indeed suppose that it was logically impossible for two different persons to have literally the same percept, but for James this is not a question of logic but of empirical fact. He sees no logical objection to the hypothesis that the separate biographies which are constituted by the experiences of two different persons should literally intersect, although, as I shall argue later on, this is hardly consistent with his own theory of personal identity. He does, however, think that there are empirical reasons against taking percepts to be such points of intersection. 'Apart from colour-blindness and such possibilities', the main reason which he gives is that different people who are looking at the same thing at the same moment see it in different perspectives.[2] This is not conclusive even in all cases of visual perception, since the difference in the situation of two observers relatively to the thing they are both looking at may not be great enough to cause any difference in the quality of their respective percepts, but it is enough to show that the fact that two people perceive the same object does not entail that they share a common percept. There must, therefore, be some other way of accounting for their knowing the same world.

There are passages in *The Principles of Psychology* where James appears to entertain the view that our perceiving the same objects

[1] *The Meaning of Truth*, p. 36. [2] *Essays in Radical Empiricism*, p. 82.

consists in the fact that our separate percepts have a common external cause. This would just be possible to reconcile with his saying that we perceive the fact with which we are acquainted through sensation as an immediately present outward reality, if he were prepared to hold that this 'perception' was erroneous. There is, however, no indication that he ever considered taking this step, and in his later work he consistently adheres to the view that the physical objects of common sense, the houses and trees and stars and books and tables, which we suppose ourselves to perceive, so far from being the external causes of our percepts, are constituted out of them. He admits that we can have a 'notion of imperceptibles like atoms or ether',[1] but maintains that such notions are empty unless they can be 'cashed' in terms of sense-perception. 'Scientific theories', he says, 'always terminate as definite percepts.'[2] These percepts, or to speak more strictly, the sensations out of which they are elaborated, are 'the only realities we ever directly know',[3] and since the realities that we know indirectly must be reducible to them, they are, in a sense, the only concrete realities that we can know at all.

This still leaves the problem of explaining how the contents of the experiences of different people can serve to construct a common world. As will be seen when I come to criticize James's theory, he does not undertake this task in any detail. He tends to rely, in a rather uncritical way, on what he takes to be the fact that one's perception of other people's behaviour usually gives one good reason to believe that they are having percepts which resemble one's own. There is, however, one passage in which he puts forward a thesis which could form the basis of a more thoroughgoing solution to the central problem. It occurs in an essay entitled 'A World of Pure Experience', which first appeared in the *Journal of Philosophy, Psychology and Scientific Method* in 1904 and is reprinted in the *Essays in Radical Empiricism*. Having argued, in a passage from which I have already quoted, that the objections to supposing that we have common percepts are not logical but empirical, he goes on to ask whether our minds have

---

[1] Ibid., p. 83. [2] *The Meaning of Truth*, p. 40.
[3] Ibid., p. 39.

any common object. His answer is that 'they certainly have *Space* in common'.[1] To illustrate this, he takes the example of a situation in which he and another person are looking from different points of view at the Harvard Memorial Hall. 'The percepts themselves', he says, 'may be shown to differ: but if each of us be asked to point out where his percept is, we point to an identical spot. All the relations, whether geometrical or causal, of the Hall originate or terminate in that spot wherein our hands meet, and where each of us begins to work if he wishes to make the Hall change before the other's eyes. Just so it is with our bodies. That body of yours which you actuate and feel from within must be in the same spot as the body of yours which I see or touch from without: "There" for me means where I place my finger. If you do not feel my finger's contact to be "there" in *my* sense, when I place it on your body, where then do you feel it? Your inner actuations of your body meet my finger *there*: it is *there* that you resist its push, or shrink back, or sweep the finger aside with your hand. Whatever farther knowledge either of us may acquire of the real constitution of the body which we thus feel, you from within and I from without, it is in that same place that the newly conceived or perceived constituents have to be located, and it is *through* that space that your and my mental intercourse with each other has always to be carried on, by the mediation of impressions which I convey thither, and of the reactions thence which those impressions may provoke from you.'[2]

This is in many ways an attractive thesis, but it encounters serious difficulties. The first of them is to make clear exactly what it implies. There is no question about the facts which James adduces to support it. If I am speaking to another person about an object within my field of vision, one of the recognized tests by which I can decide whether he has correctly understood me is to ask him to point to it or handle it. If it then appears to me that his finger points in the direction of, or comes into spatial contact with the object to which I was referring, I conclude that there has been no misunderstanding, at any rate with regard to

[1] *Essays in Radical Empiricism*, p. 84.   [2] Ibid.

the spatial position of the object in question. But what this proves is that we locate the same physical object in the same region of physical space: it is not at all clear that it implies anything whatever about the spatial location of our respective percepts. James argues that 'on pragmatic principles we are obliged to predicate sameness wherever we can predicate no assignable point of difference' and applying this to his example says that 'there is no test discoverable, so far as I know, by which it can be shown that the place occupied by your percept of Memorial Hall differs from the place occupied by mine'.[1] But the answer to this is that there are two distinct kinds of reason why we may be unable to assign any point of difference. The first is that, knowing what would constitute a difference, we fail to find one; the second is that we have no criteria for deciding whether or not a difference exists. In the first case we are justified in predicating sameness, but in the second we are not. In the second case, we have yet to give a meaning to speaking either of identity or difference. Now it would seem that the present instance falls into the second class. Surely no spatial relation between the percepts of two different observers could ever be perceptible; for who could be in a position to perceive it? But if no such spatial relations are perceptible, then, on James's own principles, we can have no criteria for determining what they are or indeed whether they exist. And if we can have no criteria for determining whether or in what way the percepts of two different observers are spatially related, it follows that we can have no criteria which will enable us to decide that they are spatially coincident.

To this James might have replied that he has a criterion. He could contrast the case in which two people are looking directly at an object, and there is no reason to suppose that either one's vision of it is in any way impeded or distorted, with the case in which one of them sees it directly but the other sees it reflected in a mirror. In the second case both may agree in their judgement of where the object is, but the location of their percepts will be different. The first observer's percept will be where the object is judged to be, but the second observer's percept will be in, or a

[1] Ibid.

little behind, the mirror. Accordingly it might be decreed that percepts of different observers were to be regarded as occupying the same place when the observers were simultaneously perceiving the same object, and there were no reasons, like the one just mentioned, for concluding that their percepts were differently located. This proposal will indeed run the risk of circularity, since it is not clear how it would be possible, on James's principles, to 'construct' either the observers or their common object, without already postulating a common space; but it might at least be held to meet the objection that the assumption of the spatial coincidence of the percepts of different observers is one to which no meaning has been attached.

But now we come to a logical difficulty, which I find it strange that James should have overlooked. It is admitted that when different persons perceive the same object at the same time, and perceptually locate it in the same place, their percepts may be qualitatively incompatible. An object, or the same part of an object, which looks round to one person may look elliptical to another: if a person's colour vision is affected, he may see as yellow what others see as green; and so forth. Now since James refers to differences of perspective, as well as to the possibility of colour-blindness, as reasons for denying that the percepts of different observers are identical, I take it that he must hold that, in cases of this kind, the qualities which the objects look to the different observers to have are the qualities of their respective percepts. So one man's percept of a given object is round and another's elliptical; one man's percept is yellow and another's green. But is it not a plain contradiction to say that the same region of space is wholly occupied both by a round thing and by an elliptical one, or both by a green thing and by a yellow one? It would certainly be a contradiction if the things in question were physical objects; so that if the contradiction is to be avoided, the sense in which percepts occupy space must be different from the sense in which physical objects do. But now it is altogether unclear what this sense can be. It may indeed be feasible, as we have seen, to assign percepts an artificial location in terms of the location of physical objects, but this will not serve James's purpose.

Even if the use of such a method could be shown not to be viciously circular in itself, it would not permit him, in his attempt to construct the physical world out of percepts, to start with the assumption that the percepts of different observers can occupy a common space.

This is not to say that James's programme is necessarily frustrated at the outset. It remains to be seen whether any satisfactory way can be found of cashing our concept of physical space in terms of spatial relations between percepts, and whether, if this were achieved, it would then be possible without circularity to link the percepts of different observers through their common relation to physical space. But if any such procedure is to be successful, it will have to take a more complex form than that of straightforwardly assuming that when different observers see the same physical object in the same place, their respective percepts are spatially coincident.

2. The Genesis of Space

It is indeed doubtful whether this assumption is consistent even with the psychological account which James gives of the genesis of our concept of space; and this for the reason which I have already indicated, that his account makes no provision for the existence of spatial relations between the percepts of different observers. James says that his empiricism requires that spatial and temporal concepts should have direct application to our sensations: and it is for this reason that he insists upon the fact that 'the relations between things are just as much a matter of particular experience, neither more so nor less so, than the things themselves'.[1] In fact, he maintains that even though a newly born child knows nothing about the ways in which his sensations are spatially related either to each other or to anything else in the world, he nevertheless feels them as being at a place. He does not consciously discriminate these sensibly known places from one another, but they remain in his memory as 'the places *where those sensations were*: and his only possible answer to the question

[1] *Essays in Radical Empiricism*, p. 84.

where anything is would be to say "there" and to name some sensation or other like those first ones, which shall identify the spot. Space *means* but the aggregate of all our possible sensations. There is no duplicate space known *aliunde*, or created by an "epoch-making achievement" into which our sensations, originally spaceless, are dropped. They *bring* space and all its places to our intellect, and do not derive it thence.'[1]

There is no question as yet of the child's sensations being arranged in any spatial order. What they possess is a 'vague form or quale of spatiality'[2] and this is identified by James with 'the element of voluminousness' which is present, in varying degrees, 'in the sensations of hearing, touch, sight and pain'.[3] It is out of this single element that 'all the exact knowledge of space that we afterwards come to have is woven by processes of discrimination, association and relation'.[4] This is not a field in which it is easy to distinguish between the raw material and the manufactured article, but James in fact attributes to sensation what would seem to involve a modicum of judgement. Thus he speaks of 'rightness and leftness, upness and downness' as pure sensations, and in obedience to his general principle that 'in the field of space the relations are facts of the same order with the facts they relate' he derives the relation of direction from the sensation of a line that joins two points together and the relation of distance obtaining between a point and a horizontal line below it from 'the sensation, ideal or actual, of a perpendicular drawn from the point to the line'. In this way he is able to satisfy himself that 'all space-relations except those of magnitude are nothing more or less than pure sensational objects'; and magnitude is brought in through the combination of the primitive sensation of *more* with actual or ideal sensations of 'particular outstanding portions of space after two figures have been superposed'.[5] How pure these sensations really are is perhaps not a question of the first importance. What is essential for James's theory is that even if they are relatively impure, in the sense that they already display the influence of 'processes of discrimination, association and relation', the material

---

[1] *The Principles of Psychology*, II 35.   [2] Ibid., p. 145.   [3] Ibid., p. 134.
[4] Ibid., p. 135.   [5] Ibid., pp. 149-52.

on which these processes are brought to bear is purely sense-given. And this, I think, may fairly be conceded to him.

Having thus, as he believes, accounted for all space-relations, James has little difficulty in tracing the sensory origin of our concepts of locality, shape and size. The next steps are not so easy. Up to this point he has not only confined himself, as he does throughout, to the experience of a single person, but he has made no attempt to link up different sense-modalities. The most he can claim is to have outlined the genesis of private independent spaces of sight, hearing, touch and organic sensation: and even these independent spaces have not as yet been systematically ordered. The two main problems, therefore, with which he next has to deal are, in his own words, first: 'How is the subdivision and measurement of the several sensorial spaces completely effected?' and secondly: 'How do their mutual addition and fusion and reduction to the same scale, in a word, how does their synthesis, occur?'[1]

In answering the first of these questions James draws upon the physiological fact that different points of the surface of the skin or the retina, 'differ in the quality of their immanent sensibility' with the result that external stimuli awake 'local differences of feeling';[2] a further condition is that the stimuli should be selective, in the sense that they operate on certain parts of the surface without exciting the rest. But what he regards as the main factor in developing our powers of spatial discrimination is 'the feeling of motion over any of our surfaces'.[3] He is referring here not to the muscular sensations which accompany our own movements but to our awareness of the apparent displacement of an object within a given sense-field, an appearance which may indeed be produced in certain cases by movements of our own. It might be thought that this would have to be a consequence rather than a source of spatial discrimination, on the ground that in order to have the feeling that an object moves from one place to another one must already have discriminated the two places, as a condition of being able to perceive that the object occupies them at different times. But James dismisses this as 'only another example

<hr>

[1] Ibid., p. 166.   [2] Ibid., pp. 167–8.   [3] Ibid., p. 171.

of what I call "the psychologist's fallacy" in thinking that the
mind he is studying must necessarily be conscious of the object
after the fashion in which the psychologist himself is conscious of
it'.[1] His own view is that 'it is experimentally certain that we
have the feeling of motion given us as a direct and simple *sensation*'.[2] He can, therefore, maintain, without circularity, that
places are initially discriminated through being perceived as the
starting or terminating points of motions which are simply sensed.

The measurement of sensory spaces, involving as it does the
comparison of magnitudes, depends fundamentally on our ability
to superpose one surface on another. Where this is not possible,
we are likely to be at a loss. In the case of visual sensation, for
example, we have little or no idea of the respective sizes of
different retinal images. When we are dealing with a distant
object like the moon, we find it very difficult to say how large
it looks. Our judgement tends to be affected by what we know
or believe the real size of the object to be: and here James makes
the interesting point that the way in which the real size of an
object is determined is rather arbitrary. '*Out of all the visual
magnitudes of each known object we have selected one as the* REAL *one
to think of, and degraded all the others to serve as its signs*. This "real"
magnitude is determined by aesthetic and practical interests. It is
that which we get when the object is at the distance most pro-
pitious for exact visual discrimination of its details. This is the
distance at which we hold anything we are examining. Farther
than this we see it too small, nearer too large. And the larger and
the smaller feeling vanish in the act of suggesting this one, their
more important *meaning*. As I look along the dining-table I
overlook the fact that the farther plates and glasses *feel* so much
smaller than my own, for I *know* that they are all equal in size;
and the feeling of them, which is a present sensation, is eclipsed
in the glare of the knowledge, which is a merely imagined one.'[3]

Whether the farther plates and glasses would even feel smaller
is debatable. The experiments conducted by *Gestalt* psychologists
suggest that they would not. But, however that may be, there is
no doubt about the result; the magnitude which is judged to be

---

[1] Ibid., fn.   [2] Ibid.   [3] Ibid., pp. 179–80.

real sets the standard to which apparent magnitudes are made to conform. I believe also that the account which James gives of the way in which the real magnitude is selected is substantially correct, though rather over-simplified. It applies very well to medium-sized objects in one's immediate neighbourhood, but not so well to very large or very small objects, and not at all, or at least not directly, to the case of remote objects like the moon, where our judgements of magnitude are derived from a fairly elaborate theory. It must be remembered also that in making judgements of magnitude we do not rely solely, and perhaps not even primarily, on the sense of sight. James himself allows that when we have succeeded in equating visual spaces with the spaces given to touch, 'it is probably the touch-feeling which prevails as real and the sight which serves as sign',[1] the reason being not only 'the far greater constancy of felt over seen magnitude'[2] but also the greater practical interest which we take in the sense of touch because of the discovery which we made as children that it was mainly through physical contact that things benefited or harmed us. This is in line with James's general principle that 'when two sensorial space-impressions, believed to come from the same object, differ, then *the one most interesting*, practically or aesthetically, is *judged to be the true one*'.[3]

The question still remains: how are the spaces of sight and touch equated and fused with the spaces of the other senses? As James puts it, 'how are the various sense-spaces added together into a consolidated and unitary continuum?'[4] Initially, he thinks, there is no connection between them. Before we carry out our work of discrimination, even objects which are simultaneously presented to the same sense organ may be felt to have only a vague spatial relation to each other, and objects which are presented to different sense-organs are not felt to be linked by any spatial relation at all. How then are we able to arrive at our concept of a single spatial system in which we are able to assign every real object a place, no matter by which of our senses we perceive it?

What we do, according to James, is to apprehend some of our

[1] Ibid., p. 180.   [2] Ibid.   [3] Ibid., p. 181.   [4] Ibid.

experiences as existing 'out and alongside' of each other, and
others as interpenetrating. But how is this effected? In the first
place, he thinks, through following a principle of economy.
'Whatever sensible data can be attended to together we locate
together. Their several extents seem one extent. The place at
which each appears is held to be the same with the place at which
the others appear. They become in short so many properties of
one and the same real thing.'[1] Having grouped a number of sensations in this way, we then, in a fairly arbitrary fashion, take one of
them to be the thing, the others being regarded as 'its more or
less accidental *properties*, or modes of appearance'.[2] Here again
the factor of constancy comes into play, together with our
practical interests. On these grounds the sensation most often
chosen to represent the thing is that of hardness or weight; with
weight goes tactile bulk, and since when we handle anything we
usually also see it, tactual and visual bulk are identified, and also
taken to be part of the thing's 'essence'. 'Frequently', James
continues, 'a shape so figures, sometimes a temperature, a taste,
etc.: but for the most part temperature, smell, sound, colour, or
whatever other phenomena may vividly impress us simultaneously
with the bulk felt or seen, figure among the accidents.'[3]

James acknowledges that sensations of sound and smell are often
associated with objects that are not at the same time being seen
or felt, but he remarks that they are strongest when we do see or
touch the objects from which they emanate, with the result that
we ascribe a precise location only to their source, the properties
of sound and smell themselves being thought of as permeating
places which are occupied by other things. Here, as elsewhere,
he appears to overlook the part which is played by causal theories,
but presumably this is deliberate. His aim is to bring to light the
primitive associations on which he must hold that our causal
theories themselves are ultimately founded.

The assumption which lies behind this account of the first
steps that are taken in fusing the spaces of different senses is that
we can attend to different sensations simultaneously only when
they come to us from different sense-organs. In that case, as

---

[1] Ibid., pp. 183–4.   [2] Ibid.   [3] Ibid.

James puts it, they 'do not interfere with each other's perception'.[1] On the other hand, 'different impressions on the same sense-organ do interfere with each other's perception and cannot well be attended to at once'.[2] The result is that 'we do not locate them in each other's spaces but arrange them in a serial order of exteriority, each alongside of the rest, in a space larger than that which any one sensation brings'.[3] This applies to tactual and kinaesthetic as well as to visual space, and derivatively to the data of the other senses. But whereas the blind man has to perform the more difficult task of constructing and uniting space out of 'tactile, locomotor and auditory experiences',[4] the data which are used for this purpose by those who can see are almost exclusively visual.

In opposition to Berkeley, whose Theory of Vision was an attempt to show that the field of sight can only be two-dimensional and that we are led to see things in depth by the association of sight with touch, James argues, to my mind convincingly, that depth is no less an intrinsic property of our visual sense-field than length and breadth. He therefore has no problem in explaining how we come to conceive of space as being three-dimensional. The problem which he does have is the much more serious one of showing how space is projected beyond the actual spread of our sensations, so that we are able to think of it, and of the things which occupy it, as existing unperceived.

Once more James's explanation is very simple. Primarily as the result of our own movements, the composition of our visual fields is constantly changing. In other words, one visual field is constantly being replaced by another. But the replacement is not always total. Very often, a portion of a given field survives in its immediate successors. When, for example, we scan a row of objects from left to right, an object which is at the right-hand edge of one visual field appears in succeeding fields first towards the centre and then towards the left; new objects appear on its right, and the objects which were on its left disappear from view; but we remember that these objects which have now disappeared stood in it in the same spatial relation as it is now seen to stand to

[1] Ibid.   [2] Ibid., p. 185.   [3] Ibid.   [4] Ibid.

objects which did not figure in the previous sense-fields. In this way 'we get to conceive of the successive fields of things after the analogy of the several things which we perceive in a single field. They must be out and alongside of each other, and we conceive that their juxtaposed spaces must make a larger space.'[1]

Furthermore, since we live in a predominantly stable world, we find that these sensory routes can usually be retraced. By reversing the movement of our eyes, we can scan the same series of objects, this time from right to left. The vanished members of the series then reappear in the same spatial relations to each other in which they were seen to stand before. The result is that 'through these constant changes every field of seen things comes at last to be thought of as always having a fringe of *other things possible to be seen* spreading in all directions round about it'.[2] Finally, we abstract from the various natures of the things which occupy these sense-fields and think only of their extents, and since the extent of an object is equivalent to the space which it fills, the spaces themselves become detached in our thought from their occupants. We discover that the objects may be displaced, or cease to exist, but the places which they served to identify are now thought of as being permanently 'there', and permanently accessible to us, as the result only of our making certain movements. A strong association is thereby created between spatial extensions and the possibility of movement; so strong indeed that some psychologists have taken them to be synonymous. In James's view, this is a mistake. He insists that however large a part movement may play in the later stages of the construction, the fact which fundamentally makes the construction possible is just that our visual sense-fields are given to us as spatially extended.

For one who lacks the sense of sight the construction of the notion of space follows the same principles: 'Skin-feelings take in him the place of retinal feelings in giving the quality of lateral spreadoutness, as our attention passes from one extent of them to another, awakened by an object sliding along.'[3] The main differences derive from the fact that the tactual field is so much less extensive than the visual. In consequence, the blind man is

[1] Ibid. [2] Ibid., p. 186. [3] Ibid., pp. 186-7.

obliged to rely more upon movement, as well as upon the auditory sense which plays little if any part in the construction of visual space; and he has to perform a more considerable feat of imaginative synthesis.

Though this theory is put forward as a piece of genetic psychology, it can also be regarded as a contribution to the theory of knowledge. Without having to settle the question whether this process of constructing space is one through which every infant actually goes, we can look upon James's account of it as an attempt to show how the concept of space is capable of being 'cashed' in sensory terms. Viewing it in this aspect, I find the theory generally plausible. The dubious step in it appears to me to be the rather summary account of the way in which the spaces of the different senses are synthesized. It is certainly not true that whenever we are able to attend simultaneously to data which belong to different sense-modalities, we assign them to the same object. Not only, as James admits, is this principle often violated in the association of visual data with those of sound and smell, but it may also be violated in the association of visual data with the data of touch. For the most part when we touch things we do also see them, but sometimes we do not; and in either case there are likely to be other things which we see at the same time but do not touch. To overcome this difficulty, I think that James would have had to say that he was referring not to occasional but only to habitual concomitances. The space of sight being taken to be primary, and the problem being to insert in it the data of touch, the question is how, among the objects which we are seeing at a given time, we select those to which we ascribe the tactile properties that we are simultaneously feeling. It will not do to say that they are just those with which we observe ourselves to be in contact, for this is to assume that in the case of our own bodies the integration of tactual and kinaesthetic with visual data has already been accomplished. The answer which James would require to give is rather that we pick out those visual objects the sight of which has been habitually found to accompany tactile experiences of the kind in question. This presupposes that the object is fairly thoroughly explored by touch, and it ignores the cases in which the condition is satisfied by more than one object in the visual field, as well as those in which it is satisfied by none. These objections might, however, be met by saying that without tactual exploration the synthesis would not be possible, and that in its initial stages it is legitimate to concentrate upon the standard cases. Once we have made a certain number of straightforward correlations, we can use them as a check upon the others. In the case where two or more objects in a visual field are associated with a given tactual quale, it will be found that only one of them has the 'right' spatial relation to other visual objects which have had tactual properties assigned to them: the right relation here being that which preserves in the combined space the relations in tactual space of the unassigned property to those that have already been assigned. In the case where no candidate for the tactual property is seen, we have to rely upon established correlations for the inference that one and only one candidate would be seen, if the appropriate movements were made. The initial concentration upon standard cases carries with it the assumption that sight and touch are 'normal'. It is only when the synthesis is firmly established that it becomes possible to deal with sensory illusions. It is, therefore, on this view, a necessary proposition that such illusions are relatively infrequent.

With these emendations, I think that the theory is defensible, at least if it is viewed analytically as an account of the way in which space can be broken down into its sensory elements. Psychologically, it hardly explains why the idea of fusing tactual and visual data should ever have arisen, but once it has arisen the practical advantages are plainly very great. It must be an early discovery that tactual manipulations are systematically correlated with changes in visual aspect and position. These causal connections are very much easier to formulate if the corresponding visual and tactual objects are identified and situated in a unitary space.

Exception may be taken by some philosophers to the 'Robinson Crusoe' character of James's approach. He writes as though the construction of space was a task which we each perform without assistance from anybody else. But surely, it may be said, it is at least of some relevance that the child is taught a language in which the effects of the construction are already embodied. Psychologically, the answer to this might be that the child must already have made the construction for the language to be intelligible to him, though it is admittedly not easy to see how without any assistance from language he could perform the intellectual feats which the construction requires. But from the analytical point of view, in any case, this objection carries no weight. The fact is that however much information we may obtain from other people, each one of us has to interpret it in terms of his own experience. It follows, on James's premisses, that for anyone to be able to understand any statements which refer to the location of objects in space, his own sensations must exhibit the order which alone makes it possible, in his case, for these statements to be cashed. James is therefore quite justified in describing these sensory relations as though their owner existed in a world of his own. How one man's world is integrated with another's is a problem to which we shall return.

3. The Genesis of Time

Just as the concept of space must be capable, in James's view, of being constructed out of elements which are directly given to us in sense-experience, so must the concept of time. In many ways the derivation of the two concepts is analogous. Temporal duration, like spatial extension, is regarded by James as something of which we are immediately aware. Like the original experience of space, the original experience of time 'is always of something already given as a unit, inside of which attention afterwards discriminates parts in relation to each other'.[1] The only difference here is that the temporal duration which is contained in our elementary sensations has a much shorter span. And just as the overlapping of sense-fields enables us to project spatial relations beyond their original limits, so does it make possible our extended consciousness of time. 'If the present thought is of ABCDEFG, the next one will be of BCDEFGH, and the one after that of

[1] *The Principles of Psychology*, 1610.

CDEFGHI – the lingerings of the past dropping successively away, and the incomings of the future making up the loss. These lingerings of old objects, these incomings of new, are the germs of memory and expectation, the retrospective and the prospective sense of time. They give that continuity to consciousness without which it could not be called a stream.'[1]

The implication here is that temporal duration, again like spatial extension, is a relation between sense-contents. We can no more perceive empty time than we can perceive empty space. We may have a sense of the passage of time even when our attention is withdrawn from any distinct outward impressions, but this will then depend upon our 'twilight awareness' of such rhythmical processes as our heart-beats, our breathing, or the pulses of our attention to our thoughts. 'In short, empty our minds as we may, some form of *changing process* remains for us to feel, and cannot be expelled. And along with the sense of the process and its rhythm goes the sense of the length of time it lasts. Awareness of *change* is thus the condition on which our perception of time's flow depends; but there exists no reason to suppose that empty time's own changes are sufficient for the awareness of change to be aroused. Thus change must be of some concrete sort – an outward or inward sensible series, or a process of attention or volition.'[2] Once more, as James remarks, there is an analogy with space; for he holds, as we have seen, that the spatial discrimination which gives us 'the earliest form of distinct space-perception' depends upon movement, and movement is a species of change.

It is to be noted that James speaks of our having a sense, not only of the changing process, but also of the length of time it lasts. The difficulty here is to see how these experiences can arise at the same level. In the ordinary way, to speak of the length of time that anything lasts is to relate its duration to the duration of some other event. It need not involve anything so sophisticated as a conventional standard in terms of which lengths of time are measured, but must it not at least involve the recollection of some previous occurrences, to serve as a basis of comparison? The

---

[1] *The Principles of Psychology*, pp. 606–7. [2] Ibid., p. 620.

trouble is that in that case we have moved outside the limits of what is supposed to be directly given. James quotes with apparent approval the view of Münsterberg that when the time which separates two sensible impressions is very short we measure its extent by the amount to which the memory-image has faded; when it is longer, by the feelings of tension and relaxation in the muscles by which we adapt our sense-organs to the incoming signals; and when it is longer still, by the rhythm of our breathing. But even if this be true, it hardly seems to meet the difficulty; for how do we measure the rate at which an image fades, or the duration of our feelings of muscular tension or the rhythm of our breathing, except by comparison with similar processes which have occurred at other times? So far as I can see, the only course which is open to anyone who wishes to take the view that length of duration is immediately perceived would be to maintain that within a given sense-experience we can not only apprehend one event as being earlier than another, but also as standing to it in a more specific time-relation, such as that of being much earlier, or a little earlier. That is to say, relations like that of being much earlier would be taken, in this context, not as involving any reference even to any *ad hoc* standard of measurement, but as simple temporal qualia. There would again be some analogy with space, where sensations of magnitude, as we have seen, were held to be derived, in part, from a primitive sensation of 'more'. It is true that in the case of space-perception, we have a ready means of measuring the 'more' through our ability to compare different extensions within the same sense-field. But in a lesser degree, the same applies to our perception of time, since there may be sub-processes of change which occupy a shorter time than that of the sense-experience within which they fall.

In one important respect, the construction of time is simpler than that of space. There is no question of our having to synthesize the times, as we have to synthesize the spaces, of different sense-modalities. We apprehend temporal relations not only between data of the same sense, but also between the data of all the different senses: an auditory datum, for example, is sensed as occurring before or after or simultaneously with a visual one.

Were this not so, the synthesis of spaces would itself not be possible: for it depends, as we have seen, on our remarking that certain kinds of data, which belong to different sense-modalities, habitually occur together.

The theory that the data which are presented to us in sense-experience possess a sensible duration is technically known as 'the theory of the specious present', a term which, according to James, was introduced in a book called *The Alternative* by Mr. E. R. Clay. In most versions of the theory, it is held that what we apprehend as being present is a set of events which go back a certain distance into the immediate past. We are aware of them all as present, but also of some of them, or at any rate some parts of them, as being earlier than others. James, however, adopts a version in which 'the practically cognized present is no knife-edge but a saddle-back, with a certain breadth of its own on which we sit perched, and from which we look in two directions into time'.[1] It, therefore, looks as if he holds that we are directly aware of the immediate future as well as of the immediate past.

The idea that we can be directly aware even of the immediate future is difficult to accept. For to say that an event is future is to say that it has not yet happened, and it appears contradictory to claim that one can, in the present moment, be already aware of something that has not yet happened. It should, indeed, appear equally contradictory to speak of our being still aware, in the present moment, of something that is no longer happening: but psychologically it is easier to think of the past as retaining a foot-hold in the present than of the future as literally casting its shadow before. Logically, however, it might be argued that if the specious present really is wholly present, it must altogether exclude both the future and the past.

In fact, the contradiction here is only apparent; it seems to arise because of the misleading way in which the theory of the specious present has been formulated. What James presumably has in mind when he speaks of our looking in two directions into time is that we are sensibly aware of the inception of events as well as of their fading away; and there is certainly no logical reason why

[1] Ibid., p. 609.

this should not be so. It is, however, a mistake to express this in terms of our being aware of the future and the past; the only reason for so speaking is the assumption that what is strictly present can have no duration, so that anything taken to be present to which we ascribe duration must extend beyond the real present into the future or the past, or both. But it is just this assumption that the theory of the specious present rightly denies, though wrongly paying tribute to it by the use of the word 'specious'. The fact is that 'present' is a relative term. We use it to apply to periods which cover, or coincide with, whatever is occurring now; and to say of something that it is occurring now is to say that it is simultaneous with something that is shown in the context of our utterance, whether it be the expression of certain words, or a certain gesture, or some other event which can be demonstratively indicated. So long as it is something ostensible, in this sense, it does not matter what is taken as the standard of reference: all that is required of whatever serves as the standard is that it should not be so long as to exceed the span of a single act of attention or so short that it cannot be attended to. Anything which is strictly contemporaneous with the standard event is, therefore, strictly present; anything earlier is past, and anything later is future. Of course, with the passage of time, the standard event itself is constantly changing: or rather, to speak more precisely, there is a continuous series of overlapping standard events, but that makes no difference to the argument.

Accordingly, since any act of attention has a minimal as well as a maximal duration, it follows that no sensibly present event is instantaneous. Whatever is present, even in the strictest sense, must have some duration, however short, and this means that the distinction of earlier and later occurs within it. But this does not make it correct to speak of the earlier phases as past or the later phases as future, with reference to a present which is defined by a class of events of which the event that includes these phases is a member. On the contrary, the whole point of the argument is that all the phases of such an event are present. If we are nevertheless inclined to divide the event up into past and present, or past, present and future phases, the reason may be that we are confused by the idea of the instantaneous present, but it may also be that we unconsciously change our standard of reference. The earlier phases are past, with respect to a present which overlaps with the later stages of the original event, and the later phases are future with respect to a present which overlaps with its earlier stages. It is particularly easy to think of the earlier stages as past, because we allow ourselves to be carried along imaginatively with the flow of time; but it is a mistake none the less.

This problem of where to draw the line between the present and the past or future is of some interest in itself, but it is in no way vital to James's theory. All that he requires is that the relation of temporal priority, the earlier–later relation, be sensibly given. If this is granted to him, as I think it must be, he is in a position to define not only the other temporal relations of simultaneity, interiority and partial overlapping, but also the attributes of past, present and future. An event is present, past, or future according as it is simultaneous with, earlier than or later than an arbitrarily chosen event which is taken, in the way I have just explained, as the current standard of reference.

The projection of temporal relations beyond the specious present, which is the first step in the construction of time, operates on the same principle as the projection of spatial relations beyond a given sense-field. It is because successive presents overlap that we find it easy to conceive of events which are no longer present as being earlier than the earliest of present events and of the latest of present events as being earlier than events which are yet to come. We then conceive of these events, which lie just outside the limits of the specious present, as standing in the same relations to more remote events, and in this way come to represent the field of temporal relations as being indefinitely extended. This is not so sophisticated a notion as that of the infinitude of time, which depends upon the construction of an objective temporal order as distinct from the temporal sequence of one's own sense-experiences, but it is the foundation on which the more sophisticated notion rests. Rather surprisingly, James does not enter into the problem of the way in which we come to arrange events in an objective temporal order. As we shall see, when we come to deal with the problem of synthesizing the experiences of different persons into a common world, it is fundamentally a matter of our being able to correlate the temporal perceptions of different observers who occupy different spatial positions. It, therefore, depends among other things on our having completed the construction of space.

Although the same method of projection is used to carry us beyond our original data in the development of the concepts of space and time, there is one important difference in the conclusions to which it leads. The difference, on which James fails to remark, is that in the case of space we are led to think of the objects between which the projected spatial relations hold, and so of the positions which they occupy, as being permanently 'there': in the case of time this is not so; we think of events as occurring only when they are present, and of the moments of time as perpetually fleeting. The reason for this is mainly logical. It depends primarily upon the impossibility of our moving about in time, as we can move about in space. The permanence attributed to spatial positions depends upon our ability to occupy them at different times, but to speak of our occupying the same times at different times is just nonsensical. This in itself would not prevent us from endowing events with more than a fleeting existence, but if we tried to develop an analogy with the persistence of objects in space, we should soon run into other logical difficulties. It would, for example, be hard for us to reconcile the unobserved persistence of this morning's rain with the visible presence of this afternoon's sunshine. This still leaves the possibility of identifying this morning's rain with yesterday's. But while such a policy of treating similar events as the same is one on which we might well have embarked if our experience had been more uniform than it is, the balance of advantage, as things are, does not lie with it. It is more convenient for us to individuate events by assigning to each of them a unique position in time, and excluding the possibility of their literal recurrence.

Even on this point, however, there is a closer analogy with space than might appear at first sight. The consequence of our method of individuating events is that every event has a fixed position in time, more fixed, indeed, than the position of objects in space; for it is possible for objects to change their position in space, whereas it is not possible for any event to change its position in time. Accordingly, since periods of time are identified by the events which occupy them, so that to assign an event a position in time is a matter of relating it temporally to other events, there is a sense in which the parts of time are no less stable than the parts of space. They are equally stable in the sense that they occupy a fixed position in the temporal order – and here it makes no difference whether one is talking of an objective temporal order, or of the temporal order of one's own experiences – just as the parts of space occupy a fixed position in the spatial order. The location of moments in time depends upon the relations of simultaneity and succession which the events that occupy them bear to other events, and these relations are timeless. Even if it is only the experience of change that enables us to conceive of temporal succession, it is not logically possible that the order of terms in the succession should itself be liable to change. It just is what it is. The earlier–later relation generates the flow of time: it is not subject to it.[1]

One reason why James may have wished to speak of the earlier phases of the specious present as being past is that he saw no other way of accounting for 'our notion of past time, upon which memory and history build their systems'[2] than by supposing that 'we have a constant feeling *sui generis* of pastness'. Since he also speaks of the later phases of the specious present as being future he would seem to be committed to holding that we have a similar feeling of futurity, though this is not necessary for his purpose: if we have concepts of presentness and pastness, we can define the future as anything to which the present is related as the past is related to the present. We have, however, seen that there are logical objections to conceiving of the present as including segments of the past and future. On the view which I have put forward, the primitive 'feeling' is that of temporal succession: the

[1] Cf. my essay 'Statements about the Past', *Proc. Arist. Soc.* 1950–1. Reprinted in *Philosophical Essays*.

[2] *The Principles of Psychology*, I 605.

present, past and future can then be very simply defined in the way that I have already shown.

A possible objection to this procedure is that it makes our acquisition of the concept of the past depend upon our ability to project the relation of temporal priority beyond our present sense-experience. At any rate, it may be argued, this is inconsistent with James's theory that our ability to make the projection depends upon the fact that our sense-experiences overlap. For we should not even be aware of this overlap unless we were able to remember the parts of its earlier constituents which were no longer present; and to remember anything is already to think of it as past.

The first comment to be made on this is that there is a circle, on either view, if the dependence of projection upon overlap is taken to be logical. Even if we are given the concept of pastness, we shall need memory to take us beyond the specious present; it cannot consistently be held that this employment of memory depends upon the temporal overlap of our sensations, since in order to perceive this overlap we have to employ memory. We are bound, therefore, to regard memory as a primitive faculty of temporal projection, and to treat our perception of the overlap not as a logical condition of our power to project but merely as facilitating its operation.

But does not my view still commit us to the circle of making the notion of the past depend on memory, and memory depend upon the notion of the past? The answer is that it does not, because the notion which memory presupposes is not that of the past but that of temporal priority which is derived from our observation of the present. There would, indeed, be no objection, on the score of circularity, to defining the past as the domain of memory. The objections are that we need to make provision for the extension of the past beyond the reach of anyone's memory, and also perhaps for the occurrence of experiences which not only never are but, for psychological reasons, never could be recalled. So while it is a necessary proposition that whatever is remembered is past, it is not a necessary, or even a true proposition, that everything that is past is capable of being remembered.

4. The Analysis of Memory

The account which James gives of the phenomenon of memory is rather brief. He begins by defining it as 'the knowledge of an event, or fact, of which meantime we have not been thinking, with the additional consciousness that we have thought or experienced it before'[1] and then goes on to consider in what this knowledge consists. 'The first element', he says, 'which such a knowledge involves would seem to be the revival in the mind of an image or a copy of the original event.'[2] He admits that 'when the past is recalled symbolically, or conceptually only, it is true that no such copy need be there'. Even when we are comparing qualities of two objects, only one, or even neither, of which is present to our senses, we do not have to bring in images, and if we do bring them in their role is not essential. For 'suppose the mind does compare two realities by comparing two ideas of its own which represent them – what is gained? The same mystery is still there. The ideas must still be known: and as the attention in comparing oscillates from one to the other, past must be known with present just as before'.[3] This argument is irrefragable, and it is strange that, having seen this important point so clearly, James should still be prepared to make the presence of images an essential ingredient of memory-knowledge. His reason is that since 'all conceptual knowledge stands for intuitive knowledge, and terminates therein', he is justified in confining himself 'to those memories in which the past is directly imaged in the mind, or, as we say, intuitively known'.[4] But the trouble here is that the intuitive knowledge in which conceptual knowledge is supposed to terminate is knowledge of the contents of our present experiences, and an image, considered as a present content, tells us nothing whatever about the past. So long as we are concerned, not with what is called habit-memory, that is, the retention of skills, but with memory in the sense of conscious recall, I doubt, indeed, if one has any memory-knowledge which is not conceptual. Even at the pre-verbal stage where it may be supposed that

[1] Ibid., p. 648.   [2] Ibid., p. 649.   [3] Ibid., p. 500 fn.   [4] Ibid., p. 649 fn.

the psychological process of remembering does consist in having images, the images function as concepts, and could, therefore, be dispensed with, if there were anything else to play their psychological part.

James himself virtually admits this, since he goes on to argue that 'the revival of an image is obviously not a *memory*, whatever else it may be: it is simply a duplicate, a second event, having absolutely no connection with the first event except that it happens to resemble it'.[1] It is no more a memory than sensations 'recurring in successive editions'[2] are memories of each other. As he rightly remarks, a further condition is required and that is that 'the fact imaged be *expressly referred to the past*, thought as *in the past*'.[3] But then any symbol which is so referred will serve the purpose equally well. There is no logical reason why the symbol should be in any degree a copy of the fact.

The condition that the symbol which serves as the vehicle of memory should be interpreted as referring to the past is necessary but not sufficient. The fact which is 'thought as in the past' has to be believed and not merely imagined; if the memory is to be of any cognitive value, the fact in question has to be given a definite location in the past; it has to be associated with other facts which give it its proper setting. For James, this is another proof that memory cannot simply consist in making mental copies of the facts remembered. 'What memory goes with is, on the contrary, a very complex representation, that of the fact to be recalled *plus* its associates, the whole forming one 'object' known in one integral pulse of consciousness and demanding probably a vastly more intricate brain-process than that on which any simple sensorial image depends.'[4] But it is still not enough to constitute a memory that the fact be dated in the past. According to James, 'it must be dated in *my* past. In other words, I must think that I directly experienced its occurrence. It must have that warmth and intimacy [which characterize] all experiences "appropriated" by the thinker as his own.'[5]

Even when the mistake about images has been corrected, there

[1] Ibid., p. 649. [2] Ibid. [3] Ibid., p. 650.
[4] Ibid., p. 651. [5] Ibid., p. 650.

are several difficulties in this account. A minor objection to the initial definition of memory is that there is no reason to stipulate that the event, or fact, which is remembered should be one 'of which meantime we have not been thinking'; if this were taken literally it would entail the absurd conclusion that no event in a man's experience could be remembered by him more than once. What James presumably had in mind was that there must be an interval between the experiencing of an event and its revival in memory, but this is inconsistent with his own theory that the constituents of the specious present fade gradually out of the reach of sensation and into the domain of memory. Neither is there any reason in logic why an event which has undergone this transition should not be continuously remembered over a long period of time.

But the most serious defect in James's definition is its requiring us to be conscious that the event, or fact, which we remember is one that we have thought or experienced before. Again, this is inconsistent with his own theories. For he holds that the child's transformation of his sensations into 'things', which implies at least an elementary projection of spatial and temporal relations, precedes his arrival at self-consciousness; and we have seen that this projection is not possible without the exercise of memory. No doubt these primitive memories have the warmth and intimacy that we associate with experiences which we think of as our own, but it is impossible, on James's own view, that the child should actually so think of them.

It might be argued that there are different stages in the development of memory which call for different analyses. At the very primitive stage it may be sufficient that the child should recall his own experiences without his having to recall them *as* his own. But the position changes once he has become self-conscious. It is only those experiences, it may be held, which he recalls as his own, that he can then properly be said to remember. But this seems to me very doubtful. I believe that it quite often happens, even in adult life, that we recollect scenes which we have witnessed without recollecting our reactions to them, or indeed without thinking of ourselves at all; and I see no reason why these should not count as genuine memories. It is true that if we were asked, in such cases, whether we had been witnesses of the events in question, we should normally reply that we had; but this does not mean that when we recalled them our act of recollection included any reference to ourselves. If we were conscious of having been present at the scene, it was in a purely dispositional sense. And even this is not absolutely necessary. There are abnormal cases in which it is clear from the evidence of their behaviour that people remember events which they actually deny having witnessed. It may be said that such memories should be classified as unconscious, and therefore as falling outside the scope of James's account, but this would appear somewhat arbitrary in the cases where the subject is conscious of the past event and only not conscious of having witnessed it. What makes it tempting to maintain that we always remember events *as* experienced by ourselves is that saying 'I remember' does carry the implication that the occurrences in question entered into one's own experience. But, if I am right, it does not enter into the conditions of remembering an event that one should claim to remember it, even if the claim is made only to oneself. I have tried to show that it is not necessary, and it is obviously not sufficient.

It is not at all easy to say what is sufficient. I have argued that James requires too much, but it is also true that he does not require enough. In saying, as he does, that 'the object of memory is only an object imagined in the past to which the emotion of belief adheres',[1] he forgets that it is quite possible to believe truly that a certain event occurred, to locate it correctly in one's own past experience, to imagine it vividly, but still not to remember it. The most obvious way in which this could happen would be for one to have been told about the event by someone whom one regarded as a reliable authority. This is a well-known difficulty, but I am still not sure how it can be overcome. It has been suggested that we need only add the further condition that one's belief in the occurrence of the event be causally dependent upon one's previous experience of it. But the trouble is that this may also be true in a case where one's belief in an event which one has forgotten is caused by someone else's testimony; for instance,

[1] Ibid., p. 652.

one's informant may originally have heard the story from one-self. To exclude the effect of testimony altogether will not do, because it often has the effect of bringing memories back. It is, therefore, necessary to enter more precisely into the details of the causal connection, to stipulate, for example, that the belief must be the direct outcome of the activation of a brain-trace which was implanted by one's experience of the original event. But now it seems very implausible to read such a specific causal theory into the definition of memory. It is anyhow conceivable that the theory of brain-traces should be false, without our therefore having to conclude that nothing is remembered. Moreover, even if we adopted such a causal condition, we should still have to account for the change that takes place when we suddenly remember something which we had previously believed upon testimony. It can hardly be supposed that it consists in our becoming aware of the activation of a brain-trace. To speak of a 'feeling' of memory, which is *sui generis*, is not very satisfactory, but I confess that I do not know what else there is to say.

With this brief account and criticism of his analysis of memory, I come to the end of my survey of the materials out of which James tries to construct the world as we know it and of the very first steps that his construction takes. The next stage in our examination of his radical empiricism will be to see how out of the stuff of 'pure experience', which is all that he believes there really is, he tries to extract the conscious subject and to explain how the subject differentiates between himself, his feelings and his concepts, and the things which are external to him. We shall begin with James's analysis of self-consciousness.

B. THE KNOWER AND THE KNOWN

1. *The Concept of the Self*

In an essay entitled 'Does "Consciousness" Exist?', which appeared in the *Journal of Philosophy, Psychology and Scientific Methods* in 1904 and is reprinted as the first of the *Essays in Radical*

Empiricism, James comes to the conclusion that it does not. This conclusion is, however, less startling than it might appear. James does not mean to deny that people have thoughts and feelings; neither does he take the behaviourist view that these thoughts and feelings are reducible to the physical states and dispositions of those who own them, though, as we shall see, there is a sense in which he does hold that mental and physical 'objects' are identical. What he does deny is that the word 'consciousness' stands for an entity, while insisting 'most emphatically that it does stand for a function'.[1] The function for which he takes it to stand is that of knowing.

It will help to elucidate James's position if we contrast his analysis of this function with that which is likely to be given by philosophers who tie themselves more closely to the outlook of commonsense. Their view would be that in the analysis of a cognitive situation there are three, or perhaps even four elements to be distinguished; first, the knowing subject, secondly, his act of consciousness, and thirdly, the object of this act: a fourth element would be added by those who think it necessary to distinguish between the object of the act, or state, of consciousness and its content. James, for his part, is very much more economical. For him there is only a piece of experience, in which there is no distinction between object and content. The knowing subject and his act of consciousness are both eliminated, at least as entities. Together with the cognitive process, in the analysis of which they were supposed to figure, they are transformed into relations between experiences.

James's reasons for denying that either the self or its alleged acts of consciousness exist as entities are partly empirical and partly reasons of economy. On the subject of acts of consciousness he quotes G. E. Moore, who had based his *Refutation of Idealism*[2] upon the assumption that the distinction between acts of consciousness and their objects is not only one that we are logically bound to make but also one that we can introspectively detect. 'The moment we try to fix our attention upon conscious-

---

[1] *Essays in Radical Empiricism*, p. 3.
[2] *Mind*, XII 1903. Reprinted in Moore's *Philosophical Studies*.

ness,' Moore had written, 'and to see *what*, distinctly, it is, it seems to vanish. It seems as if we had before us a mere emptiness. When we try to introspect the sensation of blue, all we can see is the blue; the other element is as if it were diaphanous. Yet it *can* be distinguished, if we look attentively enough, and know that there is something to look for.'[1] James has no *a priori* reason for holding that this cannot be true. He just thinks that Moore, and others like him, have made an error of diagnosis. What they mistake for mental acts of consciousness are bodily processes 'for the most part taking place within the head';[2] and what may have induced them to fall into this error is the false belief that unless we were aware of acts of consciousness, or were in some other way justified in postulating their existence, we should have no means of distinguishing between our own processes of cognition and the objects which they enable us to know. How James himself makes this distinction is a question to which we shall come later on.

The question of the self is a good deal more complex. Taking the term in a very wide sense, James asserts, in *The Principles of Psychology*[3] that the constituents of the self may be divided into two classes. The first class comprises what he calls the material self, the social self and the spiritual self. The second class contains only one constituent 'the pure Ego', or whatever does duty for it. The point of this division is that the members of the first class all play the role of accusatives in one's self-consciousness. They are all parts, as James puts it, of the 'me' that is known. The pure ego, on the other hand, or its functional equivalent, is the 'I' that does the knowing. As we shall see, however, this does not mean that James does not also think it capable of being known.

One might expect that 'the material self' would be just another name for the body. But James uses the term more widely. The body is indeed 'the innermost part of the material self: and certain parts of the body seem more intimately ours than the rest'[4] but the material self also includes our clothes, our families, our houses, any pieces of property that we especially value, any product of our labour in which we take especial pride: in short, anything

---

[1] *Philosophical Studies*, p. 25.   [2] *The Principles of Psychology*, I 300.
[3] Ibid., pp. 292 ff.   [4] Ibid., p. 292.

which we regard as an extension of our personalities. The social self arises out of our relations to one another. It is formed by our personal affections, our professional standards, our code of manners, our code of honour and so forth. James does not clearly distinguish here between the impression that one desires to make on others and the impression that one actually succeeds in making, but his examples show that he is mainly thinking of the influence of what one believes to be the opinion of others both on one's behaviour and on one's opinion of oneself. So he remarks that, practically speaking, a man 'has as many different social selves as there are distinct *groups* of persons about whose opinion he cares', and notes that these different social selves may vary widely. He also remarks that the opinions to which we are sensitive need not only be those of our fellow men. We are also apt to measure our conduct by the standards which we attribute to an ideal observer. This practice is most common among those who hold religious beliefs, but it is by no means confined to them.

What James calls the spiritual self is distinguished by him both from the material self and from the pure ego, or 'basic principle of personal Unity'. He explains that what he means by it is 'a man's inner or subjective being, his psychic faculties or dispositions, taken concretely' and he goes on to speak of these psychic dispositions as 'the most enduring and intimate part of the Self, that which we most verily seem to be'.[1] This appears to be in line with the Cartesian view that we are primarily spirits who are lodged in our bodies like a pilot in a ship: a view which has, I suppose, been very largely taken over by common-sense. It is, however, one that James is very far from sharing. Not only does he hold, as we shall see, that the distinction between mind and body, so far from being a distinction of substance, is merely a matter of the different ways in which we arrange common elements, but in so far as there is any primacy he allots it to the body. Introspection convinces him that in his own case at least, which he takes to be typical, 'the part of the innermost Self which is most vividly felt turns out to consist for the most part of a collection of cephalic movements, of "adjustments" which, for want of

[1] Ibid., p. 296.

attention and reflection, usually fail to be perceived and classed as what they are'.[1]

In *The Principles of Psychology*, James does indeed allow that this may not be quite all that there is to it. He speaks of there being 'an obscure feeling of something more' without attempting to decide 'whether it be of fainter physiological processes, or of nothing objective at all, but of subjectivity as such'.[2] But this concession is withdrawn in his later writings, where he also changes his view of what the central physical fact is. Thus, in the essay 'Does "Consciousness" Exist?' he declares himself to be 'as confident as I am of anything that, in myself, the stream of thinking (which I recognize emphatically as a phenomenon) is only a careless name for what, when scrutinized, reveals itself to consist chiefly of the stream of my breathing. The "I think" which Kant said must be able to accompany all my objects, is the "I breathe" which actually does accompany them. There are internal facts besides breathing (intercephalic muscular adjustments, etc.), and these increase the assets of "consciousness", so far as the latter is subject to immediate perception; but breath, which was ever the original of "spirit", breath moving outwards, between the glottis and the nostrils, is, I am persuaded, the essence out of which philosophers have constructed the entity known to them as consciousness. *The entity is fictitious, while thoughts in the concrete are fully real. But thoughts in the concrete are made of the same stuff as things are.*'[3]

This being his view, one might have expected James to try to analyse self-consciousness, in the sense in which it implies an awareness of one's own self-identity, in terms of the identity of the body which is the locus of these perceptions of oneself. Such a procedure would indeed be circular if it consisted first in identifying a certain body as one's own, and then in making it the bearer of one's self-identity: but I believe that there is at least one way in which the circle can be avoided. This would be to begin by identifying one's body merely as the 'central' body, along the lines that Peirce suggests,[4] and then defining as one's

---

[1] Ibid., p. 305.   [2] Ibid.

[3] *Essays in Radical Empiricism*, pp. 36–7.   [4] See above, p. 120.

own those and only those experiences which stood to this body in a certain unique relation.[1] I shall show later on how a theory of this kind might be developed, and shall argue that while this definition would be too restrictive as it stands, a version of it has to be incorporated in any adequate account of personal identity.

James pays surprisingly little attention to this problem in his later writings, but in his *Principles of Psychology* he takes a different line. The reason why he does so is that he accepts Kant's assumption that our experiences have first to be 'unified' before anything like a body can be constructed out of them. There has, in short, to be an 'I' at work on one's experiences before they can yield any 'me', and although in James's case, as we shall see, this 'I' is very much attenuated, it is still required in the form of 'a basic principle of personal unity' as a precondition of our ability to construct either the material or the spiritual self. James is indeed very scornful of Kant's solution of this problem, describing the 'transcendental Ego', the mysterious entity to which Kant assigns the work of synthesizing our experiences as 'simply nothing; as ineffectual and windy an abortion as Philosophy can show',[2] but he takes the problem seriously. His account of self-identity is developed with a view to solving it.

In accepting this legacy from Kant, he was, I think, mistaken. If one speaks of the construction of objects out of the flux of experience, it is indeed natural to ask who does the constructing; and then it would appear that whatever self is chosen for this role must stand outside the construction; it would be contradictory to suppose that it constructed itself. But the metaphor of construction is here misleading. What is in question is the derivation of concepts, not the fabrication of the things to which the concepts apply. To 'construct' either the material or the spiritual self is to do no more than pick out the relations within experiences which make it possible for the concept of a self of this kind to be satisfied, and these relations exist whether or not we direct our attention to them. Since the experiences which they relate occur at different times, they could not be discerned by

[1] See the title essay in my *The Concept of a Person.*
[2] *The Principles of Psychology,* I 365.

anyone who had no power of memory; but the exercise of memory which is required is not such as to presuppose self-consciousness. Neither does it presuppose that the experiences are already unified. If one wishes to talk in this fashion, I suppose it can be said that remembering one's past experiences is a way of uniting them with their successors, but I can see no reasons to assume that this union has to be effected before they can be remembered. There is, therefore, no necessity for distinguishing between the 'I' and the 'me'. However the concept of the self is to be analysed, there is no reason why the self which acquires the concept should not be identical with the self which satisfies it.

In fact, James comes to the same conclusion, since he accounts for self-consciousness in terms of the capacity of one experience to reflect upon another. In his view, the agent which unifies the stream of one's experiences and represents them as the experiences of one and the same self is 'the real, present onlooking, remembering, "judging thought", or identifying "section" of the stream'.[1] The principles on which it operates are not made very explicit; it is said to be partly a matter of felt continuity, and partly of the present thought's finding a 'warmth' in its remembered predecessors that it does not find in its conception of experiences which it does not claim to own. James likens the experiences of a single person to a herd of cattle all of which bear the same brand: but whereas in the case of the cattle, the brand signifies that they have a common owner who is not identical with any one of them, in the case of the experiences, the 'title' of ownership is passed around among themselves. A thought which 'appropriates' those which have gone before it is itself appropriated by a later one. In fact, it is only by a later thought that any thought is cognized. 'It may feel its own existence', says James, though he does not think that introspection shows this to be more than a possibility, 'but nothing can be known *about* it till it be dead and gone. Its appropriations are therefore less to *itself* than to the most intimately felt *part of its present Object, the body, and the central adjustments*, which accompany the act of thinking, in the head. *These are the real nucleus of our personal identity*, and it is their actual

[1] Ibid., p. 338.

existence, realized as a solid present fact, which makes us say "as sure *as I exist*, those past facts were part of myself". They are the kernel to which the *represented* parts of the Self are assimilated, accreted, and knit on; and even were Thought entirely unconscious of itself in the act of thinking, these "warm" parts of its present object would be a firm basis on which the consciousness of personal identity would rest.'[1]

In view of this passage, it may seem that I was wrong to reproach James with failing to consider that personal identity might be defined in terms of the identity of the body. But the fact is that although he very largely equates one's consciousness of oneself at any given moment with one's consciousness at that moment of certain bodily feelings, and although he goes so far as to say that a man 'identifies himself with this body because he loves *it*, and that he does not love it because he finds it to be identified with himself',[2] nevertheless he does not rely on the identity of the body in his account of the principles according to which experiences which occur at different times are assigned to the same self. Even though he comes very near to rejecting the distinction between the ego, which generates one's personal identity, and the material self, he still retains a vestige of it, in that the particular features of my past experiences which make it possible for my present thought to appropriate them to my body are held by him to exist independently of my 'construction' of my body as a persistent object. Even if I identify myself with my body, as James on the whole implies that we all do, I could not make this identification unless the experiences which furnished me with the materials for the construction of my body had been appropriated by my present identifying thought. It is, therefore, to this process of appropriation and not to the construction that he looks for the source of personal identity.

2. A Theory of Personal Identity

The result is that, with one important point of difference to which we shall come in a moment, James follows Hume in regarding

[1] Ibid., p. 341.   [2] Ibid., pp. 319–20.

the self as 'a bundle of perceptions'. Like Hume, he sees no
reason to assume the existence of what is variously called a pure
ego, or soul, or mental substance. He does not claim that he
can prove that no such thing exists, but only that it is superfluous
for any scientific, or indeed any other useful purpose: and pragmatically this is as good as to say that it does not exist. The main
reasons for postulating it have not been scientific. It has been
given the function of exercising free-will, or acting as a vehicle
of immortality, or supplying God with something to reward or
punish. But even those who accept the doctrine of free-will 'will
have to admit that spontaneity is just as possible, to say the least,
in a temporary spiritual agent like our "Thought" as in a permanent one like the supposed Soul'.[1] The 'simplicity and sub-
stantiality' of the soul may indeed appear to offer a more solid
guarantee of immortality than the fluidity and diversity of a mere
series of perceptions. But if we think about it we shall find that it
is hardly the sort of immortality that we want. 'The enjoyment
of the atom-like simplicity of their substance in *saecula saeculorum*
would not to most people seem a consummation devoutly to
be wished. The substance must give rise to a stream of consciousness continuous with the present stream, in order to arouse
our hope, but of this the mere persistence of the substance *per se*
offers no guarantee.'[2] Finally, if there were any candidates for
divine retribution, they would presumably be persons; but as
Locke already saw, what makes a man the same person over a
period of time is the unity of his consciousness, whether or not it
be supported by the same substance.

From a more scientific point of view, 'one great use of the
Soul has always been to account for, and at the same time to
guarantee, the closed individuality of each personal consciousness.
The thoughts of our soul must unite into one Self, it was supposed,
and must be eternally insulated from those of every other soul.'[3]
But James regards this as a doubtful advantage. On psychological
grounds, he prefers to allow room both for the fact that 'in some
individuals, at least, thoughts may split away from the others and
form separate selves'[4] and for the possibility of such things as

---

[1] Ibid., p. 346.　　[2] Ibid., p. 348.　　[3] Ibid., p. 349.　　[4] Ibid., pp. 349-50.

thought transference. What he has in mind, presumably, is that different selves may be associated with the same body and that even when not associated with the same body they may literally share a common experience. But the first point is hardly relevant, except as an argument against the one-to-one matching of souls and bodies, and the second may not be tenable: I shall in fact argue later on that the idea that one and the same experience could belong to different selves is inconsistent with James's own theory of personal identity. I think, therefore, that what he should have said here is not that selves are not insulated, but once again that we have neither any need nor any use for the soul in accounting for their insulation. The separateness of different selves is secured by the character of the relations which have to obtain between experiences for them to belong to the same self. The postulate that souls are separate is of no assistance to us, since we do not know how experiences are to be assigned to them.

Not only then is the existence of a mental substance not verifiable, but 'the substantialist view' is not required 'for expressing the actual subjective phenomena of consciousness as they appear'.[1] It explains nothing that cannot be equally well or better explained without it. 'The Spiritualists do not deduce any of the properties of the mental life from otherwise known properties of the soul. They simply find various characters ready-made in the mental life, and these they clap into the soul, saying "Lo! behold the source from whence they flow." The merely verbal character of this "explanation" is obvious. The Soul involved, far from making the phenomena more intelligible, can only be made intelligible itself by borrowing their form, – it must be represented, if at all, as a transcendent stream of consciousness duplicating the one we know.

'Altogether, the Soul is an outbirth of that sort of philosophizing whose great maxim, according to Dr. Hodgson, is: "Whatever you are *totally* ignorant of, assert to be the explanation of everything else".'[2]

---

[1] Ibid., p. 344.
[2] Ibid., p. 347. The Dr. Hodgson referred to is Shadworth Hodgson, founder of the Aristotelian Society.

So we are brought back to Hume's theory of the self which James accepts with an essential modification. The difficulty which Hume admitted that he was unable to resolve was that of finding a way to sort perceptions into their different bundles. He could not discover any relations between perceptions in virtue of which they could be collected into a unitary self. As he saw it, 'all our distinct perceptions are distinct existences, and the mind never perceives any real connection among distinct existences. Did our perceptions either inhere in something simple and individual, or did the mind perceive some real connection among them, there would be no difficulty in the case.'[1] Since he believes that neither of these conditions is satisfied, Hume is obliged to 'plead the privilege of a sceptic' and leave the problem unsolved.

James's comment on this is that Hume has created the difficulty for himself by misrepresenting the facts. It is true that our distinct perceptions are distinct existences, in the sense that they are logically independent of one another. But this does not mean that there cannot be any factual connections between them. That they are separate does not entail that they are disunited. What unites them, in James's view, is primarily the fact that 'within each personal consciousness, thought is sensibly continuous'. That is to say, 'the changes from one moment to another in the quality of consciousness are never absolutely abrupt' and 'where there is a time-gap the consciousness after it feels as if it belonged together with the consciousness before it, as another part of the same self'.[2] So the identifying thought appropriates whatever experiences it feels to be continuous with itself, as well as any other experiences, more remote from it in time, which are marked in its recollection with a similar warmth and intimacy.

Though James did not go any further than this in the way of defining personal identity, a definition can be constructed on the lines that he indicates. Besides the relations of sensible continuity and appropriation, to which he refers in the passage which I have just quoted, we shall need to draw on the relation of sensible comprescence which is taken by him to hold between contem-

---

[1] *Treatise of Human Nature*, Book 1. Appendix.
[2] *The Principles of Psychology*, 1 237.

porary experiences. It will also be useful, for the sake of economy, to introduce the concepts of indirect sensible continuity and indirect appropriation. The relation of indirect sensible continuity is that in which two experiences stand when they are not sensibly continuous with one another but are both members either of the same continuous chain, or of different chains which are linked at one or more points by a relation of sensible compresence. For instance, in a case where two experiences E_1 and E_4 are not sensibly continuous with one another, it may happen that E_1 is sensibly continuous with an experience E_2, that E_2 is sensibly continuous with another experience E_3, and that E_3 is sensibly continuous with E_4; or it may happen that E_1 is sensibly continuous with E_2, that E_2 is sensibly compresent with E_3 and that E_3 is sensibly continuous with E_4. In either case E_1 and E_4 stand to one another in the relation of indirect sensible continuity. It is clear that so long as the chain of continuity is unbroken, there can be any number or variety of intermediaries.

The concept of indirect appropriation is a little more complex. For convenience of exposition, I shall refer to any experience which is either sensibly compresent with a given experience E or sensibly continuous with it, whether directly or indirectly, as a 'neighbour' of E. Then in a case where an identifying thought T appropriates an experience E across a time-gap, in the way that James describes, it indirectly appropriates not only any experience which is a neighbour of E, in the sense defined, but also any experience which E or any of its neighbours appropriates, and any experience which *these* experiences or any of *their* neighbours appropriate and so on. Further, since T is itself an experience which can be appropriated in its turn, E also stands in a relation of indirect appropriation to all the experiences which directly or indirectly appropriate T or any of its neighbours, as well as to all the experiences which any neighbour of T directly or indirectly appropriates. It is to be noted that among all these experiences to which E stands in the relation of indirect appropriation, there may be others which T directly appropriates, and other identifying thoughts which directly appropriate E. It follows that the relations of direct and indirect appropriation, unlike the relations of direct and indirect continuity, are not mutually exclusive.

We are now able to give a precise formulation to what I am taking to be James's definition of personal identity. The suggestion is that two experiences belong to the same self if and only if they are related in one of the following ways: either they are sensibly compresent or sensibly continuous with one another, or there is a relation of indirect sensible continuity between them, or one of them, directly or indirectly, appropriates the other. When any two experiences stand to one another in any of these relations, let us say that they are 'confamiliar'. Then a self can be defined as any class of experiences which are confamiliar with each other.

For this definition not to be circular, it is necessary that the relation of being confamiliar, which has been equated with the relation of belonging to the same self, should not have any reference to the self included in its own definition. We have in fact defined it in a way which does not carry any overt reference to the self, but it might be objected that there was a covert reference in the use of such expressions as 'sensibly compresent' or 'sensibly continuous'. For to talk of these relations as being 'sensible' is, in this usage, to imply that they are the objects of some sort of awareness; and does not this already imply the existence of a subject who is aware of them?

The answer, on James's principles, is that it does not. A self is no more needed to apprehend these relations than it is to apprehend any sensory quality. In so far as a 'subject' is required to make the introspective judgement that two experiences were sensibly compresent or continuous, or to perform the function of appropriating earlier experiences, it is supplied by the identifying thought. James's whole theory depends, as we have seen, on his making members of the series of 'perceptions' themselves do the work for which other philosophers have had recourse to a separate agency: and I see no reason *a priori* why this procedure should not be legitimate.

But even if the theory escapes the charge of circularity, it may still be open to the objection that it leads to counter-intuitive results. Since its aim is to uncover the principles on which experiences are commonly assigned to different persons, it would not be acceptable if its effect were to ascribe to one person what would ordinarily be taken to be the experiences of another, or to make a division of ownership where common-sense makes none. The assumption that only the experiences of the same person can be sensibly compresent or continuous with one another is indeed in line with common-sense, but there are difficulties in the cases where the chain is broken by an interval of time. For instance, it is not ordinarily thought that even a total loss of memory makes one into a different person, but if such a loss of memory were immediately to follow a lapse of consciousness, the theory would leave us no alternative but to conclude that the experiences which came before and after it belonged to different selves.

This is not the only type of case in which the effect of adhering to our definition might be to deprive a person of experiences to which he would ordinarily be thought to be entitled. It seems, for example, quite reasonable to suppose that people have dreams which are completely self-contained, in the sense that they neither include any thoughts which appropriate previous experiences nor have any constituents which are appropriated by subsequent thoughts. It is even conceivable that this should be true of a series of waking experiences, if, for example, they occupied only a brief interval between two periods of sleep. But then it will follow from the definition that any such series of experiences constitutes a self of its own.

The definition may also err in the reverse direction: its effect may be to credit a person with experiences to which he has no legitimate claim. For while it would, indeed, make it contradictory to suppose that my present thought could appropriate any other experiences than my own, there is no contradiction in supposing that I sometimes fall into the error of 'reviving' experiences which either did not occur at all or occurred in situations at which I was not physically present. We can deal with the first of these possibilities by stipulating that our definition of the relation of belonging to the same self is to be understood as applying only to experiences which actually occur, but the second presents more difficulty. We shall see later on that, under certain very exceptional conditions, it may be legitimate to credit a person with experiences which were attached to a different body from that which he currently occupies, but in the normal way this is not admissible. If I appropriate an experience which was attached to a different body from the one to which my present experiences belong, it will normally follow that I am appropriating the experiences of another person. It may be argued that this does not have to entail that the experience cannot also have been my own, but then it must be remembered that in appropriating this experience I may be indirectly appropriating a great many other experiences with which it is confamiliar. The result would, therefore, be an intolerable intermingling of the constituents of what would ordinarily be regarded as separate selves.[1]

This should be enough to show that our proposed definition of personal identity will not do as it stands. The most obvious way to try to repair its deficiences would be to supplement it with the criterion of bodily continuity. In certain cases, at least, we could make it a necessary, or even a sufficient condition for two experiences to be the experiences of the same person that they are attached to the same body. But while the idea of there being a unique attachment between a particular body and a particular series of experiences is commonly accepted without question, it is not at all easy to say exactly what the nature of this attachment is. Let us for the moment set aside the question whether the attachment can be taken to be universal, that is, whether there could be series of experiences which were confamiliar with one another without being attached to any body, and confine our attention to the cases in which the attachment exists. Then one way in which one might attempt to analyse it would be to start with the assumption that every experience of this class was sensibly compresent with a bodily sensation. The next step would be to characterize the body to which a given experience was attached as that which was the locus of the bodily sensation with which the experience was sensibly compresent: the problem of identifying this body would then be merely part of the general

[1] See below, p. 282.

problem of synthesizing kinaesthetic with visual and tactual data. The pairing of different bodies with the different series of experiences which, on James's view, constitute different selves would depend upon the fact that, generally speaking, experiences which satisfy the conditions of belonging to the same self are accompanied by bodily sensations which are assignable to the same body. I shall deal later on with the possible exceptions to this rule.

Before we proceed further, it is advisable to note the objection that we are not entitled to regard it as a matter of logical necessity that one's kinaesthetic sensations are all located in one's own body. It will be argued that it is at least conceivable that a person should locate, say, a sensation of physical pain in a body which is other than his own. The point is debatable but I think that we can afford to concede it, so long as we are permitted to assume that experiences of this sort occur very rarely, if they ever occur at all, and that whenever they do occur they are accompanied by bodily sensations which are normally located. The result would then be that we should have to decide which of the two bodies in question was the one to which these experiences, and any experiences that were sensibly compresent with them, were to be assigned, and the decision would go in favour of whichever body claimed the attachment of the great majority of the other experiences with which they were confamiliar. But *ex hypothesi* this would be the body which was the locus of those sensations that were, as I put it, normally located.

A much graver difficulty is that the basic assumption that every experience which is attached to a body at all is sensibly compresent with a bodily sensation is seriously open to question. It is certainly not a necessary truth, and it is doubtful if it is even a true empirical generalization. This is not an easy matter to settle, because it is not clear what the criteria are for deciding whether or not a sensation exists. It would seem that they must be introspective, but in that event the answer will remain uncertain in the cases where no process of introspection is actually carried out. It can at least be said that if all our experiences are accompanied by bodily sensations, these sensations quite often fail to obtrude themselves upon our notice, but the reason for this, it may be argued, is just that they provide a familiar, relatively constant background to other more interesting items of experience. In the face of arguments of this kind, it is hard to produce a decisive counter-example, but there is evidence that in certain trance-like states the subject loses all awareness of his body, and there seems to be no good reason why, instead of merely saying in such cases that the subject's attention is withdrawn from his bodily sensations, we should not say that he is not at these moments having any bodily sensations at all. Dreams are another possible source of counter-examples. There is indeed evidence that bodily sensations do occur while one is dreaming, in that they are some-times causally responsible for certain features of the dream, but it would be very hard to prove that every dream-experience is sensibly compresent with a bodily sensation. As I said, these examples may not be decisive, but I think that they throw enough doubt upon the general principle to make it unsafe for us to allow the assignment of experiences to bodies to depend exclusively upon it.

It is, however, possible that a weaker assumption will serve our purpose. Even if it is not true that all our experiences are sensibly compresent with bodily sensations, it can fairly be assumed that the greater number of them are. Consequently, if an experience E is one of the exceptions, it is not likely that the same will apply to all the experiences which are related to E by sensible continuity. It is also unlikely that among the experiences which are accom-panied by bodily sensations there will not be at least one that is connected with E by some relation of direct or indirect appropria-tion. Accordingly in taking it as a general rule that an experience E is attached to a living body M if and only if E is contemporary with some state of M, and there is some bodily sensation S which is assignable to M, and either E is sensibly compresent with S or there is some experience E' which is sensibly compresent with S and to which E stands, directly or indirectly, in a relation of sensibly continuity or appropriation, we can hardly fail to cover the great majority of instances.

In fact, apart from the possibility that some bodily sensations are abnormally located, for which, as we have seen, it would not be difficult to make special provision, and apart also from certain possible cases of bodily transference, with which we shall presently deal, the only type of instance, so far as I can see, which will not be covered is that in which the experience is a member of a self-contained group, no member of which is sensibly compresent with a bodily sensation. I do not know that such experiences ever in fact occur, but if we admit them to be possible, as I think we must, we have to be able to accommodate them; and it is not at all easy to see how this can be done. Of course there is no great problem if it can be assumed that at least one member of every self-contained group achieves some outward expression: for we can then make it a further criterion of the attachment of an experience to a particular body that some states of that body constitute the outward expression either of the experience itself or of one of its neighbours; the difficulty then will only be to give an adequate account of the relation between an experience and its bodily expression. I am, however, not convinced that this is an assumption which we are justified in making. In its favour one might invoke Wittgenstein's principle that an inner process stands in need of outward criteria, but if this principle is to have any plausibility at all, it must be taken as implying, not the obvious falsehood that it is necessary for every experience to be overtly manifested, but only that it is a necessary mark of any experience of which we can significantly speak that some form of outward expression should be characteristic of experiences of its kind. But this is a condition which the members of our self-contained group of experiences can be supposed to satisfy, without becoming tractable. It is of no advantage to say that experiences of their kind are outwardly manifested in some characteristic way, so long as they themselves are not.

If this resource fails us, the only other way that I can see in which it might be possible to incorporate such experiences in our general scheme would be to construe their bodily attachment as a relation of unique causal dependence upon the bodies to which we should thereby assign them. If this were feasible, it would give us an answer which could supersede the theory on which we have been working: for there is no reason why a causal analysis should apply to this particular class of experiences, unless it held good universally. But while I was once inclined to think that this was the correct solution,[1] it now seems to me very doubtful whether it can be. It is not only that it is very hard to find a form of causal relation that looks at all plausible in this role. There is also the objection of principle that if causality is to be analysed, as I believe it should be, in terms of uniform spatio-temporal relations, then since it is conceivable that two different persons should at the same moment be having qualitatively identical experiences, and since in the case of experiences and their physical causes it is only temporal relations that have to be considered, it will not be possible to pair these experiences with their respective causes unless their attachment to different bodies has already been established.[2] This is not to deny that our experiences are causally dependent upon our bodily states, but rather to suggest that the attachment of experiences to bodies is logically not the outcome of this causal dependence, but its precondition.

Accordingly, I believe that the attempt to analyse this attachment in terms of bodily sensations remains the most promising, in spite of the weakness which I have not been able to eradicate. In any event, the attachment is in fact exemplified, however it is to be analysed, and this entitles us, as I have said, to try to make use of the criterion of bodily continuity to repair the shortcomings of the process of appropriation. Thus, if we were to make it a sufficient condition for two experiences to belong to the same self that they were attached to the same body, we should be able to unite the experiences which would otherwise be sundered by a total loss of memory, and also to recapture an isolated series of experiences by assigning them to the self which owned the body to which they were attached. If we make it a necessary condition, we should acquire an effective means of dealing with the cases where one appropriates experiences which would ordinarily be ascribed to another person; for it is primarily the fact that they are attached to another body that makes

[1] See the title essay in my *The Concept of a Person.*
[2] I am indebted for this argument to Mr J. A. Foster.

their appropriation suspect. Indeed, it might be argued that provided that we were able to give a satisfactory account of the attachment of experiences to bodies which did not itself depend upon the notion of personal identity, our best course would be the one which I previously said that one might have expected James to follow; straightforwardly to define personal identity in terms of bodily continuity, and so avoid having to adopt any more of the other theory than is required to protect this definition for circularity.

Such a course would, however, be open to certain objections. In the first place it is at least not obvious that we are entitled to assume that every experience is attached to a body. We have seen that there is reason to doubt whether every experience is sensibly compresent with a bodily sensation, and even the weaker assumption that every experience is at least confamiliar with a bodily sensation, though it may in fact be true, is surely not necessary. Of course it may be argued that what is at fault here is our attempt to analyse the attachment of experience to bodies in terms of their compresence with bodily sensations; even so, it is difficult to see how any alternative analysis, which was at all conformable to James's principles, could have the effect of making this attachment a logical necessity. We could indeed exclude the possibility of there being disembodied selves, simply by writing the requirement of bodily attachment into our definition of the self; but this manœuvre would serve no useful purpose. It would still leave it open for there to be any number of series of confamiliar experiences which failed to be attached to any bodies, either before or after a certain point or throughout the whole of their length: the only difference would be that to the extent that they were not attached to any bodies we should not be permitted to speak of them as selves. But the interesting question is not what these things should be called, if they did exist, but whether we are bound to admit that their existence is at any rate logically possible.

Perhaps we ought to admit it. Certainly a great many people have seen no difficulty in the idea that a self may continue to exist in detachment from any body, however little reason there may be to believe that this ever in fact occurs. There would, I think, be rather more reluctance to accept the idea that part of a self's existence might precede its attachment to a body, or that it might never be attached to a body at any period at all, though so far as I can see, these three variations on the theme of disembodied existence are logically on a level; if we allow any one of them to be a possibility, we have to allow them all. The main argument against allowing any of them is that the existence of such 'persons' would not be detectable except by themselves. This rests on the assumption, which may itself be questioned, that for an empirical proposition to be significant it is necessary that it be publicly testable. When translated into James's terms, this means that every empirical proposition must 'work' in some degree for everyone if it works at all; more precisely, it must be capable of being supported by experiences which are neutral, in the sense that their capacity to support the proposition does not depend upon their having this or that particular owner. I am not saying that this is a principle which James either would or should have accepted in this form.

I think, however, that much the same effect can be obtained from a different principle which it seems clear that James's radical empiricism does require if its programme is to be carried through successfully. The principle is that everything which is constructed out of the elements of the system must find its place in one and the same objective spatio-temporal order. Now selves are constructs and though it would be begging the present question to demand that every self should occupy a set of positions in space, it must be demanded that every self should at least occupy a set of positions in time. But, as we shall see when we return to James's construction of the physical world, the only way in which it is possible to arrive at an objective temporal order is by determining the times of physical events by means of a correlation of experiences which are obtained from different points of view, and then dating other experiences through their temporal relation to these physical events. Since the point of view of an observer depends upon his position in space, the correlation relies upon the fact that in general experiences are attached to bodies. It does not follow that this has to be true of every series of experiences which constitute a self, but since it is required that the construction be capable of being carried out by anyone, it does follow that no such self can figure in it unless there is some way, not confined to itself, of determining how its experiences are temporally related to the physical events which set the temporal standard. But this means that some at least of these experiences must be physically manifested.

Even so, the argument against the possibility of disembodied selves is not yet conclusive. We require the further assumption that it is a logically necessary condition for experiences to be physically manifested that they be attached to a body. But while I do not doubt that this is necessary in fact, I am not sure that it is logically necessary. It seems to me that the objections to believing in the existence of such things as poltergeists, or to supposing that oral or written communications can emanate from invisible and intangible 'spirits', are scientific rather than logical. I am inclined to think, therefore, that while the necessity for every self to give physical proof of its existence attenuates the concept of a disembodied self, it does not make it logically impossible that it should have any application.

If I am right on this point, we cannot make bodily continuity a necessary condition of personal identity; but of course it is still open to us to make it a sufficient condition. The argument against doing so is that we should then have debarred ourselves from describing even the most extreme cases of multiple personality as cases in which the same body is occupied, simultaneously or successively, by different persons. This would perhaps be no great loss. It would certainly not be incorrect to describe any case of this kind as one in which a single person displayed very pronounced changes of character, or even possessed a divided consciousness. Even so, it might be preferable to allow ourselves the other option, especially in view of the possibility that the different personalities, besides displaying differences of character, might consist in mutually isolated sets of experiences each of which was internally confamiliar.

There is a similar objection to making bodily continuity a

necessary condition of personal identity, even if I am mistaken in thinking that it is logically possible for there to be disembodied selves. The objection is that even though there may never yet have been any actual instances which we should want to describe by saying that the same person occupied numerically different bodies at different times, there are no compelling reasons for refusing to admit this as a logical possibility. The fairy tales, or works of fiction, in which a character is translated into another body do not appear to be self-contradictory. And while there may be no empirical grounds for believing in the possibility of re-incarnation, it is at least doubtful if we should be justified in excluding it *a priori*.

This is again a matter of policy. If anyone has strong objections to the idea that a person's existence can be physically discontinuous, then, however strange the phenomena, he can always find some other way of describing them. He can deal with these out-of-the-way cases, whether they be real or imaginary, by saying not that one and the same person reappears in a different body, but that one person has somehow acquired the character traits and the ostensible memories of another. On the other hand, if we are prepared, as I think we should be, to allow the requirement of bodily continuity to be overriden in certain exceptional instances of this sort, we have to lay down the conditions under which this is to be permitted.

For this purpose, I think that we need to introduce a distinction between stronger and weaker forms of appropriation. In any case in which an experience E is appropriated by an identifying thought T, the experiences with which E is confamiliar fall into two groups: those with which it becomes confamiliar only through its appropriation by T, and those with which it is confamiliar independently of this appropriation. In the same way, the class of experiences with which T is confamiliar is divisible into those with which it is independently confamiliar and those with which it becomes confamiliar only through appropriating E. Now let C be the set of experiences with which E is confamiliar independently of its appropriation by T, and let D be the set of experiences with which T is confamiliar independently of appropriating E. Since experiences are confamiliar with themselves E itself will be a member of C and T of D. Then the strength with which T appropriates E may be measured by the number of members of C which are directly appropriated by members of D. This allows the appropriation to be strong even if E is not attached to the same body as T or as most of the other experiences which the members of D directly appropriate. There is, however, another factor which comes into play here. If E is attached to a body B_1 and most of the other experiences which the members of D appropriate are attached to a different body B_2, the appropriation of E will be weakened if among these other experiences there is an experience E' which is contemporary with E. How much it will be weakened will depend upon the strength with which E' is appropriated. The reason for making this proviso is that I am not supposing it to be possible that the same person should occupy different bodies at the same time.

It can now be said that the only cases in which it could be legitimate to say that a person had been translated from one body to another would be cases in which the appropriation of experiences which occurred before the transfer by experiences which occurred after it was very strong. This would apply even if there were sensible continuity at the point of transfer: unless the experiences which were attached to the previous body continued to be strongly appropriated, we should have to say not that the person had suffered translation into another body, together with a loss of memory, but that he had ceased to exist. In the cases, to which we referred earlier, where one appropriates experiences which one is mistaken in supposing to have been one's own, the appropriation is bound to be weak. Not only is it false *ex hypothesi* that one directly appropriates many experiences which are confamiliar with them, but among their contemporaries there are likely to be experiences, belonging to a different body, which one appropriates more strongly. This is in contrast with a case like that of Anstey's *Vice Versa* where the author imagines an exchange of bodies between a father and his schoolboy son. For here it has to be assumed that, after the exchange, the identifying thoughts which are attached to either body directly appropriate a considerable number of the experiences which previously were attached to the other body, and that they directly appropriate very few, if any, of the experiences which were previously attached to the body which their owner currently occupies. Without this assumption, the story does not make sense.

The case of reincarnation is even more complex. Not only does it introduce a large measure of temporal as well as bodily discontinuity, but the bodily discontinuity goes much further, since the idea is that the same person may survive a series of physical incarnations. In this case, it will not be sufficient, though clearly necessary, that the experiences of any previous 'life' be very strongly appropriated, even if it can also be shown that a continuity of character is displayed in the successive lives. At least two negative conditions must also be satisfied. The claimant to a previous life must not appropriate two or more sets of experiences which were contemporaneously attached to different bodies, and the same set of experiences must not be appropriated by two or more contemporary claimants. Though neither of these occurrences is a logical impossibility, it would strain the concept of a person altogether too far to allow two persons to merge into one in a subsequent incarnation, or one person subsequently to divide into two. It may be held that we are straining it too far already in admitting the idea of the same person's occupying different bodies at different times; but, as I said before, I do not regard the idea as one that we are bound to rule out *a priori*. I have, therefore, tried to specify the conditions under which, in my view, this way of speaking would be legitimate, without, however, implying that even if they were satisfied it would be the only way or necessarily the best way of describing the facts.

The same applies to the cases where one might wish to say that two or more different selves were simultaneously in possession of the same body. The facts which could give us a motive for speaking in this way would not be easy to establish; it would not be easy to prove that the different series of experiences were both internally confamiliar and mutually isolated: but if it were accepted that these were the facts, then again this would be one way, though not the only possible way, of describing them. The motive for adopting it would be strengthened if the 'two selves' also displayed marked differences of character, but I think that it can be regarded as legitimate, even if this further condition is not satisfied.

The admission of these abnormal possibilities does make it more difficult to deal with the case of the 'self-contained' group of experiences, which came up as one of the counter-examples to our original definition of personal identity. It will no longer be enough to say that these experiences are to be assigned to whatever self owns the other experiences which are attached to the same body as they are, since we are now allowing that these other experiences may themselves belong to different owners. In the case where the different selves occupy the body successively, the easiest course would be to assign the self-contained group of experiences to whichever one was in possession of the body at the times which immediately preceded and succeeded their occurrence. If, under this condition, the group occurs at the very beginning of the whole sequence of experiences which are attached to the body, it may be assigned to the self which owns its immediate successors: if it occurs at the very end, it may be assigned to the self which owns its immediate predecessors. In the case where it occurs at a juncture between two selves, or in the case where the different selves occupy the body simultaneously, the only reason that there could be for assigning the group to one self rather than another would have to lie in the character of its members. In default of any such reason, there would be no strong objection, in such very exceptional instances, to allowing them to constitute a separate self.

So far, our account of personal identity, though placing a stronger emphasis on the criterion of bodily continuity, adheres fairly closely to the lines which James laid down. There is, however, one point on which I think that we should be wrong to try to follow him. As we have seen, he did not think it necessary that the bundles of perceptions which constituted different selves should be mutually exclusive; he was prepared to allow for the possibility that one and the same experience should be a constituent of more than one self. He did give empirical reasons for concluding that this was never in fact true of any percepts,[1] though in at least one of his attempts to explain how two minds can know the same physical object he inconsistently treats it as a matter of their appropriating the same past experience.[2] And he appears in any case to have held that there were instances in which the thoughts of different persons were literally shared. But, as I have said, for him to allow this possibility is not consistent with his own theory of personal identity, at least in the form in which we have restated it. The reason why it is not is that the theory does not make it possible for divergent series to meet and then diverge again. The relations between experiences which make them members of the same series have been so defined that if an experience E belongs to a given series, so does every other experience with which E is confamiliar. But this means that if an experience is already a member of one such series, it cannot join a second series without bringing all the other members of the first series with it. It is, therefore, contradictory to suppose that two different selves could have any experience of whatever sort in common; for if they did have any experience in common, they would merge into one.

We might try to emend our definitions so as to avoid this consequence; but the emandations would have to be so radical that it is doubtful whether the theory could survive them. Neither is there any necessity for them. In any instances in which James might have wished to say that two different persons were having one and the same experience, we can be content to say that they are having experiences which are qualitatively identical but numerically distinct. There is no danger of our failing to do justice to the facts, since the only relevant facts that there can be on either view, apart from the quality of the experiences, are the ways in which they are related to other experiences; and these we can perfectly well describe.

In itself, this question of the sense in which different people may be said to have the same experience may not be very important, but it raises a more general problem which is of fundamental importance, not only to James's theory of personal identity but

[1] See above, p. 228.   [2] *Essays in Radical Empiricism*, pp. 130–3.

to the whole of his radical empiricism. The problem is how any experience is to be individuated. In the end experiences themselves will have to be taken up into the theory which they found and assigned their place in an objective order of time. They will then be individuated, as indeed they commonly are, by reference to the persons who have them and the times at which they occur. But this cannot be the basic way of individuating them, if persons themselves are to be defined in terms of relations between experiences; we can individuate experiences by reference to persons only if some other method of individuating them is presupposed. For a similar reason, it is not open to James to say that experiences are basically individuated through their physical manifestations. But how then can we individuate them? The only possible answers are that they are to be individuated through being identified demonstratively, or that they are identified in the first instance only as experiences of such and such a kind, and then individuated by the relations in which they respectively stand to one another.

There are two objections to the view that experiences are to be identified demonstratively. In the first place it can be argued that it tacitly implies a reference to persons. The use of a demonstrative may serve to distinguish one experience from another, so long as it is already decided whose experiences they are: but until this is decided it can hardly be said that the experiences have been identified. In short, we have to know who is speaking before the use of the demonstrative can be interpreted. To this it may be answered that one is bound to start with what are in fact one's own experiences, in which case the difficulty does not arise. It is not as if the experiences had first to be identified as one's own, before one could use a demonstrative to distinguish them. On the contrary, we have already seen that in order to be able to discriminate between one's own experiences, it is not necessary that one should even have arrived at the concept of oneself.

But this brings the second objection into play. It is, indeed, true that if we actually 'construct' the world in anything like the way that James describes, the only materials on which each of us can draw are his own experiences. But this does not mean that one is bound, or even entitled, to single out one's own experiences in giving a general account of the way in which experiences are individuated. Admittedly, an account can be given on this basis. Having identified some experience demonstratively, I can individuate all the rest of my experiences, that is to say, all the experiences which are confamiliar with this experience, by their temporal relations to it: in the case where more than one experience stands in the same temporal relation to it, they can be distinguished by their qualities. This makes it possible to identify my own body as the body to which these experiences are attached. Then, since I am able, on the basis of my own experiences, to construct a spatio-temporal system in which every other person occupies a unique position relatively to myself, I can individuate all the experiences which are not my own by reference to their respective owners, their qualities and the times at which they occur. There is no doubt that this procedure secures uniqueness of reference. What is against it, at least for our present purpose, is its egocentricity. Not only are all identifications made to include a reference to oneself, but the use of the demonstrative ties them to the present moment and to the existence of some particular experience which the demonstrative selects. But surely what is meant to be a general account of the individuation of experiences should not have to depend in this essential way upon the contingency of one's own existence, let alone the existence of some particular experience that one happens to be having.

For this reason, I think that the other method is to be preferred. It consists, as I have said, in subordinating numerical to qualitative identity. Experiences of the same kind are distinguished from one another by the differences in the kinds of experiences to which they are related. The relations in question will normally be those of sensible compresence and continuity. In the rare cases where two experiences of the same kind are not differentiated by the qualities of any of their neighbours, it will be necessary to go further afield and bring in relations of appropriation. In this way we can individuate any experience that is actually likely to occur. There are, however, two remote possibilities for which we shall not have provided. One is the case in which two or more self-contained groups of experiences, occurring either in different biographies or at different periods in the same biography, are qualitatively identical; and the other, which is even more fanciful, is that in which the qualitative identity extends over the complete biographies of different persons. In the event that these duplicate sets of experiences either constituted or formed part of different biographies, the only ground that we could have for distinguishing them would be that they were attached to different bodies: in the event of their being attached to the same body, they would be distinguishable only if they occurred at different times. It follows that they could be individuated only at a theoretical level where we were in a position to speak of bodies, as physical objects, and of an objective time-order. There is, however, no objection to this, so long as we are able, as in fact we are, to construct the necessary theory on the basis of experiences which are individuated, not in terms of the theory, but only in terms of their respective qualities and of the qualities of the experiences with which they are confamiliar.

There is another advantage to this procedure, apart from its supplying us with a neutral rather than an egocentric basis from which to operate. One of the standard objections to Hume's account of personal identity is that since the relations between experiences in virtue of which they constitute a self are admitted to be contingent, it is conceivable that they should not obtain: and from this we can derive what many people take to be the absurd conclusion that there could be experiences which were not the experiences of anyone. This objection also holds against James's version of the theory, since it remains possible that there should be experiences which exist in this isolation from any others, even if he is right in thinking that none of them ever are so isolated in fact. It is true that such experiences could not enter into our picture of the world unless they could be assigned a position in an objective time-order, but some doubt may be felt whether this entirely disposes of the difficulty. For one thing, I suppose that it is conceivable that they should be physically manifested, and for another it might be argued that since these experiences would not be constructs, this condition would not apply to them. I think that this argument can be met on the ground that it is only with respect to constructs that the question of what there is arises, but the point is doubtful and I do not need to rely on it here. The method which we have chosen to individuate experiences will do the work more simply.

This is easily shown. The reason why there cannot be unowned experiences is that it is only through being confamiliar with other experiences that any experience acquires a numerical identity. The relations in question are still contingent: it is not necessary that any experience should be related in the ways it is to just those experiences with which it is in fact confamiliar. It is, however, necessary that it be confamiliar with some experiences if it is to be particularized; and it is only as a particular that it has any title to existence. This is in line with Peirce's view that existence comes under the heading of Secondness, the category of relation.

Though I do not know that James would have approved of every step that we have taken in developing our theory of personal identity, I believe that it is the best that can be done along the lines that he sketched out. In the end, we have found it necessary to distinguish seven different types of case in which two experiences may legitimately be said to belong to the same self. The standard type is that in which the experiences are confamiliar and attached to the same body, and no set of confamiliar experiences of which they are not members is attached to that body. In the second type of case, which takes account of the possibility of there being self-contained groups of experiences within a biography, the experiences are members of a set of experiences all of which are attached to the same body but not all of which are confamiliar: it is then necessary that the set be mainly composed of experiences which but for the existence of one or more minority groups within it would constitute a self of the standard type; that the minority groups, though internally confamiliar, should in each instance be too thin to constitute a separate self; and that whenever two members of the set are not confamiliar at least one of them should belong to such a minority group. In the third type of case, which is similar to the second, a set of experiences which are attached to the same body is sundered, at one or more places, by a permanent loss of memory following a lapse of consciousness. The main difference between this and the second type is that the unity of the self is maintained, not because any one of the sundered parts is too thin to constitute a separate self, but because of the continuity of character which is displayed throughout.

If the continuity of character is conspicuously broken, a case of this sort may turn into one of the fourth type, which is abnormal in that it allows more than one self to be attached to the same body, either simultaneously or successively. It is necessary in all cases of this type that the sets of confamiliar experiences, which constitute the different selves, should be thoroughly isolated from each other, in the sense that no experience is appropriated by any identifying thought which is attached to the same body but not a member of the same set: in the case where the different selves occupy the body successively, discontinuity of character is also necessary. The abnormality in the fifth type of case also consists in its violation of one of the standard physical conditions. In this instance, the experiences are all confamiliar but not all attached to the same body. Cases of this kind are admitted only if the appropriation of experiences which are attached to one body by identifying thoughts which are attached to another is very strong and if it is backed by some continuity of character. There also have to be safeguards, which I have listed, to ensure that we do not allow it to be possible for a single self to occupy different bodies at the same time.

The admission of these abnormal cases makes it necessary to provide for a sixth type, which is that in which a self-contained group of experiences, which would normally be too thin to constitute a separate self, is attached to a body which is not uniquely owned. Under certain conditions, which I have set out,[1] the group may be assigned to the same self as one of the other sets of experiences which are attached to the body in question. If these conditions are not satisfied, and there is nothing in the character of the members of the group to favour their assignment

[1] See above, p. 281.

to one owner rather than another, they may be regarded as forming a separate self.

Finally, we have allowed the doubtful possibility of there being sets of confamiliar experiences not all or even none of which are attached to a body. For such selves to exist, it would, however, be necessary that some of the experiences which occurred in the state of bodily detachment should be physically manifested, and that they should provide enough evidence about the others to enable the self, throughout its history, to be located in an objective time-order.

So much for the exposition of the theory. How far is it viable? There is a good deal to be said in its favour, and would be still more if we had managed to give a wholly satisfactory account of the relation of bodily attachment. It is not circular: it appears to deal with every possible eventuality; and so far as I can see it does not now lead to any counter-intuitive results. Its chief weakness, to my mind, is that the concept of appropriation, on which it relies very heavily, is not sufficiently precise. It is not enough merely to refer to the 'warmth and intimacy' which the identifying thought finds in the experiences which it appropriates. A better characterization of the concept, which James also gives, is that the identifying thought looks upon these experiences as if they were related to itself by sensible continuity. But, apart from the difficulty of the 'as if', it is still not sufficiently clear how one experience can reflect upon another. We need a fuller analysis of the ways in which it is possible for any experience to refer beyond itself.

3. Percepts and Concepts

To ask how an experience can refer beyond itself is to ask how it can come to have a meaning. A point on which James repeatedly insists is that the data with which we are presented are not intrinsically meaningful. 'The perceptual flux as such', he says, 'means nothing, and is but what it immediately is.'[1] It acquires a meaning only when we subject it to interpretation, and for this we have to

[1] *Some Problems of Philosophy*, p. 49.

bring it under concepts. James remarks that here his view is just the opposite of Kant's: whereas Kant thinks of the 'aboriginal sensible flux'[1] as a discontinuous manifold which needs to be synthesized by the understanding, James looks upon it rather as a coagulated mass from which the understanding carves its objects out. Even so, we have seen that he follows Kant in assuming that 'a basic principle' is needed for unifying our experiences, and he agrees with him also on the fundamental point that if concepts without percepts are blind, percepts without concepts are empty.

But what are concepts and how deep does their difference from percepts go? James's answers to these questions are not entirely consistent. Sometimes he thinks of concepts as signs, as when he says that the concept 'man' is at once 'the word itself; a vague picture of the human form . . . an instrument for symbolizing certain objects from which we may expect human treatment when occasion arrives'.[2] More often he identifies the concept with the meaning of a sign, and speaks of it therefore as a special kind of object. The one point to which he consistently adheres is that concepts are extricated from percepts and accountable to them. This leads him to say, at one moment, that concepts and percepts 'are made of the same kind of stuff, and melt into each other when we handle them together. How could it be otherwise', he characteristically continues, 'when the concepts are like evaporations out of the bosom of perception, into which they condense again whenever practical service summons them?'[3] On the other hand, when he is thinking of concepts primarily as objects, he tends to distinguish them from percepts much more sharply. They are said to be discrete, whereas percepts are continuous: they enjoy an 'eternal' kind of being, which is real in its own way, but inferior to the temporal reality which belongs to percepts. It is this line of thought that drives James into the irrationalism which comes out most strongly in the course of lectures which were published under the title of *A Pluralistic Universe*, but also makes a more guarded appearance in *Some Problems of Philosophy*; the idea being, as I have said, that because reason has to operate with concepts, which are by their very nature static,

[1] Ibid., p. 51 fn.   [2] Ibid., p. 58.   [3] Ibid., p. 107.

it cannot give a wholly adequate account of the dynamic world of experience, which is the fundamental reality. James, therefore, sees himself as reversing the position of Plato who took the static world of concepts to be primordial. At the same time he declares himself to be an adherent of 'the platonic doctrine that concepts are singulars, that concept-stuff is inalterable, and that physical realities are constituted by the various concept-stuffs of which they "partake" '.[1]

This so-called Platonic doctrine, to which James gives the name of logical realism, does not in fact amount to very much. It is mainly a denial of that form of nominalism which consists in maintaining that things to which the same predicate is applied have nothing in common except that we attach the same name to them. Against this James argues that this position is anyhow incoherent, since it requires at least that instances of the use of the same name do have something in common: and further, that it is an undeniable fact that there are recurrent features in the course of our experience. To my mind, the whole dispute is rather idle. The nominalists are right to the extent that the regularities which we mark with our concepts are in a certain sense constituted by them; they are seen as regularities because we have chosen to pick them out. On the other hand, it is also a fact that the regularities are there; it is due to the character of our experiences that such and such concepts apply to them. It is not as though individuals were presented to us independently of their qualities. On the contrary, whether or not we enlist the help of demonstratives, it is only through their qualities that they can be individuated. Unless they had recognizable, which is to say repeatable, properties there would be nothing to which the demonstratives could serve to call attention.

I do not know what James means in this context by concept-stuff, or how far, if at all, he wishes here to distinguish it from the stuff of percepts. I do not suppose, however, that he is being so far inconsistent as to depart from his general view that experience is the unique stuff of which everything is made. Possibly he is thinking, in Kantian fashion, of experience as being the fusion of

[1] Ibid., p. 106.

two elements, the raw material of percepts and the intellectual leavening of concepts, and of the two elements as being inextricably mixed. When he speaks of physical realities as being constituted by the various concept-stuffs of which they partake, I think that, in spite of the Platonic phraseology, he in fact means no more than that physical realities are constructed out of percepts, and that what the construction puts together is a set of sensory qualities. This is in line with his saying that the pragmatic meaning of 'substance' is that 'a definite group of sensations will recur'.[1]

There is, indeed, no harm in speaking of concepts as objects, if all that is implied is that one can refer to what is normally signified by a given sign, or by a given series of signs, in abstraction from any particular occasion of their use. But if we do speak of concepts in this way, we must not forget that a sign has only the meaning that it is given. Whatever is said about concepts as objects requires to be cashed in terms of their actual occurrence in our processes of thought; and, as James himself puts it, 'conception as an *act* is part of the flux of feeling'.[2] Moreover, if any act of this kind is to refer beyond itself, it cannot simply consist in the evocation of an abstract object, even if it could be assumed that such objects exist. For if the abstract object is not a symbol, then, whether it enters into or stands apart from the flux of feeling, it cannot endow the act which evokes it with any symbolic force; on the other hand, if it is a symbol, the mere mention of it tells us nothing to the purpose. We learn that a thought becomes symbolic through somehow employing an abstract object as a symbol. But what is implied by the use of a symbol is just the question at issue; and merely to entitle the symbol an abstract object is no answer to it at all.

In fact, there is only one answer to this question that James can consistently give. Since he holds that the only way in which an experience can be self-transcendent is by modifying the course of future experience, he must take the reference of a thought beyond itself to consist in the character of the further thoughts, feelings and percepts to which it tends to give rise. The standard case, on which all others are modelled, is that of belief. To hold a belief,

<hr />

[1] Quoted above, p. 201.   [2] *Some Problems of Philosophy*, p. 48.

where it is not simply a tendency to action, is in the first instance to be disposed to produce an assent to certain signs. But if the analysis is not to be circular, these signs have here to be taken only as marks or noises, which tend to initiate the production of further marks or noises, and so on indefinitely. It may again be objected that a sign does not acquire an interpretation merely by being associated with a string of other uninterpreted signs, but, as we remarked when discussing the views of Peirce, this objection can be met by stipulating that the string must be linked at some point, either actually or conditionally, with some form of action. In James's case, the action is narrowed down to the process by which the beliefs are verified. But in what terms is this to be analysed?

James goes into the question fairly thoroughly in a series of essays, respectively entitled 'The Function of Cognition', 'The Tigers in India' and 'The Relation between Knower and Known', all of which are reprinted in *The Meaning of Truth*. That on 'The Relation between Knower and Known' also appears in the *Essays in Radical Empiricism*, where it forms part of the essay on 'A World of Pure Experience', to which we have already referred.[1] James addresses these essays to the analysis of knowledge, but it will be seen that so far as his arguments go, he might equally well have been speaking of belief. In all of them, his principal aim is to eliminate what he calls the 'epistemological gulf' which might be thought to exist between states of cognition and their objects by showing that the processes in which knowledge consists entirely 'fall inside the continuities of concrete experience'.[2]

The assumption being, as we have seen, that all purely conceptual transactions have at least to be cashable in terms of percepts, whether or not they are ever actually cashed, James confines his analysis of the relation between knower and known to the types of instance in which the object known is perceptible. In this field he asserts that there are just three possible forms that the relation can assume. 'Either the knower and the known are: (1) The selfsame piece of experience taken twice over in different contexts; or they are (2) two pieces of *actual* experience belonging to the same subject, with definite tracts of conjunctive transitional

---

[1] See above, p. 229.   [2] *The Meaning of Truth*, p. 41 fn.

experience between them; or (3) the known is a *possible* experience either of that subject or another, to which the said conjunctive transitions *would* lead, if sufficiently prolonged.'[1]

The first case is supposed to be that in which the knowledge consists in the perception of some present object. We shall deal with it when we come to discuss James's view that one and the same experience can be, in one aspect, a constituent of a physical object and, in another, a constituent of a self, according as it is classed with one or other of the different groups of experiences to which it is variously related. It is the other two types of case that interest us at present because they are the cases in which, as James puts it, 'the mind has "knowledge about" an object not immediately there'.[2] The difference between them is that in the one case the claim to knowledge is eventually substantiated by the perception of the object, while in the other it is not; but the lines on which they are analysed are essentially the same. In neither case does James attempt to give a formal analysis. He assumes that an elementary example will be enough to make his meaning clear. In the essay on 'The Relation between Knower and Known' from which I have been quoting, he is content with an example in which the relation obtains between items of actual experience, on the ground that the case where the experience which is known is merely possible can always be reduced 'formally or hypothetically' to the case where it is actual. He supposes himself to be sitting in his library at Cambridge and 'thinking truly' of the Harvard Memorial Hall which is ten minutes walk away. The problem is to explain how this thought can be cognitive. In the essay on 'The Function of Cognition' which was written twenty years earlier, James had attempted to deal with examples of this kind by taking the cognitive thought to be what he called the feeling of a quality q and then laying it down that 'the feeling of q knows whatever reality it resembles, and either directly or indirectly operates on'.[3] He took the factor of resemblance to be primary and brought in the causal factor mainly as a means of determining which of the several realities that the feeling of q might resemble was the one that it knew. He now

[1] Ibid., p. 103.   [2] Ibid.   [3] Ibid., p. 28.

sees, however, that for a thought to be cognitive of an absent object, it is neither necessary nor sufficient that there should be any qualitative resemblance between them. It is not necessary because the object may be thought of only by name or description, without the accompaniment of any image; and even if there is an image, it does not have to be clear or accurate in order to fulfil its cognitive function. It is not sufficient because, as we have repeatedly seen, the mere fact that two things are similar or even identical in quality in no way entails that they stand in any relation of reference. So even if one does take the cognitive thought to be an image 'certain *extrinsic* phenomena, special experiences of conjunction, are what impart to the image, be it what it may, its knowing office'.[1]

In the example chosen, James remarks that if he could not describe the Hall that he was thinking of, or direct someone to it, or recognize it when he came upon it, then even though his thought consisted in an image which in some degree resembled it, the resemblance would be no more than a coincidence. 'On the other hand,' he continues, 'if I can lead you to the hall, and tell you of its history and present uses; if in its presence I feel my idea, however imperfect it may have been, to have led hither and to be now *terminated*: if the associates of the image and of the felt hall run parallel, so that each term of the one context corresponds serially, as I walk, with an answering term of the others; why then my soul was prophetic, and my idea must be, and by common consent would be, called cognizant of reality. That percept was what I *meant*, for into it my idea has passed by conjunctive experiences of sameness and fulfilled intention. Nowhere is there jar, but every later moment continues and corroborates an earlier one.'[2] In short, what makes the thought cognitive of the object is that one leads to the other by an experiential path which feels 'right' at every stage. As James puts it, 'there is experience from point to point of one direction followed, and finally of one process fulfilled'.[3]

In most cases, indeed, the path is not actually traced, but this makes no essential difference, so long as it is traceable. James's

[1] Ibid., p. 104.   [2] Ibid., p. 105.   [3] Ibid., p. 106.

treatment of the example of the tigers in India, in the essay with that title, is in fact rather slap-dash. He asks what can be meant by saying that we mentally point at the tigers when we are not perceiving them, and answers that 'the pointing of our thought to the tigers is known simply and solely as a procession of mental associates and motor consequences that follow on the thought, and that would lead harmoniously, if followed out, into some ideal or real context, or even into the immediate presence, of the tigers'.[1] He does not, however, attempt to describe these 'mental associates and motor consequences' in any greater detail, and the further conditions which he lists, such as that of our being able to distinguish tigers from other animals and to 'utter all sorts of propositions which don't contradict other propositions that are true of the real tigers', are at most necessary conditions of our knowing that the tigers exist. They provide no evidence at all that the tigers are actually being thought of.

It is, I think, a fault in both examples that James does not sufficiently distinguish between a set of experiences which would constitute what Peirce called the 'development' of the thought of an object and a set of experiences which would lead to the actual perception of the object. It is, indeed, possible that the two should coincide; talking of the Memorial Hall might immediately lead one to take one's friend to see it; thinking of the tigers might set up an immediate disposition to book a passage to India. But even in these cases what fixes the reference is not just that the train of experiences leads to the perception of the object, but rather that the perception is, or would be, taken as the fulfilment of the thought. This applies also to the experiences which come between the thought and the perception. In the example of the Memorial Hall, James makes much of the fact that these intervening experiences themselves correspond to previous images, but this is clearly not necessary except in so far as the correspondence satisfies the criteria which one must have for locating the object; if one did go to hunt for the tigers, one might have very little idea of what one would encounter on the way. The intervening experiences only come into the picture to the extent that they

[1] Ibid., pp. 44-5.

also develop the thought, and this they may do without having any tendency to lead to the perception of the object.

To see that this must be so, one has only to consider that in a great many cases, there is no possibility of our ever getting to perceive the objects to which our thoughts refer. Sometimes the impossibility is only practical, as when we think of things or events which are located in the distant future or very far away in space, but very often it is logical. Even if we leave abstract objects and fictitious objects out of account, and confine our attention to what is perceptible, not everything that is in its own nature perceptible is capable, even in theory, of being perceived by everyone who may chance to think of it. There is a sense in which we cannot perceive the thoughts and feelings of others, and, what is more important in the present context, we cannot now perceive events which are located in the past. This does not mean, however, that we cannot think about them.

But how then do these thoughts acquire their reference? To use another of James's examples, how can a present thought be interpreted as referring to Julius Caesar? His answer is that the 'effects' of the thought and of Caesar have to 'run together'. 'The real Caesar, for example, wrote a manuscript of which I see a real reprint and say "the Caesar I mean is the author of *that*".'[1] The implication is, presumably, that the thought initiates a series of experiences which terminates in a perception of some copy of *De Bello Gallico*. Being unable to perceive Caesar himself, we make do, as in magic, with something that emanates from him. Once more, however, this puts the emphasis in the wrong place. It is indeed necessary that any reference to Caesar should be capable of being cashed in terms of something which is now perceptible, though this need not be anything which is causally related to Caesar in the simple way that James suggests; any present object will do, so long as it can be linked with an identifying description of Caesar by a spatio-temporal designation. But the fact that this condition is satisfied shows only that the reference to Caesar is possible: it is not a ground for saying that it has actually been made. If the object to which the description of Caesar is anchored

[1] Ibid., p. 222.

is to endow a thought with a reference to him, it must feature in the development of the thought. But what the development of the thought must mainly consist in is a disposition to have further thoughts which are 'appropriate' to Caesar, to reply in the proper way to certain questions, and so forth, rather than the perception of objects which serve to link Caesar with the present time. One sign certifies another; the role of perception is simply to give security to the system of credit as a whole.

This being so, the process of appropriating a past experience, which plays so large a role in James's theory of self-identity, must be taken to consist in the setting up of a disposition to accept this experience as having been one's own. This will imply not only that the revival of it carries with it a similar feeling of 'warmth' to that which attends one's awareness of present events, but, more importantly, that one is prepared to acknowledge it, to accept responsibility for it, if that is called for, and in the normal way to think of it as having been sensibly continuous or com-present with other experiences which one also claims to own. The content of the identifying thought will be, essentially, that this was something that happened to oneself.

It is clear that such an account is very wide open to the charge of circularity. If appropriating an experience comes down to acknowledging it as having been one's own, it would seem to follow that this concept of appropriation itself depends upon the concept of self-identity and cannot therefore be legitimately used to define it. The only way of escaping from the circle would be to show that the claim to ownership of a past experience can be made in such a way as not to involve the concept of self-identity. This would be achieved by construing the making of the claim as the production of certain signs which would sooner or later be interpreted by experiences which could be described without any reference to their owner. The signs in question would have to exhibit the use of the first person, or something which did duty for it, but the assumption would be that the reference to oneself could be analysed out. Whether this assumption can be made good depends upon the answer to the more general question whether it is possible to account for the reference of signs without having to credit them with intentional 'objects'. I am inclined to think that it is possible, but cannot claim that what I have been able to extract either from James's rather summary account of the relation of knower to known or from Peirce's more sophisticated but far from lucid theory of signs comes anywhere near proving it to be so. In my own view, the position stands or falls with the behavioural theory of belief to which, as we have seen, there are very serious objections. I wish that I had been able to do more in the way of showing how they can be met.

C. THE CONSTRUCTION OF THE PHYSICAL WORLD

1. *Experiences in Their Double Aspect*

As we have seen, James upholds the thesis that 'there is only one primal stuff or material in the world, a stuff of which everything is composed'.[1] In itself, this primal stuff, to which he gives the name of 'pure experience' is neither mental nor physical: the distinction between 'thoughts' and 'things', like the distinction between the knower and the known, is to be analysed wholly in terms of the different relations in which its elements stand to one another. Just as the same geometrical point can lie at the junction of two intersecting lines, so the same item of experience can be a member of two different groups of experiences, one of which constitutes a physical object and the other a mind.

To illustrate this, James invites us to consider a typical case of sense-perception; for instance, that of the reader's present perception of the room in which he is sitting. Philosophers may tell him that the physical objects, which he takes himself to be perceiving, are not directly presented to him; the immediate data of perception are subjective impressions to which it is inferred that external objects correspond. But the trouble with such theories is that 'they violate the reader's sense of life, which knows no

[1] *Essays in Radical Empiricism*, p. 4.

intervening mental image but seems to see the room and the book immediately just as they physically exist'.[1]

On this issue James sides with common-sense. The reason why philosophers have had recourse to representative theories of perception is that they have thought it impossible that 'what is evidently one reality should be in two places at once, both in outer space and in a person's mind'.[2] But this difficulty is illusory. The paradox disappears, once it is realized that the object's being in two different places is simply a matter of its belonging to two different groups, or, as James here puts it, entering simultaneously into two different processes. His account of these processes is worth quoting in detail.

'One of them', he says, 'is the reader's personal biography, the other is the history of the house of which the room is part. The presentation, the experience, the *that* in short (for until we have decided *what* it is it must be a mere *that*) is the last term of a train of sensations, emotions, decisions, movements, classifications, expectations, etc., ending in the present, and the first term of a series of similar 'inner' operations extending into the future, on the reader's part. On the other hand, the very same *that* is the *terminus ad quem* of a lot of previous physical operations, carpentering, papering, furnishing, warming, etc., and the *terminus a quo* of a lot of future ones, in which it will be concerned when undergoing the destiny of a physical room. The physical and the mental operations form curiously incompatible groups. As a room, the experience has occupied that spot and had that environment for thirty years. As your field of consciousness it may never have existed until now. As a room, attention will go on to discover endless new details in it. As your mental state merely, few new ones will emerge under attention's eye. As a room, it will take an earthquake, or a gang of men, and in any case a certain amount of time, to destroy it. As your subjective state, the closing of your eyes, or any instantaneous play of your fancy will suffice. In the real world, fire will consume it. In your mind, you can let fire play over it without effect. As an outer object, you must pay so much a month to inhabit it. As an inner content, you may

<hr />

[1] Ibid., p. 12.　　　　[2] Ibid., p. 11.

occupy it for any length of time rent-free. If, in short, you follow
it in the mental direction, taking it along with events of personal
biography solely, all sorts of things are true of it which are false,
and false of it which are true if you treat it as a real thing experienced, follow it in the physical direction, and relate it to associates
in the outer world.'[1]

If this passage is intended to show that the results of viewing
experiences under a double aspect are not paradoxical, it proceeds
very strangely. Were we to take it literally, we could only
conclude that it consists of a series of contradictions. Whatever
may be said about different operations or different aspects, it
cannot possibly be true of one and the same entity both that it
has just come into existence and that it has existed for many years
past, both that it needs an earthquake to destroy it and that it
can be destroyed by a play of fancy, both that it can and that it
cannot be consumed by fire, both that you must and that you
need not pay to inhabit it. The existence of anything which had to
satisfy these conditions would be a logical impossibility.

In fact, it is not necessary for James's argument that anything
should satisfy them. He runs into contradictions because he does
not take the trouble to distinguish between a given experience
and the different groups of which it may be a member. The
experience is ephemeral and at the mercy of a play of fancy: the
persistent object which it would take an earthquake or a gang of
men to destroy is not any single experience but, at best, a group of
experiences of which the given experience is one. In fact, everything that James here says about the experience in its physical
aspect should be construed as applying not to the experience but
to this group which it helps to form. On the mental side also, he
travels outside the experience in saying such things as that it can
be occupied for any length of time rent-free or that fire can play
upon it without effect; for these are picturesque ways of referring
to what may be subsequently remembered or imagined. In these
instances, the reference is not to the mental group as a whole, but
to other actual or possible members of it. Had James bothered to
make these distinctions, which are evidently required by his

[1] Ibid., pp. 13-15.

theory, his account of the dual function of an everyday experience might have lost some of its vividness: but it would at least have been free from self-contradiction.

This is not to say, however, that it would have been free from difficulty. The idea that physical and mental 'objects' are constructs which may have common elements is not one that can be accepted or rejected out of hand: it has to be seen how it works in detail. We need to know exactly how the experiences, the neutral items, which enter into one or other type of construct are supposed to be related. James's account of the composition of the mental group is to be found in his theory of personal identity, which we have already examined. We have seen that while there are obvious lacunae in the theory as James states it, some theory of this kind may be tenable. The question which we have now to consider is whether an equally good case can be made for his conception of the physical world.

It must be admitted that at this point James himself gives us very little help. He must be presumed to hold that physical objects, at least of the common-sense variety, can be explicitly defined in terms of items of pure experience, but so far from supplying any such definitions, he does not offer any suggestion as to the form which they could take. He deals with the whole problem only at a very general level, and even at this level his remarks are very sketchy. For instance, one of his fundamental assumptions is that the difference between two experiences in virtue of which one is a merely subjective thought, while the other is the perception of an objective physical thing, is not a difference of quality. A mental image, a hallucinatory sensation, a constituent of a dream, may have the same felt qualities of extension, temperature, colour and so forth as physical objects are perceived to have. 'Why, for example, do we call a fire hot, and water wet, and yet refuse to say that our mental state when it is 'of' these objects, is either wet or hot? "Intentionally", at any rate, and when the mental state is a vivid image, hotness and wetness are in it, just as much as they are in the physical experience.'[1] James's answer to this is that the difference lies in the respective consequences of the two

[1] *Essays in Radical Empiricism*, pp. 31–2.

experiences. One of them is 'energetic' in a way in which the other is not. 'Mental fire is what won't burn real sticks; mental water is what won't necessarily (though of course it may) put out even a mental fire. Mental knives may be sharp, but they won't cut real wood. Mental triangles are pointed, but their points won't wound. With "real" objects, on the contrary, consequences always accrue; and thus the real experiences get sifted from the mental ones, the things from our thoughts of them, fanciful or true, and precipitated together as the stable part of the whole experience-chaos, under the name of the physical world.'[1] In short, what distinguishes a 'physical experience' from a merely mental one is the regularity of the association of experiences of its sort with other experiences of the appropriate type; but exactly what these associations are and what are the salient characteristics of the experiences which they are supposed to relate are questions which James leaves unanswered. He does see that our actual percepts are too fragmentary to be the sole architects of the stable order in which he takes the physical world to consist. In their capacity as 'the originally *strong* experiences', they form the nucleus of this order, but they have to be supplemented. 'We add a lot of conceptual experiences to them, making these strong also in imagination, and building out the remoter parts of the physical world by their means, and around this core of reality the world of laxly connected fancies and mere rhapsodical objects floats like a bank of clouds.'[2] But this is as far as he goes. He does not explain how 'conceptual experiences' are used to build up the physical world, nor does he provide any criteria for distinguishing merely rhapsodical objects from those which belong to the core of reality. He just gives the hint that 'in the clouds, all sorts of rules are violated which in the core are kept'[3] and leaves it at that.

I shall not attempt to make good all the omissions in this account. Nor shall I embark on an independent defence of the strong phenomenalist thesis that everything that can significantly be said about physical objects can be translated into statements about actual and possible experiences. For reasons which I have

[1] Ibid., p. 33.   [2] Ibid.   [3] Ibid., pp. 33-4.

given elsewhere,[1] I no longer believe that this thesis is tenable. The most that I shall try to do for James's 'neutral monism' is to make out a very general case for the weaker thesis that our conception of the physical world can be exhibited as a theory with respect to our experiences. This thesis is weaker inasmuch as it does not imply that physical objects are 'reducible' to sense-experiences. It does, however, imply that the 'positing' of physical objects, to borrow a useful expression from Professor Quine,[2] is a means of organizing our experiences in a systematic fashion. In James's own metaphor, the bank-notes which are required for the theory to operate are not exchangeable for hard coin; but it is only as representatives of the hard coin of experience that they fulfil their function. This is not perhaps quite so far as James would have wished to go, but I think that it gives him most of what he wanted.

But does not the use of this metaphor beg an important question? Many philosophers would deny that there is any such thing as the hard coin of experience, if this is understood to imply that our knowledge of the world around us is derived from more primitive data than the perception of physical objects. If we follow Quine in thinking of physical objects as 'cultural posits', we have to admit, as he does, that we could have used posits of a quite different order, which, though no doubt inferior in explanatory value, would have been equally consonant with the bare facts of experience. But this is to imply that we are presented with un-interpreted data which we are free to work up in any way that we find convenient. How far, and with what justification can this be taken to be true?

2. The Basis of the Construction

I shall not, in fact, say anything more about the notion of pure-experience than I have already said in my discussion of James's

[1] See 'Phenomalism' in my *Philosophical Essays* and *The Problem of Knowledge* (1956), ch. iii.
[2] W. V. Quine, 'Two Dogmas of Empiricism' in *From a Logical Point of View* (1953), p. 45.

starting point. My reason for leaving the matter there is that the data which we require for our present undertaking cannot be the data of James's 'blooming, buzzing confusion'. If they are to serve as materials for the construction of the physical world, they must have recognizable properties. They must be capable of figuring in what I propose to call experiential statements; a technical term, the use of which I shall presently explain. But, according to Peirce and others, this is already to interpret them. I have no objection at all to admitting this. If any way of bringing data under concepts is to count as interpreting them, then clearly the only data with which we can actually work are data which have been interpreted. I do not mind going still further and admitting that the way in which these data are interpreted is conditioned by the use to which they are going to be put; that their serving as a basis for the theory of physical objects accounts to a very large extent for the way in which they are discriminated and classified, so that although there is a sense in which the theory exists only for them, there is also a sense in which they exist for it. All that I require is that their interpretation, at this primitive state, should contain no formal commitment to the existence of physical objects. The theory may, as it were, be visible in the background, but it must not be entailed by the way in which the data are described.

Many philosophers nowadays would deny that even this condition could be satisfied. I do not claim to be able to demonstrate that they are wrong, but I can produce what seems to me a highly persuasive argument. It is based on the fact of there being a very good sense in which even the simplest of our ordinary judgements of perception goes beyond the evidence, in that it claims more than is contained in the experience which gives rise to it. Here again it can be said that the use of this sort of language begs the question. Against this, all that I can do is to try to make as clear as possible what I have in mind.

The easiest course will be to take an example. I look up from where I am sitting and see a door a few yards in front of me. I have no doubt of its being a door. Even if I had not seen it many times before, I should have no difficulty in identifying it. But now consider what very large assumptions even this simple judgement makes. In the first place, there are the assumptions which are involved in taking anything to be a solid three-dimensional object of this general type, the most important of them being that the object can be touched as well as seen, that it is perceptible to other people besides myself, and that it continues to exist whether or not anyone actually perceives it. In a case of this kind, it is assumed also that the object has parts which are not visible to me, or at any rate not visible to me on this occasion; it is assumed that it is not hollow and that it has a back as well as a front. Finally there are the assumptions which are involved in its identification as a physical object of a certain specific sort; in this instance as a door, rather than a piece of stage scenery, or a painted part of the wall to which it is attached; and these may relate not only to the appearance of the object, but to its origin, the materials of which it is made and the uses to which it is put.

Now I am not saying that these assumptions are not warranted or even that in this particular instance I do not know that they are satisfied. What I do say is that this knowledge, if I have it, is indeed founded on the data which are visibly presented to me but is not covered by them. Merely by inspecting the content of my present visual field, I cannot, without the help of other premises, deduce that the object, which I identify as a door, is tangible as well as visible, that it is perceptible to other observers, that it exists when no one is perceiving it, that it has parts which are hidden from my sight, that it is made of wood, that it can be used to bar entry to the house. To make the same point in another way, it is logically consistent with my having the visual experience that I am now having, considered by itself, that all these propositions should be false. But if this is so, there is a clear sense in which in making such a judgement as that I see a door, I am going beyond my present evidence: I am claiming more than is contained in the experience on which the judgement is based. In this sense, my judgement can, I think, quite properly be said to be the outcome of an inductive inference.

I find this conclusion so obvious that it is hard for me to understand why so many philosophers are unwilling to accept it. One of the main objections to it, as set out, for example, by Professor J. L. Austin,[1] is that it is just not true of sentences about 'material things' as such that they must be supported by or based on evidence. I take his reason for this to be that we do not commonly speak of having evidence for a proposition like 'that is a door' unless the observations which lead one to accept it in some way fall short of the highest standard. If I could not see the door, but thought that I heard it banging, or someone described it to me, I might be said to have evidence of its existence; I might be said to infer that it existed if in default of direct observation I were merely going by the fact that doors of this kind usually are fitted to houses of this type. But this just shows that the cases which are describable in this sort of way are contrasted with cases of direct observation, when the point is precisely that we do not rely on evidence. There is no question of my having evidence, or of my making an inference, when I am looking at the door from a few yards away in broad daylight, and I have no reason to suppose that the conditions are in any way abnormal.

This may well be correct, as an account of ordinary usage, but it is still a bad argument. The fallacy in it lies in the assumption that if, in a given set of circumstances, it is not good usage to assert some proposition p, it follows that p is false. For instance, if I think that I know that something is the case, it is not good usage for me to say that I believe that it is the case. The reason why it is not is that if I say only that I believe it I convey the impression that I do not think I know it. But the explanation of this is just that it is not our habit to make a weaker claim when we think that we are in a position to make a stronger one. It certainly does not follow that when one knows something one does not believe it. So, in the present instance, when one talks of having evidence for a proposition p, it will commonly be understood that one is not in a position to pronounce authoritatively on its truth or falsehood. If my grounds for asserting p are such as to put its truth beyond reasonable doubt, I am underplaying my hand, and

[1] In his *Sense and Sensibilia* (1962). This book contains a number of arguments against the kind of position which I am defending, none of which I find cogent. Cf. my article 'Has Austin Refuted the Sense-Datum Theory?' in *Synthese*, 17, 1967.

so being misleading, if I say only that I have good evidence for it. But of course it does not in the least follow that when I am in a position to assert *p* without qualification, I do not have evidence for it. The true conclusion may rather be that my evidence is very strong.

Even so, it may be objected, this still does not entitle me to say that my judgement that I see a door is the conclusion of an inductive inference. There are circumstances in which this could be said. If my eyesight were very bad, or the light were very poor, or the object were of a kind with which I was unfamiliar, or my capacity for recognizing objects had ben impaired by a brain injury, I might have to go through a process of reasoning in order to identify what I saw; in very exceptional circumstances I might even have to reason myself out of the suspicion that I was dreaming. But again the point is that these circumstances are abnormal. In a normal case, like the present one, I do not have to engage in any reasoning. I just look up and see that there is a door in front of me.

Once more all this is true but irrelevant. I am not maintaining that it is never possible for us, even in the most favourable conditions, to identify the things that we perceive, without working through the stages of an argument. I am quite willing to admit that it is only in exceptional instances that we are conscious of making any inference. All that I mean when I speak of our everyday judgements of perception as being inferential is that they are based on observations which do not entail them. That they are based on observations cannot seriously be questioned; that these observations do not entail them is what I have been trying to show. I could multiply examples, but the one that I have given should be enough to make my meaning clear.

But now, if judgements of perception are, in this special sense, the conclusions of inductive inferences, it ought to be possible to formulate the premisses. It ought to be possible to describe the data on which they are based, not necessarily in a way that is free from all interpretation, but at least in a way that is non-committal with respect to the question whether one is perceiving a physical object and *a fortiori* to the further question what kind of physical object it is. The statements that we are looking for are statements which fit the data, in the sense that they do not attempt to go beyond them. If they are false it must be through their misdescribing the content of the experiences which they monitor, and not through their carrying any implications which further experiences fail to honour.

It is statements of this kind that I propose to call experiential statements. There are several conditions that they must fulfil if they are to do the work that we require of them. To begin with, the fact that they are limited to the description of what is sensibly presented must be understood to carry the consequence that they do not prejudge the question whether or not the assumptions which we have seen to be involved in our ordinary judgements of perception are satisfied. Let us, for convenience of exposition, call an experiential statement an E-statement and a statement to the effect that some physical object is perceived a P-statement. Then what is required of E-statements is that they support P-statements without entailing them. Collectively they must be such that our construction of the physical world can be exhibited as an interpretation of the data which they describe; individually they must be consistent with either the truth or falsehood of the particular P-statements which are based upon them. They must, finally, be framed in such a way that they can count as being descriptive of the actual contents of our perceptual experiences.

At this point, there are various ways in which one might proceed. The course which I propose to follow is to start, like Berkeley, with sensible qualities, but not to treat them as particulars. That is to say, I shall not differentiate, initially, between different occurrences of the same quality. For this purpose I shall follow the example of C. I. Lewis and Nelson Goodman in making a technical use of James's term 'Quale'. I shall, however, give it a rather different extension from that which it is given, at least by Professor Goodman, in his excellent book *The Structure of Appearance*. One reason for this is that our aims are different. Professor Goodman is not committed to James's thesis that the primary system, for the theory of knowledge, must be a system with a phenomenal rather than a physical basis. In his view, no case has been made out for saying that either type of system is primary; he does not think that the question of epistemological primacy has yet been formulated clearly enough to permit of there being any definite answer to it. The result is that while the elements of his system belong to sense-modalities, he is not saddled with the admittedly vague requirement of preserving fidelity to the actual character of our sense-experience; he is able to escape it because he is not committed at the outset to holding that the physical system is an interpretation of the phenomenal. His concern is to construct a language which could be used by people who were looking at the word phenomenologically, and only then consider whether and to what extent a physical language could be developed out of it. In the constitution of his phenomenal language he is guided by logical considerations. He insists that every term which figures in the system be explicitly defined on the basis of its primitive terms, and in the case of visual phenomena, on which he mainly concentrates, the elements which the primitive terms denote are colours, places and times, where places are places in the visual field and a time-quale is a moment of phenomenal time which has no other as a part.

The conditions which I have imposed upon my E-statements make things harder for me in some ways, but in one way they make them easier. Since my qualia have, as it were, to present themselves as being candidates for physical objects, I have to conceive of the phenomenal field in which they occur as being already fairly highly organized. This means that I am able to take as primitive a great deal of what Goodman, if he arrived at it, would have been obliged to construct. It may well be, of course, that my primitives are wholly constructible out of his materials. In that case I shall anyhow be protected from the charge of making assumptions to which I am not entitled, and be only at worst susceptible to the charge of laziness.

My qualia, then, are visual or other sensory patterns. I conceive of their range as being very wide. Anything counts as a quale that a person is able to pick out as a recurrent or potentially recurrent feature of his sense-experiences, from a two-dimensional colour expanse to a complex three-dimensional *gestalt*. Suppose, for example, that my cat is curled up in a chair beside me. Then if I look towards him, the quale which is presented to me may be that of a light brown expanse, a light brown expanse against a green background, an animal pattern, a feline pattern, a Siamese-cat pattern, a cat-in-a-chair pattern, and so forth. I borrow these expressions from ordinary speech to avoid the labour of devising a special vocabulary. There would, I believe, be no insuperable difficulty in constructing such a vocabulary, or even in teaching it as a primitive language. After all, a child does not need already to have the concept of a physical object in order to identify patterns. Still, for our present purpose, there is clearly a practical advantage in trading on expressions the meaning of which is already known. It must, however, be borne in mind that these borrowed expressions do not carry all their usual implications. Though it may often be the case that a cat-pattern indicates the presence of a cat, this is not a deductive inference. The expression 'cat-pattern' is not defined as a pattern which is typical of the appearance of a cat, since its use does not imply that there are any cats. In the same way the expression 'bird-note', in this vocabulary, does not carry the implication that there are birds. The reference is solely to the quality of the sound, irrespective of its provenance. In short, these are purely ostensive terms like colour-words, used phenomenally: a term like 'cat-pattern' differs from a colour-word only in denoting a quale of a more complicated type.

Expressions which denote simple qualia may also serve to denote the attributes of more complex ones. For the visual modality, which is the most important, these attributes will be colours, sizes and shapes. They provide a means of distinguishing between qualia which answer to the same general description. For instance, there are many different ways in which a quale which falls within the range of a cat-pattern can be further specified. I do not, however, assume that this is necessarily true of all such complex qualia. I think it possible that someone should signal the presence of some visual pattern without being disposed to signal the presence of its attributes. That is to say, he would register the pattern, without registering its particular shape or size, or perhaps even colour. I am in some doubt whether this could happen but I think it best to allow for the possibility. If I am wrong, no harm is done; so long as we are concerned about fidelity to the appearances, the important thing is that no type of fact should be excluded. It does not matter if provision is made for possibilities which are not actually realized.

Like James, I assume that the qualia are given to us as spatially and temporally related. I follow him also in assuming that sense-fields have some temporal duration. Temporal relations may obtain between qualia of the same or different sense-modalities, on condition that they occur within the same specious present. Spatial relations occur only within visual or tactual sense-fields.

It is by their spatial and temporal relations that qualia are particularized. At the primitive level, this particularization is not complete, since we have no right to exclude the possibility that the total contents of two different specious presents are qualitatively identical. It is completed only in the course of the construction of the physical system. There is no circularity in this, since it is not necesssary for the construction to proceed that its elements should be fully individuated. It is enough that if any ambiguity should arise we can always resolve it by extending the context in which the rival groups of qualia are located.

An experiential statement is formed by coupling a designation of a quale, or of a group of qualia, with some sign of instantiation: an exclamation-mark would be as good a sign as any other for this purpose. The rule which governs the use of these statements is that they can refer only to present qualia, and only to qualia which are presented to the speaker. No provision is made for their use in any other way. So if a dialogue were conducted at this level, each speaker would assent to or dissent from the other's statement according as he found or failed to find the designated qualia occurring within his own contemporary experience.

3. The Question of Privacy

This does not entail that qualia are private entities. They are not confined to my experience or to that of any other given observer. On the contrary, since they are universals there is no theoretical limit to the incidence of their instantation. It is, indeed, a necessary and sufficient condition of the truth of an E-statement that the quale to which it refers should be presented to some person at the relevant time, but this condition is not contained in the E-statements themselves: it is not expressible at their level. The game, if we may so call it, is just that the player greets a pattern when it appears with the appropriate sign, and this greeting carries no further implication whatever, not even that the pattern is perceived by him, let alone that it is or is not perceived by others.

The reason why nothing of this sort can be implied is that persons do not enter into this universe of discourse. Consequently, the question of privacy or publicity does not arise for qualia, since this antithesis makes sense only at a level where one not only has the means of referring to different persons but is also able to distinguish between their 'inner' experiences and the 'outer' world which they perceive in common. I shall try to show later on how this distinction can be made. It must, however, be admitted that our E-statements do possess the feature which is the main source of Wittgenstein's objection to what he considers to be a private language. There is no criterion by which the player of the language-game can determine that he is abiding by its rules, except his own recognition of the qualia which he picks out. There is no way in which the accuracy of his recognition can be independently checked.

The result is that what constitutes the same quale is something which the speaker simply decrees. Let us suppose that an anthropologist comes across a tribe in which this primitive language is spoken. The supposition is highly improbable but not contradictory. Let us also suppose that the anthropologist catches on to the principles of the language. Then, on the assumption that these people's sense-experiences are not significantly different from his own, he will be able to make conjectures about their use of these 'phenomenal' expressions and may very well find that his conjectures are confirmed. His position will not, in fact, be very different from that of an anthropologist who is investigating a 'physical' language of an unfamiliar type. However, when one of his conjectures comes to grief, he will not always be able to decide between the hypotheses that his interpretation has been at fault, that the speaker's perceptions diverged on this occasion from his own, that the speaker has made a verbal mistake or that from the point of view of the anthropologist he has modified his usage. Neither will this difficulty be wholly due to the fact that the anthropologist is looking at the performance from the outside. Even for the speakers of the language there is no distinction at this level between linguistic innovations and linguistic mistakes.

It does not follow, however, that such a language would have no rules at all. The speakers would have their habits of classification and these would constitute the rules. It is only that as yet there is no such thing as a speaker's infraction of a rule. We can, however, find an analogue even for this at the very next stage when the speaker is credited with memories and expectations and he has begun to associate qualia in a more elaborate way than we have yet provided for. There will still be cases when it will not be possible to say whether the deviation lies in the speaker's usage or his experience, but at least there will be occasions on which he can be judged to have made a mistake. They will be those in which he rescinds an identity decree.

Moreover, even at the most primitive level, the position of the speaker, in this respect, differs only in degree and not in kind from our own. For, as I have pointed out elsewhere,[1] we too are bound to rely in the end on what I call primary recognition. Being in possession of the concept of persistent objects, including that of other observers, we are able in many cases to point to specimens which can provide us with standards for the application of our words, and we can also check our usage by that of other people. But the specimens themselves have to be recognized: if they are labelled the labels have to be recognized in their turn. If we consult other people, the signs which they make, their words or gestures, have to be identified if we are to learn anything from them. One decision corroborates another, and although we enjoy the advantage of having a very wide area in which to look for corroboration, it still comes down to a matter of decision. For all the complexity and publicity of our language,

[1] Cf. *The Concept of a Person*, pp. 41–3.

its operation entirely depends on our continually just taking something to be an instance of an identifiable quale. Here too what the speaker does when he admits to having made a verbal error is rescind a decree.

If this argument is valid, it shows us the way to meet a further objection to the possibility of our experiential language. One of the conditions which we have imposed upon E-statements is that they be neutral with respect to P-statements, in the sense that the assertion of an E-statement leaves it an open question whether any P-statement is true or false. But here it may be objected that while this may hold good with respect to the particular P-statements to which particular E-statements give rise, it does not hold with regard to P-statements in general. For it is only through their relation to P-statements that E-statements derive their meaning. We can strip away the assumptions that ordinarily go with judgements of perception, but it is with these judgements that we have to start. Otherwise nothing that we could say in our phenomenological language would be intelligible.

Now it is quite true that our explanation of the use of E-statements does depend upon the understanding of P-statements: but that is not what is in question. In talking *about* an experiential language we are free to draw on any resources that we possess. The question is whether the reference to ordinary judgements of perception occurs implicitly *within* the E-language, and this is quite a different matter. The ground for saying that it does is that qualia are supposed to be ostensible and that nothing is ostensible unless it is public. If we are able to talk intelligibly about our private thoughts and feelings, it is only because they are logically connected with objects or processes which are publicly observable. Now, admittedly, qualia have not been introduced as private entities, but this does not avoid the difficulty. For it is a feature of the language-game into which they enter that each player is allowed to have an authoritative voice with respect to the existence and character of the qualia with which he is presented. In other words, it makes no difference to the conduct of the game whether there are many players or only one, and if there are many players, whether they apprehend the same qualia or not.

But this is inconsistent with the assumption that qualia are ostensibly definable. For it is essential to ostensive definitions that the same object be shown by one person to another.

This objection is, I think, just a variant of the one which we considered before it: for if we ask why it is thought that our ability to talk intelligibly about private experiences depends upon their being logically connected with public events, or why it is thought that only what is publicly observable can be ostensively defined, we shall come upon the argument that it is necessary for all uses of language to conform to some public standard of correctness: and then my previous rejoinder holds. I want, however, to look a little further into this question of ostensive definition. How clear cut is the distinction between public objects which can be shown to others, and private states which cannot?

Again, it will be simplest to start with a commonplace example. Consider what happens when one teaches a child the meaning of a word like the English word 'table'. One shows him a table, or a picture of a table, pronounces the word, and hopes that he will somehow come to understand that the type of word of which this is a token is to be used to stand for the type of object of which we are showing him a picture, or a specimen. But what exactly is involved in our showing him the specimen? Our bringing him into a situation where we expect that he will see the same object as that to which we are referring, and directing his attention to it. But what then counts for us as his seeing the right object, the one that we also see and wish him to attend to? His reacting in a way that we consider appropriate. And how do we establish that he has learned his lesson? Again, by observing that he reacts in the proper way and in particular that he comes out with the word on what we consider to be the right occasions, that is, mainly the occasions on which we should say that there was a table there and that he was looking at it, or in contact with it.

But now in what way does any of this differ from the case in which we teach a child the meaning of a word like 'pain'? Here too we bring him into, or, more humanely, find him in the appropriate situation, observe his reactions and accordingly make an assumption about what he is feeling, just as in the case of the table we make an assumption about what he is seeing, and are satisfied that he has learned his lesson if he subsequently comes out with, or assents to, the word when we judge that he is in pain, or when we judge that he is observing some other creature who seems to us to be exhibiting signs of pain. This case is, indeed, a little more complicated. The context is more elaborate and the child has somehow to catch on to the fact that the word refers to the feeling rather than to the thing which causes it, a distinction which very young children are said to find it quite difficult to make. Nevertheless the two sorts of cases are fundamentally alike.

But, it may be said, we can point to the table and cannot point to the pain, or at least not in the same straightforward way. What does this come to? That you accompany your utterance of the word 'table' with a gesture, the purpose of which is to direct the child's attention to the object to which you wish him to take the word to refer. Well, you could also make a gesture as part of the process of teaching him what the word 'pain' meant. But it would not have the same effect, because it would direct his attention not to the pain but to its cause, or to the part of his body in which he felt it, or to his tears. Well, it might or it might not. How can one be sure? A great deal would depend on what other words the child already understood. In any event, there cannot be more to this than a slight difference in the technique of teaching.

The moral which I wish to draw is that if there is a problem about the attribution of experiences to others, it arises just as much with respect to the observation of public objects as with respect to inner processes. If I have any reason to doubt whether the feeling which another man has when he says that he is in pain is at all analogous to the feeling that I have when I am in pain, or whether he has any feeling at all, I have just as much reason to doubt whether what he sees when he says that he sees a table is at all analogous to what I see when I see a table, or indeed whether he sees anything at all. I am not saying that there are serious reasons for doubt in either case, nor yet that there are not, but only that they are on a level. It is therefore a mistake to think either that one removes the threat of solipsism by insisting that inner processes should have outer criteria, or that one increases it by bringing experiential statements into the analysis of judgements of perception. Perhaps the introduction of experiential statements makes sceptical doubts concerning our common world a little easier to formulate, but it will always be possible to formulate them so long as one is able to raise the question whether there are any counterparts to one's own experiences. To remove this possibility, we should have to outlaw any reference to any form of consciousness, resolve thoughts into utterances, feelings into behaviour, beliefs into actions and perception into the acquisition of beliefs. There would then be no question of our seeing the world differently because there would be no question of our *seeing* the world at all.

If we are not going to these lengths, there is no reason, on the score of publicity, why we should not start with qualia, rather than with the physical objects of common-sense. It is not as if this committed us to denying the assumptions which are contained in our ordinary judgements of perception; by not making them at the outset we give ourselves the opportunity to show how they are warranted. Otherwise, the main difference is that the standing of an E-statement is not so precarious as that of a P-statement. In particular, it is not exposed in the same way to the verdict of other people. This does not mean, however, that I am debarred from holding any beliefs about the character of the qualia which are presented to other people, or that these beliefs do not play a vital part in the fixation of my beliefs about physical objects. I am handicapped only in the sense that the best warrant that I can have for my belief that the qualia which are presented to some other person, on a given occasion, are similar to those which are presented to me is that it fits in with my overall interpretation of his words and actions. But that I should find his words and actions appropriate, in the sense that I can rely on my interpretation of them for predicting my own experiences, is all that matters to me. I take this to be the point that philosophers like Schlick are concerned to make when they say that only structure is communicable, and not content. More-over, as I have just tried to show, exactly the same applies in the case of the P-statements which are made by another person. I have only this indirect way of testing my belief that the things which we both say that we perceive look at all the same to him as they do to me, and again this does not matter to me so long as I am able, in terms of my own experience, to rely on my inter-pretation of what he says.

But if we do not know that we are presented with the same qualia, surely each of us is imprisoned in his own world. Well, each of us *is* imprisoned in his own world, in the harmless sense that I have my experiences and other people have theirs, and any knowledge of the world which any one of us acquires is bound to be based upon his own experiences. But this does not prevent us from operating with criteria of identity which ensure that we perceive the same physical objects; it is just that we have separately to determine that these criteria are satisfied. Neither does it offer any bar to our conceiving of these physical objects as 'constructed' out of qualia. What is required here, as we shall presently see, is that the relations which are found between qualia should be projected and supplemented in such a way as to expand into the framework of a physical system. The question who 'owns' the qualia does not enter into it. If we are pressed to say who carries out the construction, our answer must be that it can be carried out by anyone who has access to the necessary materials.

The trap into which many empiricists have fallen is that of attempting to construct a common world out of 'my' private sense-data: not only do they find themselves in the contradictory position of having to treat the personal pronoun as standing both for a constant and a variable, but the brand of privacy which is placed upon the data at the outset is never removed. It is equally impossible to construct a common world by putting together the private data of different subjects; for here one does fall foul of the objection that no one could be in a position to perform the synthesis. We have also seen that James comes to grief in trying to arrive at a common world by giving experiences a common ownership. All these troubles arise from the initial mistake of raising the question of privacy or publicity at the primitive level. Not only is it not necessary to introduce qualia as private entities, but the very question of their ownership, or, to speak more strictly, the ownership of their instances, makes no sense except at a level of theory where persons, and therefore physical objects, have already been introduced.

Once we have arrived at such a theory, the problem takes on quite a different aspect. We can then look back on our starting point, and as it were pull the ladder up after us. That is to say, we can determine the status of qualia in the light of the theory, in much the same way as having arrived at physics through common-sense, we can reinterpret the world of common-sense in terms of physics. At this stage we can determine the privacy or publicity of qualia in accordance with the rules of identity which are adopted at the higher level. In giving qualia a place within the theory which they served to introduce, we are free to decree whether or not we are going to say that the same instance of a quale can be presented to different people. And at *this* stage no trouble would arise from our choosing to regard the instances of qualia as private, since the theory already puts us in a common world in which, as we shall see, allowance can be made for private sectors. The point is that questions of privacy or publicity, objectivity or subjectivity, arise only within the theory, and can therefore be directed to our primitive data only when these have been taken up into the theory; but once the data have been taken up into the theory, they have only a subordinate status. There is no inconsistency there, because there is no logical reason why we should identify the elements on which our conception of the world is founded with the elements of which we conceive the world to be composed. I hope that what I shall subsequently have to say about our adoption of criteria of reality will help to make this clear.

One further objection remains to be met before we can be satisfied that our primitive data are fit to play the part that we are assigning to them. I have not said that P-statements entail E-statements because I do not know how to set limits to the range of E-statements on which a given P-statement may be founded:

things do not always have their characteristic looks and I see no way of legislating *a priori* for every possible oddity or form of disguise. On the other hand, I am maintaining that in every case in which any P-statement is true, it must be based upon some true E-statement. No physical object can be perceived unless a quale of some sort or other is presented. But now the only criterion that I have given for the truth of an E-statement is that the corresponding quale be recognized; and from this it seems to follow that whenever one believes a P-statement to be true, one also believes some E-statement to be true. But surely, it may be objected, this is just contrary to the facts. People constantly believe that they perceive things but when, if ever, do they recognize qualia? Except for a very few philosophers, who even believes that they are recognizable?

One might try to escape from this difficulty by saying that the basis for the perceptual judgement is to be found in the character of the experience which gives rise to it, whether or not this character is recognized. But the trouble with this suggestion is that it leaves us without any means of determining what the character of the experience is. We should have no other resource than to identify qualia by reference to the perceptual judgements which are based upon them. But this would mean that the condition that E-statements be logically independent of P-statements could not be maintained.

In fact, it would not be fatal to our undertaking if this condition were not maintained. To characterize a quale as being of a kind which is commonly taken to be an aspect of a physical object of such and such a sort, is consistent with its failing to convey any object of this sort in this particular instance: and that is all that we strictly require. Even if in order to specify our data we have to make use of the theory which we are trying to base on them, it will still be illuminating to show how the theory is constructed: we can still regard it as a contingent fact that the data stand to one another in the relations on which the theory depends. Nevertheless, it ought to be possible, as I have said, to specify the data without making use of the theory: and clearly if this stronger position is tenable it is the more satisfactory.

I propose, therefore, to face the objection. It would, indeed, be unanswerable, if we had to maintain that qualia were recognized *as* qualia, or that in every case in which a P-statement was accepted, some E-statement was explicitly formulated and assented to. But we do not need to go nearly so far as this. The most that we have to claim is that in order to be in a position to make a judgement of perception we have at least to take note of the way that the object in question looks or, as the case may be, feels or smells or tastes or sounds. But if this is so, then I think that we are entitled to say that the acceptance of a P-statement does implicitly involve the acceptance of an E-statement. The reason why the E-statement is very seldom formulated is that we are usually not interested in the appearance of things except as a means to their identification. It is, however, on the basis of the unformulated E-statement that the identification is made. This is confirmed by the fact that when the P-statement is challenged, one does fall back upon an E-statement. I may be wrong, one says, but that is how it looks to me, or that is how it feels, or that is how it sounds. One does not speak in terms of qualia but one is in fact referring to them.

4. *The Construction Outlined*

Having given a rough sketch of the form which an experiential language might display, and having tried to meet the more serious objections which might be taken both to the possibility of a language of this kind and to the use to which I wish to put it, I shall now give an equally rough account of the way in which we organize qualia in order to arrive at what I have been calling the common-sense physical theory. I shall proceed all the more summarily, as a great deal of the ground has already been covered in our discussion of James's treatment of the development of our concepts of space and time.

Following James, I shall adopt the traditional method of fictive construction. I shall try to trace the steps by which a single person might arrive at such a theory, on the basis of his experience. This is, as I have said, a piece of fiction. I am not implying that each of us has gone through such a process in his infancy, or that it was gone through by any of our remote ancestors; I do not claim that the common-sense conception of the physical world, in whatever was its primitive form, was consciously adopted as a theory. My procedure, like James's, is also artificial in that I place my subject in a situation where he has to do all the work for himself; a situation in which it is, in fact, very unlikely that anyone would acquire the use of any language at all. None of this matters, however, since, as I have already explained, this tale of construction is only an expository device. If I can make the story sound plausible, in its own terms, I shall have given what may pass as phenomenal analysis of the way that physical concepts function.

The question which I am trying to answer may be put in the Kantian form: How is the physical language possible? Since I shall confine myself almost exclusively to the domain of visual perception, the answer, besides being highly schematic, will cover only an attenuated version of even the physical language of common-sense: but this will be enough to illustrate the main principles on which I believe that a more thoroughgoing analysis could proceed.

As I have already indicated, in dealing with James's construction of space, the empirical fact on which everything depends is that qualia form relatively stable clusters. If we consider any fairly elaborate *gestalt* there will, as a general rule, be only a small number of contexts in which our observer comes upon it. The reason for this, in physical terms, is that although things change, they mostly change gradually and indeed imperceptibly, and that although things move, they mostly stay put, in the sense that they preserve constant spatial relations to a large number of other things. In the case of qualia we also have to reckon with changes which are dependent on the observer, though the observer in our story is, of course, not yet in a position to make any such distinction. The spatial relations of qualia will vary with his own spatial relations to them; for instance, at one time one quale will be beyond another, at another time this relation will be reversed. There will also be variations among the qualia themselves as the result of changes in the light or in the observer's condition.

Nevertheless he still finds that his qualia form numerous configurations which are persistent, in the sense that when one or two members of the configuration are reinstated, the remainder are also reinstated, or at any rate reinstatable, by an overlap of sense-fields, that is, as we should say, by the observer's slightly altering his angle of vision. This fact enables our subject to pass from qualia to individuals, not of course to physical objects but to phenomenal individuals of a purely visual type. An individual of this sort is constituted by the occurrence of a visual quale as a member of a stable configuration.

It is to be remarked that the fact which makes this initial step possible is only contingent. It is imaginable that the appearances of things should be constantly undergoing abrupt processes of change, or that all the things that we observe should be continuously in motion relatively to one another, or that the condition of the observer should always be like that of one who is drugged to the point where his experience, as we should say, becomes quite phantasmagoric. Admittedly, if these were the facts, we should not be able to describe them in this way, because we should not have the standard from which they can be represented as deviations. We should not under these conditions possess the concepts which we have of physical objects, or if we somehow came to possess them we should have no use for them. There would not even be any application for the concept that we have of ourselves. It does not follow, however, that such a world would necessarily be indescribable; only that it would be resistent to the forms of description that we most commonly employ.

Having constructed phenomenal individuals out of the primitive qualia, the next major step which our subject has to take is to conceive of these individuals as being continuously latent. This is equivalent to their existing unperceived, though this way of putting it is not yet within our subject's reach, since he has still to acquire the notion of himself as a percipient. The material for this step is already at hand in the projection of spatial and temporal relations beyond the presented field, in the manner that James describes. It depends, as we have seen, upon the possibility of reinstating a given configuration by traversing one or other of a limited number of relatively stable sensory routes. Since this process takes time, the projection is initially into the future. Our subject is therefore required to extend his original E-language in a way that enables him to refer to qualia which are indeed linked to the contents of his present sense-field, but are not themselves constituents of it. This extension seems quite natural, and I do not think that it raises any difficulty of principle. We may then suppose him to make the decisive move of locating his spatial projections not in the future but in the present. In other words, he regards the potential spatial extension of his visual field as being contemporaneous with it. A stable configuration of qualia is turned into a persistent entity through its being attached to every member of a continuous series of sense-fields either as a constituent or as a simultaneous spatial projection. In this way our subject arrives at the notion of a visual continuant.

The construction of tactual continuants follows the same principles, as indicated in James's theory.[1] As we have seen, this theory, when suitably amended, provides also for the fusion of visual and tactual data and for the ascription to the resulting constructs of properties which belong to the other sense-modalities.

There is one individual which comes to be recognized as a visual continuant, not because the visual qualia which enter into its construction are set in a stable environment, but because they occupy a series of spatial positions which, in relation to the positions occupied by other overlapping sets of qualia, differ only minimally in successive sense-fields. This individual has the distinctive property of being almost totally pervasive. A complex principally of visual, tactual, and kinaesthetic qualia, it has a representative or set of representatives in every one of the observer's tactual sense-fields and in the vast majority of his visual sense-fields. It is, of course, the observer's body, not characterized by him as such, since he cannot as yet distinguish himself as a subject from the objects which he perceives, but marked out as what, following Peirce, we may call the central body. The concept of the central body, allowing as it does for the observer's

[1] See above, pp. 240–1.

movement, assists, as we have seen, in the process of fusing visual and tactual space.[1]

Our observer can now take the first step towards making the distinction between his own subjective experiences and the objective world which he perceives. He forms a rudimentary picture of the way the world works, on the basis of the concomitances which he discovers between different states of his phenomenal continuants. He allows these continuants to change within certain limits without losing their identity, the stability of the context being taken to override a slight variation in the qualia, and he also allows them to move, in this case taking the stability of the qualia as overriding a gradual diversity in the context. He then finds that these changes and movements of different continuants can be cross-correlated. There are, however, a number of presentations which do not fit into the general picture. They are, as we should say, his dreams, his hallucinations and his fantasies. He tries to accommodate them, to conceive consistently of things as behaving not only in accordance with his perceptions of them but also with the ways in which he imagines them, but this proves too difficult. I am of course speaking in our terms and not in his. For him all experiences are alike in status: it is just that there are certain complexes of qualia which he finds unmanageable. He therefore distinguishes a main story, the one which, as we should say, describes the objective world, from a number of subsidiary stories. There is nothing against the subsidiary stories in themselves. It is just that they do not fit in with the main story or with one another. We may suppose that he puts a special mark on the statements which go into the main story, as we might say, his sign for objectivity.

At this point we need to introduce a second observer, a Man Friday for our Robinson Crusoe. The importance of Man Friday, so far as Crusoe is concerned, is that he also makes use of signs. What this means for Crusoe is that qualia, in the form of sounds or marks or movements, which he is able to associate causally with the Friday-continuant, can be interpreted by him as

[1] This process is well described by Henri Poincaré in his essay on 'L'Espace et la Géométrie' in *La Science et l'Hypothèse* (1902).

fairly reliable indicators of the course of his own experience. He then discovers that while the great majority of Friday's indications of the presence of various configurations of qualia fit in with the main story, there are a certain number which fit in neither with the main story nor with any of the subsidiary stories. He therefore forms the idea of a further set of subsidiary stories, namely those told by Friday, and distinguishes them both from the main story and from the subsidiary stories which are told by himself, the important point being that it is only with the appearance of another sign-using continuant that sense can be attached to his identifying the central body with himself.

Let us now suppose that other observers, other sign-using bodies, come upon the scene. They not only provide our Crusoe with further corroboration of his main story, but also enable him to acquire the idea of himself, identified still through the central phenomenal continuant, not only as a figure in the main story which is accepted by other sign-makers, but also as a maker of signs corresponding to nothing that the others recognize and so as a recorder or spectator of worlds existing only for him. So the private-public distinction is made, from which self-consciousness arises, permitting by the same route the attribution of consciousness to others, and the eventual development of the distinction between mind and matter.

The final result is that the main story becomes autonomous. The objects which figure in it are credited with an existence of their own, independently of the contribution of any of the story-tellers. This goes with the assumption that they are all telling the same story, even though their versions of it may differ. The variations in detail are attributed to differences in the equipment of the story-tellers or in their point of view. But once the distinction is made between the story as it is in itself and any particular versions of it, including one's own, the position is reached where all one's experiences, not only those which furnish the subsidiary stories, but even those which furnish the main story, are considered to be subjective. The theory becomes dominant; and, in the way that I have tried to explain, the elements out of which it has been constructed are taken up into it and assigned a subordinate position.

I am very well aware that this is only a rude sketch of a construction, and that it involves some very audacious leaps. An unkind critic might say of it that it abundantly illustrated what Russell has called the advantages of theft over honest toil. The most that I can claim for it is that it may contain an outline of the truth. There remain one or two general comments that I wish to make on it.

The first is that the ordering of events in time is a slightly more complicated matter than the ordering of objects in space. Both depend ultimately, as we have seen, upon the projection of relations which are sensorily given to us. But whereas these relations are sufficient in themselves to generate a spatial system, without our having to make any special assumptions about the objects which they relate, beyond the fact that they are relatively stable, they are not quite sufficient for the ordering of events in time. The reason for this is that the positions which we assign to events in an objective time order depend, roughly speaking, on our assessments of the relative positions that they would appear to have to observers at different points in space, and in making these assessments we appeal to scientific laws, such as those concerning the velocity of sound and light. It is in this way that we come to distinguish between the objective temporal order of events and the subjective order of our experiences. This was the distinction on which Kant relied, in the 'Second Analogy' of the *Critique of Pure Reason*, where he attempted to prove that phenomena are necessarily subject to a principle of universal causation. But the attempt is unsuccessful: his principle is much too general, too empty of content, to do the work that he requires of it. What we need are more specific laws which we are not obliged to regard as holding *a priori*. Thus, our dating system depends on the assumption that the earth's revolutions, on its own axis and around the sun, are uniform processes in the sense that they always occupy equal periods of time. Indeed, this sets our standard of temporal equality. To speak of any other processes as being equal in their duration is to imply that they take up the same quantity of hours or days, or whatever the unit may be, upon this temporal scale. But this standard is not sacrosanct. It could be abandoned if it led to unsatisfactory results; that is to say, if it were found to assign equal durations to processes which we had other and better reasons for regarding as unequal. We should then rely upon some different law, for instance the law that the velocity of light is constant, and so be left free, on this new basis, to conclude that the earth's revolution was not the uniform process that we had taken it to be. Our standards of measurement are always cross-checked and this in itself prevents them from being sacrosanct. We are not in the position of having to regard any single one of them as infallible.

Something of the same flexibility extends, indeed, to the entire construction. Not only is it conceivable that the primitive data themselves should have been differently selected, but even given our present stock of sensory predicates, and the patterns in which they are instantiated, we could have erected a different structure on them. For instance the fact that qualia occur in stable clusters, which makes it possible to construct phenomenal continuants, would equally well support a theory in which the only persistent individuals were regions of perceptual space. Another possibility would be to have only momentary individuals, consisting of what would be described in our present theory as the phases of phenomenal continuants, or even to create a 'static' world by ascribing predicates not just to regions of space but to stretches of space-time. And if it is possible, as I have suggested, to eliminate singular terms, we could dispense with individuals altogether and make our physical language, like our experiential language, wholly predicative. It must, however, be admitted that these alternatives are all more complex and psychologically less natural than the physical theory of common-sense.

In the popular sense, in which pragmatism is thought to lay stress upon the primacy of action, my development of James's empiricism has not been pragmatic. Like him, I have followed the classical empiricists in treating the observer as a passive recipient of qualia, or rather as one who is active only in the sense that his past experience and present interests and expectations may make a difference to the character of the qualia with which he is presented. I have not started off with infantile agents. I make no apology for this. I am quite prepared to accept it as an empirical fact that children are players rather than spectators and that without this activity they would not acquire the use of ordinary language as readily as they mostly do. This is not to say, however, that they begin with the concept of themselves as agents, still less that this concept has to be taken for granted in any theory of perception. To say that one is bound to start with it is to assume that a programme like James's cannot be carried out. If the scheme which I have outlined is acceptable, I have shown that the concept of the observer as an agent need not be taken as a starting point. This does not mean that I am unable to accommodate it, at least in its physical aspect. It seems to me to depend rather simply on the correlation of movements of the central body with changes in the phenomenal environment. In its psychological aspect, it raises once more the difficult question of intentionality, which we encountered in our discussion of belief.

4. On What There Is

The aim which I set myself was to make out a general case for the thesis that our conception of the physical world can be exhibited as a theory with respect to our experiences. I said that if I were successful, as I hope I have been, it would give James most of what he wanted, though not all. The question which remains to be considered is whether it would justify his taking 'pure experience' to be 'the one primal stuff or material in the world, a stuff of which everything is composed'.[1]

This is a difficult question to answer, mainly because it is not clear what the issue is. If James is contending only that the world is constructible out of experiences, the answer would depend upon the conditions which the construction is required to satisfy. The form of phenomenalism which I have been defending may appear rather weak, but it is the strongest programme that I

[1] See above, p. 298.

believe to have any chance of success. Even if I am right, however, the matter does not rest there, since James's thesis is capable of another interpretation. He might be thought to be claiming, and probably himself meant to claim, that pure experience is all that there is. But when it is interpreted in this way, the thesis is very dubious indeed.

To begin with, it is not clear what a claim of this kind amounts to, outside the framework of a given system. We know that there is no greatest prime number, because this is a conclusion for which we can give a mathematical proof. We know that there are protons, because of the part which they play in a well-established scientific theory. We know, on the basis of historical evidence, that Julius Caesar was a real and not a mythical person. We know that there are many kinds of insects, because we can observe them. We do not know whether there are abominable snowmen or whether the man in the iron mask really existed, but we do know what sort of information would lead us to accept their existence. In all such cases, there are acknowledged criteria for deciding whether objects of the kind in question exist; and these criteria operate within a theoretical system.

But now if we look at the theory which I have constructed, so far as possible along the lines that James laid down, it gives us no licence at all for saying that only experiences exist. The fact is rather that experiences, so far from being all that exists, have only a secondary title to existence, since it is only through their association with living bodies that they gain the necessary foothold in an objective time-order. Experiences are attributed to persons, or to other sentient beings: but not only is it logically possible that the world should not contain any sentient beings, but there is good empirical evidence that it did not do so at some time in the past and will no longer do so at some time in the future.

It must be made clear that there is no contradiction between what I have just said and the thesis that the world is constructible out of experiences, in the way that I have outlined. When I speak of the world I am speaking of what is represented by the true propositions of the theory. The theory is indeed reached by generalizing and extrapolating from the data of human experience, but it is not just a summary of these data. It contains no predicates that are not cashable at the experiential level, but it does not carry the implication that they are actually cashed in every instance in which they are exemplified. On the contrary, the fact that no limits are set within the theory to the projection of spatio-temporal relations, whereas the region of space-time which is occupied by sentient beings may be taken to be limited, ensures that there are more occurrences than are actually observed. It is essentially this spatio-temporal projection that enables the theory, as it were, to live a life of its own. Not only does it gain independence of its origins but, in the way I have tried to explain, it obtains sovereignty over them.

But why, it may be objected, should the question of what there is be decidable only within a given system? Why should one not put the system itself in question, at least to the extent of assessing the claims to existence of the entities which it admits? Surely this is quite a common philosophical procedure. For example, one may do mathematics and yet raise the question whether there are numbers; one may make moral judgements and still find a point in discussing whether there are values; one may discourse in abstract terms and dispute whether there are universals; one may accept current physics and doubt whether there are atomic particles; one may even discourse at the level of common-sense and yet raise the question whether there are physical objects. Are we simply going to dismiss all such questions as meaningless or contradictory?

I do not think that we can simply dismiss them. Nevertheless they are also not to be taken quite at their face value. The interest which they present is to be found always in the negative thesis, or rather in the reasons for which the negative thesis is put forward. What is it that makes a philosopher want to say that such and such a type of entity does not exist? The reason may be that he thinks that he has found a logical flaw in the concept under which the entities in question fall.[1] More frequently, it is that he

[1] Cf. my essay on 'Metaphysics and Common-Sense' in *Metaphysics*, ed. Kennick and Lazerowitz.

is engaged in the advocacy of some form of reductive analysis. So, for example, the denial that there are values is most probably to be construed, not as a profession of moral nihilism, but as the expression of a belief in the validity of a prescriptive or even a naturalistic analysis of moral judgements, as opposed to the safe but unilluminating 'realistic' procedure of simply taking value predicates to stand for value properties. Similarly, to deny that there are atomic particles is a way of committing oneself to an operationalist treatment of scientific concepts; to deny that there are physical objects, even of the common-sense variety, is a way of professing phenomenalism. It is interesting to note that just as the apparently negative thesis turns out to have a positive content, so the converse also holds. The point of insisting that there are values, or physical objects, or whatever type of entity may be in question, is just to deny that the concepts under which they fall are susceptible of any such analysis.

There may be some question as to the conditions which the analysis has to satisfy for it to be seen as eliminating the entities on which it operates. For instance, Professor Quine has suggested that we should regard ourselves as committed to acknowledging the existence of any set of entities over which we quantify.[1] This means in effect that entities are to be regarded as eliminable only if it can be shown that whenever we appear to be talking about them our statements can be translated or paraphrased in such a way that no mention is any longer made of them. In the case of physical objects, this condition would be satisfied only if phenomenalism were tenable in its strongest form: it is plainly not satisfied by the weak reduction for which I have been arguing. On the other hand, one might be prepared to take a less stringent view of ontological commitment. An opponent of Platonism might still think himself entitled to deny the existence of abstract entities even though he had not, for example, found a method of translating statements about numbers into statements about numerals. He might be content with an informal explanation, along some such lines as Wittgenstein follows in his *Remarks on the Foundations of Mathematics*, and he might take this, rightly or

[1] W. V. Quine, 'On What There is', in *From a Logical Point of View* (1953).

wrongly, as being enough to show that doing mathematics 'came down' to operating with numerals. If we found his explanation satisfactory, we should then have to consider whether we were prepared to count it as a proof that numbers are eliminable.

The point to notice here is that, when they are viewed in this light, ontological questions are questions for decision. A good illustration is to be found in the problem of the relation between the 'world' of science and the 'world' of common-sense. Is what is really there before me the solid continuous coloured table of common-sense or a set of discrete colourless physical particles? It has been argued that this is a false dilemma, on the ground that descriptions of chairs and tables belong to a different order of discourse from the propositions of a scientific theory.[1] Since the members of either order can in their different ways be shown to be true, there can be no conflict between them. This is quite correct, in so far as all true statements must be mutually compatible, but it misses the point. There is no conflict so long as we concern ourselves only with questions of truth or falsehood, without venturing into ontology. But if we insist on posing the ontological question, then the scientific and common-sense descriptions of the world do come into conflict, if only because they compete for the same regions of space. We can consistently accept the common-sense statement that there is a table here, together with the scientific statement that there is a set of particles here, because there are independent ways of testing both statements, and these different groups of tests can each be satisfied. But if we are constructing a picture of the world, then I do not see how we can consistently think of this area as being exclusively occupied by a solid, continuous, coloured object and as being exclusively occupied by a set of discontinuous, volatile, colourless, shapeless particles. In this position we have to opt for one view or the other. At the same time we must not be misled into thinking that we are pronouncing on a question of fact. One is tempted to say: Never mind how we choose to regard the world. How is it in itself? What is *really* there, the table or the particles? What does God see? But this is to forget that we have not supplied any

[1] Cf. G. Ryle, *Dilemmas* (1954), ch. v.

criteria for determining what there really is, in this sense. We are no longer raising a question which can be settled by a recognized experimental procedure. Given two different orders of discourse, we are asking which of them we want to reify. This is not a purely arbitrary question. One can give reasons for going one way or the other. But they are not compelling reasons. In the end it comes down to a matter of choice. The word 'really', in this special usage, calls for the expression of an ontological decision.

It is not indeed necessary that this demand should be met. It may very well be that the best course is to take no ontological decisions at all. If we adopt this policy, we shall construe questions about the reality of different sorts of objects only as asking whether the statements which figure in different types of theory are true. We shall take up a position outside the different theories only for the purpose of asking how the sets of statements of which they respectively consist are logically or epistemologically related. Questions like 'Are there numbers?' 'Do numbers exist?' 'Are numbers real?' will be construed either as questions which can be answered affirmatively by giving examples of numbers or as questions about the possibility of reducing numbers to numerals. Otherwise they will not be admissible. In the same way, we shall ask how E-statements are related to P-statements and how they are both related to the statements that occur within physics, but we shall not admit as a further question the question: Do colour-qualia, or tables, or protons, or only qualia and protons, but not tables, or only tables and protons but not qualia form part of the real furniture of the world? Our reason for refusing to countenance any such question will be that if we are able to determine which statements at each of these levels are true and how statements of different kinds are related to each other, there are no matters of truth or falsehood left to be decided.

Nevertheless we can hardly prevent people from taking up ontological positions, if they are so minded. And in that case why should they not decide, with James, to look upon experiences as the stuff of reality and treat the physical objects which figure either in ordinary or in scientific discourse as merely 'entities of reason'? In favour of this decision it can be argued that it keeps to the epistemological priorities and that both kinds of physical objects are in fact theoretical constructs with respect to qualia. Even so, I do not think that this course is to be recommended. After all, the only point of having an ontology is to obtain a viable picture of the world, and this is something that qualia are not equipped to furnish. The E-language game is too rudimentary. So far as anything can be, qualia are pre-theoretical, and as we are now construing it, the question what there is comes up for decision only with respect to theories, in the special sense in which any system that allows one to distinguish between what is real and what is not real is a theory. This being so, the only serious candidates are naïve realism, considered, of course, as a form of ontology and not as theory of perception, and scientific realism. I shall not here attempt to adjudicate between them.

Whichever choice is made, it will leave no room for qualia as substantial entities. They will be buried in descriptions of the way things look to people and the way people are affected by various forms of stimulation. But this does not detract from their epistemological priority. We could not intelligently opt for the ontology of naïve or even of scientific realism, if the assumptions which are carried by the common-sense view of the world were not vindicated in our experience. In other words, it is only the character and the arrangement of qualia that make these decisions possible. But this is quite consistent, as I have shown, with their being assigned a subordinate adjectival position in the picture of the world which they make it possible to construct.

In dissenting from James on this aspect of his thesis that experience is the primal stuff of the world, I have taken a pragmatic view of ontology. It is pragmatic in the sense that once it has been established by the appropriate criteria that a given set of propositions is true, and there being no means of translating out the entities which figure in them, the question whether these entities are to be reified is treated as a matter of convenience. The thesis, which is often attributed to James, that truth is a matter of convenience is not acceptable: and in fact we have seen that James did not hold it, except in the domain of morals and theology. He did think that pragmatism afforded a means of solving metaphysical disputes, though he did not apply it to the metaphysical side of his own radical empiricism. The idea that practical considerations can be allowed to determine what there is, rather than to determine what is the case, is a modern development of pragmatism. The distinction is finely drawn, but I hope that I have succeeded in bringing it out. On this view, the question of reality becomes pragmatic just at the point where it goes beyond the question of truth.

INDEX